THE CAMBRIDGE COMPANION TO AMERICAN LITERATURE AND THE ENVIRONMENT

This *Companion* offers a capacious overview of American environmental literature and criticism. Tracing environmental literatures from the gates of the Manzanar War Relocation Camp in California to the island of St. Croix, from the notebooks of eighteenth-century naturalists to the practices of contemporary activists, this book offers readers a broad, multimedia definition of "literature," a transnational, settler-colonial comprehension of America, and a more-than-green definition of "environment." Demonstrating links between ecocriticism and such fields as Black feminism, food studies, decolonial activism, Latinx studies, Indigenous studies, queer theory, and carceral studies, the volume reveals the persistent relevance of literary methods within the increasingly interdisciplinary field of environmental humanities, while also modeling practices of literary reading shaped by this interdisciplinary turn. The result is a volume that will prove indispensable both to students seeking an overview of American environmental literature/criticism and to established scholars seeking new approaches to the field.

SARAH ENSOR is Assistant Professor of English at the University of Wisconsin, Madison, where she is also a Faculty Associate at the Center for Culture, History, and Environment in the Nelson Institute for Environmental Studies. She works at the nexus of American literature, environmental studies, and queer theory.

SUSAN SCOTT PARRISH is Arthur F. Thurnau Professor of English and the Program in the Environment at the University of Michigan, where she is also Chair of the Michigan Society of Fellows. She researches the history of how races and environments have been mutually constituted in North America since the colonial period, with a special emphasis on the plantation zone understood in an Atlantic context. She has written two prize-winning books: *The Flood Year 1927: A Cultural History* (2017) and *American Curiosity: Cultures of Natural History in the Colonial British Atlantic World* (2006).

T0381676

THE CAMBRIDGE COMPANION TO AMERICAN LITERATURE AND THE ENVIRONMENT

EDITED BY

SARAH ENSOR
University of Wisconsin, Madison

SUSAN SCOTT PARRISH
University of Michigan, Ann Arbor

CAMBRIDGE
UNIVERSITY PRESS

CAMBRIDGE
UNIVERSITY PRESS

University Printing House, Cambridge CB2 8BS, United Kingdom

One Liberty Plaza, 20th Floor, New York, NY 10006, USA

477 Williamstown Road, Port Melbourne, VIC 3207, Australia

314–321, 3rd Floor, Plot 3, Splendor Forum, Jasola District Centre, New Delhi – 110025, India

103 Penang Road, #05–06/07, Visioncrest Commercial, Singapore 238467

Cambridge University Press is part of the University of Cambridge.

It furthers the University's mission by disseminating knowledge in the pursuit of education, learning, and research at the highest international levels of excellence.

www.cambridge.org
Information on this title: www.cambridge.org/9781108841900
DOI: 10.1017/9781108895118

First published 2022

A catalogue record for this publication is available from the British Library.

ISBN 978-1-108-84190-0 Hardback
ISBN 978-1-108-81527-7 Paperback

This Companion is dedicated to our students

Contents

Figures

Contributors

RICK CROWNSHAW teaches American literature in the Department of English and Comparative Literature, Goldsmiths, University of London. He is the author of *The Afterlife of Holocaust Memory in Contemporary Literature and Culture* (2010), as well as numerous articles on American literature, memory studies, and trauma studies. He is the editor of *Transcultural Memory* (2014), and co-editor of *The Future of Memory* (2010, 2013). He is currently working on a monograph, *Remembering the Anthropocene in Contemporary American Fiction*, which focuses on, among other things, the potential of cultural memory and trauma studies in analyzing literary narratives of climate change, extinction, pollution and toxicity, the resourcing of war, American petrocultures, and post-oil imaginaries. He is the coeditor, with Stef Craps, of a 2018 special edition of *Studies in the Novel* on climate change fiction.

WAI CHEE DIMOCK is William Lampson Professor of English and American Studies at Yale University, and editor of *PMLA*. Her books include *Residues of Justice: Literature, Law, Philosophy* (1996); *Through Other Continents: American Literature Across Deep Time* (2006); *Shades of the Planet* (2007); *Weak Planet: Literature and Assisted Survival* (2020); and a team-edited anthology, *American Literature in the World: Anne Bradstreet to Octavia Butler* (2017). Other writings have appeared in the *New York Times*, *New Yorker*, *Los Angeles Review of Books*, and *Chronicle of Higher Education*.

SARAH ENSOR is Assistant Professor of English at the University of Wisconsin, Madison. Her research engages the intersections between queer and environmental thought in American literature from the nineteenth century through the present. She is currently completing her first book, "Terminal Regions: Queer Environmental Ethics in the Absence of Futurity," which reads queer sites of provisionality in order to trace how temporariness and (apparent) futurelessness can engender, rather than preclude, forms of commitment, community, intimacy, and care.

URSULA K. HEISE is Chair of the English Department at UCLA and cofounder of the Lab for Environmental Narrative Strategies (LENS) at UCLA's Institute of the Environment and Sustainability. Her research and teaching focus on contemporary literature and the environmental humanities; environmental literature, arts, and cultures in the Americas, Germany, Japan, and Spain; literature and science; science fiction; and narrative theory. Her books include, among others, *Sense of Place and Sense of Planet: The Environmental Imagination of the Global* (2008) and *Imagining Extinction: The Cultural Meanings of Endangered Species* (2016), which won the 2017 book prize of the British Society for Literature and Science. She is coeditor of *The Routledge Companion to the Environmental Humanities* (2017), coeditor of the series *Natures, Cultures, and the Environment* with Palgrave, and coeditor of the series *Literature and Contemporary Thought* with Routledge. She is also producer and writer of *Urban Ark Los Angeles*, a documentary created as a collaboration of LENS with the public television station KCET-Link.

MATT HOOLEY is Assistant Professor of Literature and the Environment at Clemson University. He writes and teaches across Indigenous, colonialism, American, and environmental studies and is a founding member of Decolonize Clemson.

ANGELA HUME's research intervenes in multiethnic American poetry/ poetics; gender, women, and sexuality studies; ecocriticism and the environmental humanities; and the feminist medical humanities, a field she is working to develop. Her articles appear in *Contemporary Literature* and *ISLE: Interdisciplinary Studies in Literature and Environment*, among others. She is currently at work on a monograph about the roles American poetry has played in radical feminist and queer health movements. Hume is Assistant Professor of English, creative writing, and environmental literature at University of Minnesota, Morris.

CHRISTOPH IRMSCHER is Distinguished Professor of English and Director of the Wells Scholars Program at Indiana University Bloomington. Among his many books are *The Poetics of Natural History* (2nd edition, with photographs by Rosamond Purcell,

2019), *Louis Agassiz: Creator of American Science* (2013), and the Library of America edition of John James Audubon's *Writings and Drawings* (2nd edition, 2011).

MIKA KENNEDY is Visiting Assistant Professor in the Department of English at Kalamazoo College (2020–2022). Her current academic book project examines narratives of Japanese American incarceration, and the ways these narratives are in conversation with questions about the environment, the seductions of the "frontier," and Native sovereignty. She is also a cocurator of the JACL Detroit Chapter's museum exhibit, *Exiled to Motown*, which explores the history of the Japanese American community in metro Detroit.

PAUL OUTKA is Associate Professor of English at the University of Kansas, with a scholarly emphasis on nineteenth- and twentieth-century US literature and culture, critical race theory, science studies, and the environmental humanities. He served as President of the Associate for the Study of Literature and Environment (ASLE) in 2013, and his first book, *Race and Nature from Transcendentalism to the Harlem Renaissance* (2008, 2013) won ASLE's 2009 biennial prize for the "Best Book of Ecocriticism." He is currently working on a monograph examining the structures in which the human was defined in the nineteenth century, and their parallels in contemporary discourses about technology.

SUSAN SCOTT PARRISH is Arthur F. Thurnau Professor in the English Department and the Program in the Environment at the University of Michigan. Her research addresses the interrelated issues of race, the environment, media, and knowledge-making in the Atlantic world from the seventeenth century up through the present, with a particular emphasis on southern and Caribbean plantation zones. She has written two award-winning books, *The Flood Year 1927: A Cultural History* (2017) and *American Curiosity: Cultures of Natural History in the Colonial British Atlantic World* (2006), and is currently editing the Norton Critical Edition of Faulkner's *Absalom, Absalom!*

NICOLE SEYMOUR researches the roles that queer styles and affects play in environmental movements, as seen in recent publications such as *Bad Environmentalism: Irony and Irreverence in the Ecological Age* (2018). She is Associate Professor of English and Graduate Advisor for Environmental Studies at California State University, Fullerton. In 2019–2020, she was on sabbatical as an Alumni Fellow at the Rachel

Carson Center in Munich, Germany, working on a project about the (im)possibilities of vegan satire and a book about glitter for Bloomsbury's "Object Lessons" series. One day, she hopes to pursue research on the role of humor in the contemporary classroom.

MIN HYOUNG SONG is Professor of English at Boston College, where he specializes in Asian American literature and environmental humanities. He is completing a new book manuscript entitled "Climate Lyricism," and is the author of *The Children of 1965: On Writing, and Not Writing, as an Asian American* (2013) and *Strange Future: Pessimism and the 1992 Los Angeles Riots* (2005). He is the general coeditor (with Rajini Srikanth) of the four-volume Cambridge University Press series Asian American Literature in Transition, the coeditor (with Rajini Srikanth) of *The Cambridge History of Asian American Literature*, and the former editor of the *Journal of Asian American Studies* (*JAAS*). He has authored numerous journal articles, book chapters, and essays in public-facing venues such as *The Washington Post*, *The Los Angeles Review of Books*, *The Massachusetts Review*, and *The Chicago Review of Books*.

HARILAOS STECOPOULOS is Associate Professor of English at the University of Iowa. He is the author of *Reconstructing the World: Southern Fictions and U.S. Imperialisms, 1898–1976* (2008) and is currently finishing his second monograph, "Telling America's Story to the World: Literature, Internationalism, Cultural Diplomacy." He has also edited the "Cambridge History of the Literature of the U.S. South" (forthcoming in 2021).

TIMOTHY SWEET is Eberly Family Distinguished Professor of American Literature at West Virginia University. His publications include *Traces of War: Poetry, Photography, and the Crisis of the Union* (1990), *American Georgics: Economy and Environment in Early American Literature* (2002), and an edited collection, *Literary Cultures of the Civil War* (2016). His latest book, *Extinction and the Human: Four American Encounters*, was published in 2021.

SARAH D. WALD is Associate Professor of Environmental Studies and English at the University of Oregon. She is the author of *The Nature of California: Race, Citizenship, and Farming since the Dust Bowl* (2016) and coeditor of *Latinx Environmentalisms: Place, Justice, and the Decolonial* (2019).

Acknowledgments

We would like to heartily thank our contributors for their energy, generosity, and brilliance. They found the time to brainstorm together at ASLE in 2019, to group-Zoom about their chapters-in-progress, and to listen to our queries about knotty places in their work. Most dramatically, everyone kept working and thinking clearly, despite a global pandemic. We also want to thank Surabhi Balachander, a PhD student at the University of Michigan, and Americanist ecocritic, for her clear-eyed help with the manuscript. Finally, we appreciate the chance that Ray Ryan gave us to create this volume, and the assistance of Edgar Mendez, Natasha Burton and Felinda Sharmal in bringing it home.

A Note on the Cover Image

The book's cover image – Sand Dunes at Sunset, Atlantic City – was painted by Henry Ossawa Tanner around 1885. Made while Tanner was completing his study with Thomas Eakins at the Pennsylvania Academy, it is the first work by an African American to be collected by the White House, which purchased the painting from the artist's descendants in 1995. Tanner's mother was born into slavery, escaping north via the Underground Railroad, and his father was a bishop of the African Methodist Episcopal Church. They gave the artist his middle name, Ossawa, to reference the place where John Brown began his militant abolitionism: Osawatomie, Kansas. Though Tanner moved to Paris in 1891 to avoid racism in the US, he wrote that "deep down in my heart I love it and am sometimes sad that I cannot live where my heart is." To make Sand Dunes, the artist mixed sand into his pigments, raising questions about the relation of art to nature, his painting being indexical, archival, and figural all at once. Also noteworthy is Tanner's indirect representation of the unseen: we see the illuminations and shadows of the sun while looking at a rising moon, and the force of the invisible wind, as we look at the slanting grasses. Other forms of the unseen – this time historical – may be present here too. Might the ship, sailing on the horizon, suggest Frederick Douglass's description of standing, in bondage, on the shores of the Chesapeake while watching "beautiful vessels, robed in purest white, so delightful to the eye of freemen," but which were to him "so many shrouded ghosts"? This tactile near shore, these elusive boats, and this eastward-looking view of the Atlantic Ocean, orient us as we prepare to think about the American histories of environmental attachment and human dislocation that subtend US history and inform so many of our essays.

Introduction

Sarah Ensor and Susan Scott Parrish

In the last days of May, 2020, Scott Edwards dipped one of his bicycle tires in the Atlantic Ocean off of Newburyport, Massachusetts and began a westward journey across the continent. A professor of organismic and evolutionary biology and curator of ornithology at the Museum of Comparative Zoology at Harvard University, Edwards found he had time to bike to the Pacific when his laboratory was shut down by the COVID-19 pandemic. One context for his road trip, then, is the zoonotic pandemic, whose opportunistic spread revealed a globe whose once-separate evolutionary locales now dangerously overlap. Another context is the pair of events that took place on May 25: the police killing of George Floyd in Minneapolis and the spurious 911-call made by a white woman who had been asked to leash her dog in a protected area of Manhattan's Central Park by a Black birder, Christian Cooper. While the murder provoked global demonstrations against police violence and a resurgence of the Black Lives Matter (BLM) movement, the framing of Cooper as a Black menace (while it was he who was trying to protect birds from roving dogs) stirred up a public conversation about the whites-only exclusions of public green spaces in the US and launched the campaigns: #BlackInNature, #BlackBirdersWeek, and #BlackAFinSTEM. As a citizen, birder, and STEM researcher of biodiversity, who is also Black, Edwards designed his cross-country trip, chronicled on Twitter, as a mobile investigation of American environments – not only physical, but also historical and social – in a time of instant global messaging. His posts, and the posts they generate in turn, are a signature example of how American environmental literature is being produced today.

Edwards records the sights and sounds of many nonhuman species and land features: an Osprey nest in New York, wild coneflowers in Indiana, and the headwaters of the Missouri River. He details his body's interactions with its environment as he is being dive-bombed by red-winged blackbirds, feeling the rise of hills in his legs and lungs, and sensing in his body's vibrations the make of the road. Place names, museums and, on July 11, a major Supreme Court ruling on Muscogee (Creek) sovereignty in Oklahoma, have him noting the ongoing presence of Indigenous human life, alongside the history of "brutal westward expansion."[1] And he is testing, with every new human interaction, what it means to be a Black man outdoors today. On Juneteenth, as he was riding through western New York with a BLM sign attached to the back of his bicycle, he heard barking dogs, and recalled the 1973 Elton John song, "Have Mercy on the Criminal."[2] He comments: "I'm not a runaway slave, but I am a black man riding solo through 2020 conservative America." Despite this historical haunting, which also included two Confederate flags (NY and Idaho) and a racist comment in Indiana, he and his BLM sign otherwise elicit mostly "small acts of kindness": positive honks, gifts of water, truckers stopping to share their support. Not only, then, is Edwards "birding by ear" as he rides and listening to the avian "soundscape," getting to know the natural and human-made landscape by feeling it in his lungs and legs, but he also is a mobile probe of the US racescape.

As he moves west, making these mostly positive face-to-face connections on the public thoroughfares, giving interviews to radio and print journalists along the way, gathering more than 11,000 followers on Twitter (who identify specimens he's photographed or discuss diversity in STEM), the purpose of the journey becomes increasingly clear: against a history in which Black Americans have been denied a sense of belonging or safety in the American outdoors (whether in the Central Park Ramble or a Minneapolis street), Edwards is "creating" biotic, virtual, scientific, and social "community" as he moves.[3] If "whiteness" has naturalized its worth by associating itself with the ascribed freedom, majesty, and innocence of the heartland and the western wilderness, and if "blackness" has, since the early twentieth century, been conflated in the white supremacist imagination with a pathological and menacing urban setting, then Edwards's cross-continental ride, and its dissemination through social media, confounds the definitions that are based upon such symbolic mapping.

We open with Scott Edwards's travel tweets as a way to mark our moment in history, but also as an opportune way to approach and assess the three terms of this Companion's title: "American," "Literature," and "Environment." First: how is his journey, and journal, American? His ride simultaneously traverses both the continent of North America and the nation of the United States. Certain features and species that Edwards encounters – the Mississippi River watershed or the Osprey, for example – have ranges that extend north and south of the US, respectively. Many of the materials that make his ride, and its publicizing, possible – from rubber tires on his bicycle to rare earth elements in his cell phone – originate outside of the US. The occasions for his trip – both COVID-19 and anti-Black police brutality – are global in origin, scope, and response. His online community stretches internationally. Therefore, while Edwards's movement is entirely within the nation, and he meditates on national histories of territorial dispossession and slavery – and so is *of* the US topically and geographically – it also involves histories, materials, systems, and people that exceed the bounds of nationhood.[4] It is precisely this understanding of "American" that informs the contributions to this volume: all address texts written in North America, including the Caribbean, and all are aware that the US is a settler nation of still-contested sovereignties which has an outsized global footprint (carbon, waste, and media emissions) but is also susceptible to and dependent on global flows (of germs, minerals, consumer goods, and capital). As soon as we try to identify something uniquely "American" about Edwards's journal/journey – its epic romantic westering, its creation of political belonging through territorial survey, for example – we must admit those practices precede and exceed the nation. Ultimately then, what "American" signifies is how global, transhistorical cultural practices and materials dynamically meet with North American space.

That we call Scott Edwards's Twitter stream – a participatory, multi-authored travelogue whose audio-visual element is as important as its verbal composition, and whose content is driven by location as much as by authorial imagination – "literature" is a sign of the widening boundaries of that category. If English departments traditionally focused on belletristic and imaginative forms written or printed on paper, they have in recent decades come to consider digital, visual, and material cultures, the social performance of everyday life, and so on. While environmental literature – in the forms of georgic poem, travel narrative, natural history, or almanac – was immensely popular before 1900, it took the increasing green activism of the 1960s and the early stirrings of the field of ecocriticism in the 1970s, to define it as a category of widespread academic interest. The American environmental literature receiving attention at this early stage tended to describe human interaction with rural and wilderness locales. Since the 1990s, and amid a growing sense that "nature" does not only exist in patently green spaces, but is also in our faucets and our weapons, on monoculture plantations and poultry plants, texts that were *not* initially seen as "environmental" – urban novels, slave narratives, labor exposés, cancer diaries, horror films – have become visible as such. Because almost every cultural production involves embodiment and place, or some kind of interplay between consciousness and its material foundations, it has in fact become hard to say what *isn't* environmental literature. Indeed, in as much as our environments mediate human capacity, *they* themselves are now understood to be media producers, or "ecomedia."[5] Edwards's narrative draws both from traditions we have long seen as green (the wilderness narrative or the natural history account) as well as from sources more newly recognizable as environmental (mobile performances of civil rights protests or Black autobiography). Moreover, as we've said, rubber, titanium, and rare earth elements mediate his experience. In the chapters to follow, you will find genres such as natural history and cli-fi (climate fiction), but also Jazz Age fiction and western film noir; you will find cotton and wood pulp paper, but also silver-coated film and digital transmission; you will see the human at the center and also on the edge.

While an "environment" is crucial to any culture's formation and mythicization, environments play an especially active role in settler nations where the material changes settlers bring drastically alter the existing world. After peoples, pathogens, species, and land practices from Africa, Europe, and America collided in North America, each of these peoples responded culturally to make sense of these material novelties and changes, even if access to what became the dominant recording medium – alphabetical print – was drastically unequal. In post-contact literature, attention to nonhuman nature was constant. Environments appeared in surveys for extractable goods and scientific dispatches, but also in divine warnings, migration stories, and captivity tales. For all writers, faced either with diminishing or expanding sovereignty, and with challenged cosmologies, nature mattered.

As we have suggested, the category bundle that is "American environmental literature" is always subject to change, because of its experimental practitioners and its always shifting media, and because of scholars who keep redefining it. Before previewing what the ecocritics in this Companion are doing here and now, we want to situate them in their evolving field. Scholarly commentators seeking to define what the nation was, or could be, have long looked to nonhuman American land and space – its immensity, its "emptiness," its "virginity" – for clues. Beginning in the 1970s, ecofeminists built on this long attention as they brought a more critical eye to how imperial powers' figuration of American nature – as female and virgin – justified white patriarchal possession.[6] Ecocritics in the 1980s and 1990s wrote of wilderness seers such as Thoreau, Leopold, and Dillard, who, while part of settler culture, lovingly mucked about in the tangible and divine particulars of nature to reveal it as a guide for a more biocentric nation.[7] Since the 1990s, ecocritics have gradually absorbed the commitments of numerous preexisting environmental and social justice movements as well as a variety of critical orientations. Cesar Chavez and the United Farm Workers' movement for unionization, fair wages, and working conditions begun in the 1960s; the environmental justice movement, which brought attention to environmental racism starting in 1987; decolonization and postcolonial studies; anti-nuclear activism and urban ecology: all these have opened up the field of ecocriticism to attend to the ways in which environments, resources, and spatial design subtend issues of social justice, labor, urban living conditions, global politics, and modern technology.[8] The sometimes frictional, sometimes playful encounter between queer theory and environmental thought has encouraged ecocritics to consider everything from the pleasures of environmental contact to how to grieve ungrievable losses in the face of climate change.[9] Awareness of human-caused, planetary-scale environmental alteration in the form of global climate change, ocean acidification, sea level rise – captured in the redefinition of the post-1800 era as "the Anthropocene" – has more recently swept across the practices of ecocriticism, forcing the field to work at the scale of both the bioregion and the planet, and to consider the gravity but also the incapacities of human agency.[10] Animal studies, plant studies, actor-network-theory, posthumanism, and other fields attending to the interactive mesh of materialities constituting existence have introduced new texts, methods, and ontological models in recent years.[11] Finally, as suggested earlier, critics are now attending to how media themselves have environmental impacts, while environments mediate human life.

Emerging out of this history of ecocriticism, what distinguishes and unifies the chapters collected here? We've already suggested that it is a broad, multimedia definition of "literature," a transnational, settler-colonial comprehension of "America," and a more-than-green definition of "environment." Beyond these parameters, perhaps the common thread is an insistence that we face *the trouble with the human* – or that version of humanity figured so aptly in 1726 by Jonathan Swift in his giant, Gulliver, who assumes a tremendous wrecking power when he takes his English norms and engines out into the seas.[12] Although our contributors generally share this understanding of the conceptual and behavioral source of the trouble, they perform but also move beyond historical diagnosis and condemnation. They consider how the authors and artists they study provide alternative models for dwelling in the world we have made, and are making. Many of these chapters – like Scott Edwards's journey – are thus surprisingly hopeful, tracing epistemological habits, practices of community, and paradigms of resilience forged within the trouble itself. And for us, as editors, some of the hopefulness comes from the critical methodologies of – and the methodological surprises in – the chapters themselves.

Our contributors are unafraid to tackle the challenges of the present – which are also the challenges of America's ongoing histories – head-on; at the same time, they trust that ethical, efficacious responses to these challenges may be necessarily indirect. After taking stock of the sheer scale, depth, and spread of the trouble that unequally confronts us, they often place their faith in small things: in early American naturalists' attention to insects too miniscule to be seen individually, or in a single word hovering on a contemporary poet's page. In the face of challenges whose urgency often encourages people to focus on the present, or set their sights on the solutions and catastrophes that the future might yet bring, the Companion's contributors often turn their attention to the past: to historical genres, to eighteenth- and nineteenth-century habits of thought, to events that, while nominally "over," continue to wield their effects today. And, while never underestimating the power of direct action, they model alternate forms of ethical engagement, whether poking fun at the most serious problems or lingering in library archives as part of the project of restoring the environments and communities outside. Indeed, such faith in indirection may be as much a part of what makes this volume "literary" as is the training of its contributors or the object(s) of study at its core.

The collection unfolds in three parts: Environmental Histories; Environmental Genres and Media; and Environmental Spaces, Environmental Methods. The opening section turns to the plural histories of American environmental literature, so as both to describe forms of ecological engagement exemplified in eighteenth- and nineteenth-century texts and to offer us a present rendered unfamiliar via its uncanny intimacies with the past. Whereas the first three chapters in this section analyze the contemporary relevance (and persistence) of particular historical periods and texts, its final two pieces track key environmental paradigms – extinction and pastoral, respectively – across a sweeping historical scope.

Christoph Irmscher's "Scenes of Human Diminishment in Early American Natural History" reads work by William Bartram, John James Audubon, and Susan Fenimore Cooper, identifying "a strand of early American natural history writing that challenges [human] exceptionalism" by shrinking the observer and enlarging the natural world. The resulting ethical implications are startling, both within an early American context which often looked to nature for reassuring lessons about human experience, and in the context of the contemporary environmental movement, which often renders the planet familiar/familial (think "Mother Earth") and encourages stewardship predicated on empathy, recognition, and love. By modeling the limits of human understanding and human power,

Irmscher suggests, early American natural historians can train us in humility and "critical self-consciousness," helping us learn to "withhold our power to dominate" and perceive the world anew.

In "Slavery and the Anthropocene," Paul Outka argues for placing US chattel slavery at the center of how we comprehend the Anthropocene. By analyzing how the institution of slavery "naturalized the absolute dominance of those considered fully human over whatever they considered natural," he demonstrates both how "racial and environmental politics [are] inseparable" and how the very ability to assume a categorical distinction between natural and human history is a marker of whiteness, and a tool of white supremacy. Through readings of slave narratives by Frederick Douglass and Harriet Jacobs, he not only traces how the ideological relationship between humanity and nature was foundational to the brutal power dynamics of slavery, but also traces the contemporary ethical implications of this fact, demonstrating how many of the conventionalities of Anthropocene discourse become untenable when we reckon thoroughly with chattel slavery.

Sarah Ensor's "(In)conceivable Futures: Henry David Thoreau and Reproduction's Queer Ecology" refracts contemporary environmentalism's preoccupation with reproductive futurity – a topic that appears repeatedly in this collection – through Henry David Thoreau's engagement with nurse insects and trees in his journals. Arguing that Thoreau's complex, multispecies understanding of reproduction distinguishes him from both twenty-first-century environmentalists, whose rhetoric often relies on normative logics of reproductivity, and queer theorists, who often critique such logics, Ensor theorizes an environmental ethic informed by the extant queerness of reproduction itself. In contrast to the organization "Conceivable Future," which helps women decide whether to have children in a time of climate catastrophe, Ensor's reading of Thoreau offers possibilities for solidarity and social change that customary definitions of reproduction have rendered inconceivable.

In "Narrating Animal Extinction from the Pleistocene to the Anthropocene," Timothy Sweet uses three case studies – of the mammoth, the passenger pigeon, and the monarch butterfly – to track extinctions linked to Pleistocene and post-Columbian colonizations. Engaging a range of cultural objects – among them, Thomas Jefferson's *Notes on the State of Virginia*, artist Maya Lin's multimedia project *What Is Missing?*, Penobscot historian Joseph Nicolar's *Life and Traditions of the Red Man*, and Donna Haraway's "The Camille Stories" – Sweet historicizes the complex relationship between Indigenous life and species death, reads the colonial violence of North American history via animal extinction (and vice versa), and tracks not only elegiac responses to species loss but also their alternatives. Ultimately, he demonstrates that even in the global context of the Anthropocene, North America remains "a critical theater for understanding extinctions, ... not least because here we often find narratives from two pulses of colonization in dialog."

Wai Chee Dimock's "Pastoral Reborn in the Anthropocene: Henry David Thoreau to Kyle Powys Whyte" responds to contemporary crisis via historical genre analysis, offering pastoral as a "poetry of desperation" (William Empson's phrase) that has achieved persistence precisely through its attention to loss. By reading scholars and practitioners of pastoral from the seventeenth century to the present, and engaging Thoreau's "Indian books" alongside contemporary Indigenous cultural production, she identifies a version of pastoral for the twenty-first century: "an indigenous pastoral, not a hide-bound genre but a crisis-responsive mode, intimate with the forces of catastrophe and able to project hope out of the company it keeps." In finding such "pastoral reborn" – exemplified by the work of Indigenous artists and activists – in music and live performances, in political campaigns and educational programs, in resistance to the Dakota Access Pipeline and the work of academic philosophy, she offers us a genre reimagined, one brimming with "sights, sounds, and tastes" and political promise alike.

The second section of the volume further expands the volume's range of genres and media – turning to petrofiction, cli-fi, metafiction, poetry, and photography, as well as activist practices, cookbooks, and blogs – in order to trace the many shapes of American environmental literature. Offering both keen rereadings of texts already within the environmental canon and ecocritical readings of texts often considered beyond the purview of environmental thought, our contributors not only expand our sense of what is germane to the field but also blur the boundaries between environmental literature and environmental criticism, insisting upon the self-reflexivity and theoretical power of literary and cultural objects themselves.

Lingering over the references to driving, automobiles, and oil that famously suffuse *The Great Gatsby*, Harilaos Stecopoulos's "The Heat of Modernity: *The Great Gatsby* as Petrofiction" not only manages to give a familiar book back to us in new terms, but also alters our understanding of petrofiction itself. Indeed, through close readings of *Gatsby* and its historical context (specifically the Teapot Dome Scandal of 1921–1923), Stecopoulos insists that "resource capitalism can incite an aesthetic vision [and] a social critique," and demonstrates the extent to which the novel "engages with petroculture at the level of character." For Stecopoulos, oil, far from simply an object appearing in the text, is a discourse, a relational mode, a way of "comprehend[ing] ... characters' relationship to the possibilities and dangers of twentieth-century life." Under his critical gaze, oil becomes a resource not only for the exploitative structures of extractive capitalism but also for the ethical practice of literary criticism itself.

Min Hyoung Song's "Children in Transit/Children in Peril: The Contemporary US Novel in a Time of Climate Crisis" takes the (real and figural) Child as a site at which to examine the relationship among migration, race, futurity, and the environment in contemporary fiction. Song focuses on two post-apocalyptic novels, Cormac McCarthy's *The Road* and Métis writer Cherie Dimaline's *The Marrow Thieves*, demonstrating how both works – for all of their important differences – throw the figural Child into a state of crisis. Song finds in *The Marrow Thieves* characters who, in being excluded from the normative future, focus on caring in the present; he finds in *The Road* language that draws readers outside their "ordinary notions of time," and insists upon a common "now" as the realm in which meaning is made. Indeed, amid its attention to displacement, the chief contribution of Song's chapter might be to our understanding of the temporality of care, which, if we heed his readings, involves less protecting the planet for future generations than trusting the transformative power of "bonds of love in the here and now."

Richard Crownshaw picks up on Song's interest in the Child in "Meta-Critical Climate Change Fiction: Claire Vaye Watkins's *Gold Fame Citrus*," this time putting reproductive futurism in conversation with questions of nonhuman agency and scale. Making a case that Watkins's novel is as theoretically informed as it is self-reflexive, Crownshaw argues that we read it as a form of meta-critical cli-fi, engaged with not only the socioenvironmental challenges of our present but also the ways in which critical theory tends to respond to them. In readings that recall Song's engagement with the racialization of childhood and Stecopoulos's interest in extractivism and the gendered body, Crownshaw demonstrates how Watkins's attention to the "histories of colonialism, settlement, and expansion" – as inscribed both in the land and on the bodies that inhabit them – resists the abstracting, dehistoricizing tendencies of some Anthropocene discourse.

Nicole Seymour's "*Junk* Food for Thought: Decolonizing Diets in Tommy Pico's Poetry" lingers with the politics of embodiment, reading the queer Kumeyaay poet Pico's collection *Junk* as a complex engagement with the "deep intersectionalities of eating" and demonstrating how, for Pico, food is "a source of comfort, ... a source of shame, ... an indicator of settler colonial trauma – and a related, explicit engagement with queer sexuality." As the juxtaposition of comfort and shame begins to indicate, Seymour lingers over the critical use to which Pico puts his ambivalence; throughout, Seymour traces Pico's simultaneously serious and satiric response to the interrelated problems of food insecurity, queer body image, Indigenous dispossession, and environmental degradation. Together, poet and critic perform an ecocriticism willing to veer from the earnestness so long at its core.

In "Tender Woods: Looking for the Black Outdoors with Dawoud Bey," Susan Scott Parrish traces the emergence of "a Black environmental imaginary" (Carolyn Finney's term) simultaneously attentive and irreducible to the legacies of harm of settler colonialism, chattel slavery/the plantation, and environmental injustice. She demonstrates how photographer Bey tinkers with specific visual technologies – as well as the technology of vision itself – in order to alter his audience's understanding of racialized bodies, natural spaces, and the historical and ideological relationship between the two. Attuning our attention to the ethics of tenderness – as noun and verb and adjective, as site of vulnerability and source of mutual aid, as a practice of vision and care, as "the act of offering," as the soreness after a blow – Parrish offers a heuristic for understanding both the histories and the many possible futures of Black environmentality.

The contributors in the final part of the volume, Environmental Spaces, Environmental Methods, find the ground for environmental criticism in a wide range of locations, including the city, the "outdoors," public lands, the refuge, the internment camp, the settler nation, the family, the archive, the island, the desiring body, and the queer home. In the process, they "trouble" not only the conventional sense of where the environment is but also ecocriticism's historical interest in locality itself. For our authors turn as often to transit as to stasis – not only because, as Song reminded us, we live in a time increasingly populated by climate refugees, but also because the history of American place has always been the history of Indigenous displacement and dispossession. Placemaking, in other words, can never be separated from the forcible unmaking of communities. In order to inhabit this dialectic, and to understand its implications for environmental thought, these chapters engage methods drawn from literary studies, political ecology, Indigenous studies, Black feminism, Latinx studies, Asian American studies, comparative race studies, and queer theory. Altering the "what" and "where" and "who" of environmental criticism, they insist, has significant implications for its "how" – and vice versa.

Mika Kennedy's "Japanese American Incarceration and the Turn to Earth: Looking for a Man Named Komako in *Bad Day at Black Rock*" demonstrates how John Sturges's 1955 (post)western makes Japanese incarceration "physically and hauntingly manifest ... even in the absence of human forms" and how "the film's environment, its landscape, speaks what the script will not." By "follow[ing] the water" and reading the rocks, and by intertwining approaches from ecocriticism and comparative race studies, Kennedy dilates her attention well beyond the film's single "bad day," demonstrating the connected histories of Japanese internment, Indigenous dispossession, and water wars in the "larger and longer" frontier West. The resulting reading reveals how "the warp of the Western and the weft of the incarceration film," far from being an unlikely intersection, are bound together in the "mythic afterlives of the frontier."

Ursula Heise's "Urban Narrative and the Futures of Biodiversity" takes us to the city – which, as she details, has long "pose[d] a problem for the American environmental imagination," but is fast characterizing our planetary future. Reading the status of the urban in environmental thought over the past three decades, she traces a shift from "nature in the city" to "nature for the city" to "cities as nature." She then considers the literary critical implications of such a transition, focusing primarily on the emergence of the urban interspecies narrative across several templates. Asking how such narratives make room for "new urban ecologies and communities, even if they are ecologies of migration, displacement, and uprootedness," Heise echoes Dimock's interest in the evolution of genre and anticipates Matt Hooley's interest in the literary and political stakes of displacement.

Sarah D. Wald's "Leisure over Labor: Latino Outdoors and the Production of a Latinx Outdoor Recreation Identity" returns us to a type of space – public lands – and a set of practices – outdoor recreation – that may feel like the familiar domain of ecocriticism, but does so in order to analyze the Latinx community's evolving claims to outdoor belonging. Her primary object of attention is the work of Latino Outdoors, an organization which "responds to the historical and ongoing exclusion of people of color from outdoor recreation and the conservation movement, challenging the racial construction of nature, the environment, wilderness, and public lands as white space." Ultimately, she demonstrates how contemporary Latinx recreationists and activists are propelling a shift from a Latino outdoor identity predicated on labor to one predicated on outdoor recreation, leisure, and enjoyment.

Hooley's "Sanctuary: Literature and the Colonial Politics of Protection" analyzes the violence undergirding colonial orders of protection and the sanctuary logics that often accompany them. At the heart of his argument is what he deems the "sanctuary interval," a spatiotemporal form that, far from being external to colonial power, is supplemental to it, both demonstrating and facilitating its recurrence. Seeking an alternative to such a model, Hooley asks how we can "imagine and practice care beyond the colonial politics of protection" – and, relatedly, what literature can "provide at the end of international orders of protection, other than their reenactment." He finds an answer to both questions in the work of Inupiaq poet Joan Naviyuk Kane, who refuses colonial logics of protection, passage, and recovery in favor of an intentional practice of waiting and forms of "immeasurable and impermanent intimacy."

The volume concludes with Angela Hume's "The Queer Restoration Poetics of Audre Lorde," whose argument interweaves the collection's over-arching interests in history, genre, space, and method. Focusing on Lorde's attention to the intersections among human illness, environmental damage, and social power, especially in the journals that she kept in the wake of Hurricane Hugo, Hume offers an account of the environmental justice movement routed through Black feminism and models a historical approach to "the emergence and evolution of environmental justice in literature." Moving among the space of the archive, the island (St. Croix), the queer home, the body, and the page, Hume theorizes what she deems Lorde's queer restoration poetics. Queer restoration – unlike more familiar ecological models of resilience or resurgence – does not "necessarily entail a lively rebounding, robustness, or increase" but rather "entails looking backward in order to heal and go forward, despite uncertainty."

It is not despite, but precisely because of, its attention to irrevocable damage that Hume's work (like Lorde's) is so galvanizing. Amid the intersecting public health – and environmental – crises of a global pandemic and structural racism, we offer this volume as a backward (and sideways) glance that may enable us to "go forward, despite uncertainty." Our hope is that, amid the many forms of harm that constitute our present, these chapters can help readers to acknowledge others' (and our own) tenderness (Parrish), to meet each other in the complex here and now (Song), to remain with possibility and loss (Hooley), to laugh as we cry (Seymour), to practice queer restoration (Hume), to build a future that, rather than reproducing the injustices of the present, realizes the ethical possibilities that too often remain inconceivable (Ensor) within it.

Note on the text

In order to respect the fact that the conversation about when to capitalize key terms related to race, ethnicity, and indigeneity is ongoing, unsettled, and often site-specific, we have allowed our authors to make their own decisions about these matters rather than imposing a set style on the volume as a whole. There is thus consistency of capitalization within chapters, but variation across them.

PART I

Environmental Histories

CHAPTER I

Scenes of Human Diminishment in Early American Natural History

Christoph Irmscher

In *Nature* (1836), the foundational text for the movement that would later come to be known as Transcendentalism, Ralph Waldo Emerson wrote:

> The instincts of the ant are very unimportant considered as the ant's; but the moment a ray of relation is seen to extend from it to man, and the little drudge is seen to be a monitor, a little body with a mighty heart, then all its habits, even that said to be recently observed, that it never sleeps, become sublime.[1]

Emerson was uncomfortable around animals, even if they were household pets. His daughter Edith reports that once, when she had left her pet parrot outside during a thunderstorm and the bird wanted to get in, her father, realizing that there was no one else to help, reluctantly went out and saved the frightened creature. When Edith returned from wherever she had gone, he reprimanded her: "Your green cat [*sic*] was much troubled by the storm . . . I offered her her cage, and she stepped into it with gratitude."[2]

No wonder that the ant receives even more condescension from Emerson. Viewed by itself, the tiny insect doesn't amount to much, a fragile little body, easily ignored or destroyed, driven by "very unimportant" instincts. Once we relate it to our own world, though, these same instincts suddenly become important, and "the little drudge" becomes a monitor, that is, a kind of mirror, reflecting what is best in us: our ability to work hard, even to go without sleep if needed.[3] Once we marry it to human history, and only then, natural history makes sense. As a former minister, Emerson would have been familiar with Proverbs 6: 6–8: "Go to the ant, thou sluggard; consider her ways, and be wise: Which having no guide, overseer, or ruler, provideth her meat in the summer, and gathereth her food in the harvest." But it seems that he is turning that advice around, telling the ant to go to man if it wants to be wise. In fact, the reader gets the feeling that there is more than a little irony behind Emerson's elevation of that "little drudge," with "*all* its habits" (my emphasis), to sudden, undeserved sublimity. Let us anthropomorphize if we must, he seems to be saying, but let us also remember that it's just a metaphor, and metaphors are not made by ants but by humans.[4]

In this chapter, I am interested in a strand of early American natural history writing that challenges such human exceptionalism, which was the norm in much of nineteenth-century science until the publication of Charles Darwin's *On the Origin of Species* (1859) and even after that. My focus will be on moments in which comfortable anthromorphisms break down, the direction of the "ray of relation" is disturbed, reversed, or ruptured, and nonhuman living beings are recognized as inhabiting a world of their own, not because they lack something humans have ("mechanomorphism," in Greg Garrard's typology) or because they are – the rarer option – considered superior to us (Garrard's "allomorphism").[5]

Arguably, even the most categorical rejection of anthropomorphic thinking takes place within the general framework of the human need to make sense of the world. Current discussions of the Anthropocene acknowledge, despite lingering disagreements over when it all began, the irreducible, ubiquitous, and irreversible impact of human actions on the planet.[6] "We live," Alfred Russel Wallace, the co-discoverer of evolution, had observed as early as 1876, "in a zoologically impoverished world, from which all the hugest, and fiercest, and strangest forms have recently disappeared."[7] My examples, drawn from the work of William Bartram (1739–1823), John James Audubon (1785–1851), and Susan Fenimore Cooper (1813–1894), offer an important, if perhaps ultimately futile, corrective to the trend identified by Wallace. Shrinking the human observer as they enlarge the natural world, imagining human diminishment amid scenes of natural wonder, they also imagine, pace Emerson, human history as firmly circumscribed by natural history and not the other way around.[8] Charlotte Porter and Thomas Hallock, among others, have shown that natural history provided a forum for outsiders such as the failed indigo farmer William Bartram, the Haitian-born French immigrant John James Audubon, and the self-taught nature enthusiast Susan Fenimore Cooper to raise questions about the expansionist ambitions of the early American republic.[9] But they did more than that: this chapter argues that, in asking such questions, early American naturalists adopted an epistemological model significantly different from academic natural history, with its insistence on the centrality of the human point of view as it had been imported from Europe.[10]

***

On July 8, 1851, Thomas Carlyle wrote to Ralph Waldo Emerson, "Do you know *Bartram's Travels*? This is of the Seventies or so; treats of *Florida* chiefly, has a wondrous kind of floundering eloquence in it; and has grown immeasurably *old*."[11] Carlyle wasn't right about the publication date or the geographical range of Bartram's book, but his characterization of Bartram's eloquence still rings true today. There is no evidence that Emerson took the bait and read what the literary historian William Hedges would later call "the most astounding verbal artifact of the early republic."[12] When *Travels*, or, to quote the complete title, *Travels through North and South Carolina, East & West Florida, the Cherokee Country, the Extensive Territories of the Muscogulges or Creek Confederacy, the Country of the Chactaws*, appeared in 1791, it defied easy categorizations. The book was based on the four years Bartram had spent traveling through North Carolina, Georgia, Florida, and Louisiana, through swamps, prairies, and subtropical forests, paddling across lakes, hiking along coastlines and river banks, fighting off water-belching alligators and interacting with deadly rattlesnakes (he did "dispatch" one of them but only reluctantly so, insisting that they were "magnanimous" creatures and would cause no injury unless attacked). But the finished book, weighed down by the sheer mass of exuberant paeans to the beauties of southern nature, stuffed with incantatory lists of plants and animals as well as admiring descriptions of encounters with members of the Creek, Choctaw, and Cherokee nations, far exceeded the genre of the travel report. Billy Bartram's talents as a draftsman had long been known – that is why the wealthy British plant enthusiast John Fothergill had agreed to sponsor his southern sojourn in the first place – but with *Travels* he had emerged as an American writer of the first order.

Bartram's remarkable eye for detail is particularly evident when he turns his attention to the smallest things in nature, such as the "ephemera" or mayflies (likely *Hexagenia orlando*) he noticed along the banks of the lower St. Johns River in East Florida in 1774. As he recalls it, the scene has a self-consciously staged quality, but the irony of the set-up is evident from the beginning. For what is Bartram – or the persona he has created for the purposes of this narrative – watching from his convenient vantage point on the shore? Animals so tiny that they can barely be seen, except in bulk. As Bartram describes them, the mayflies, appearing in a never-ending stream, emerge in the morning "from the shallow water near shore," taking flight immediately or, more commonly, creeping up the grass along the shore, "where remaining for a short time, as they acquired sufficient strength, they took their flight also, following their kindred to the main land."[13] And then Bartram doesn't really see them anymore. In the evening, though, he returns to appreciate what he calls "the closing scene of the short-lived

Ephemera."[14] He has anticipated that scene before, those "clouds of innumerable millions" of little flies, "swarming and wantoning in the still air,"[15] the water of the river churning with the agitated bodies of fish and frogs straining to catch them as they are about to land. But now, as he sits down in the shade of magnificent live oaks, lush magnolias, and sweet-smelling orange trees, the spectacle acquires new intensity for him and, presumably, for the reader, as we are invited to sit down beside him. There's even a kind of overture, as in a film score written to accompany a nature documentary: the "feathered songsters" in the trees gradually cease their music, retiring for the night. Now cue the final act, in which the mayflies have sex and die.

Though this is not, of course, how Bartram puts it. "As if insensible to their danger, gay and tranquil each meets its beloved mate, . . . inimitably bedecked in their new nuptial robes, . . . bounding and fluttering on the odoriferous air."[16] The almost comically humanizing language wears its inappropriateness on its sleeve, as it were. After all, Bartram is talking about insects here, about behavior he cannot really see, as he readily admits ("what eye can trace them"), thus reminding the reader, in passing, of the unbridgeable distance between the observer and his subject. When the mayflies die (the females after depositing their eggs in the river), their entire winged life has lasted barely a day. In the primordial, oozy slime of the riverbed, enveloped in scum and mud, the eggs hatch; over the coming months, the nymphs, "caviar to all the other inhabitants of the stream," as a contemporary fishing guide remarks, fight to stay until they're ready to emerge and the whole cycle begins again.[17]

The mayfly episode is most commonly read as a memento mori, illustrating, through the analogy of insect life, the vanity of all human aspirations, or, put more positively, as an encouragement, since our time is short, to "seize the day" and to appreciate, even in that short amount of time we're given, the glory of God's works. Let us contemplate the ephemeral mayflies, he admonishes the reader, ever so gently wagging his finger, "and communicate to each other the reflections which so singular an exhibition might rationally suggest to an inquisitive mind."[18] The latter remark especially appears to have been intended as a counterpoint to the effusive poetry of other parts. In its studied, almost boring vacuousness, Bartram's interjection is an example – one of several similar ones inserted, at strategically important points, into the book – of Bartram delivering what his contemporaries would have expected him to say: a reminder that one should never look at nature without deriving some uplifting lesson from it. Scholars have, for the most part, been content to follow Bartram's prompt, virtually ignoring the exciting double-voicedness of his writing.[19] "In the life cycle of these flies," writes Larry Clarke, "Bartram finds a moral lesson on the transience of life's pleasures."[20] Matthew Wynn Silvis similarly argues that, in following the brief course of the mayfly's life cycle, Bartram wanted to impart to us a vision of a holistic world, one in which everything is interconnected and the mayfly and the man exist to shed light on each other.[21] One particularly creative reading sees in the precariousness of the mayflies' existence a comforting reminder to Bartram himself that the dangers facing the solitary traveler in the wilderness – a memorable example is the napping Bartram's hair's-breadth escape from an alligator's jaws[22] – are nothing compared to the troubles experienced by the mayfly.[23]

Yet there are enough indications in the mayfly episode that such readings, in which the flies are interesting only in terms of how they relate to the human world, fall short. There is the swampy riverbed from which they emerge and to which at least their eggs return, a troubling hint of dark, swampy, maternal fecundity, the world of slimy things, as S.T. Coleridge would later describe it.[24] There's the one and only purpose of the mayfly's existence, to have sex (with "pleasure and enjoyment"!) and to thus propagate the species, a somewhat unexpected reminder coming from the childless bachelor Bartram. And, finally, there's the sheer mind-boggling mass of flies (creating a powerful contrast with Bartram the solitary wanderer and observer), "a number greater than the whole race of mankind that have ever existed since the creation."[25] And that assessment, mind you, pertains only to what Bartram had witnessed in that small spot on the St. Johns River, which, as he points out, with a wonderful rhetorical flourish that would have done Thoreau proud, in the context of all the rivers on the North American continent is "but a brook or rivulet."[26]

And now the analogy that the reader has been led to believe this passage proposes becomes wobbly indeed. Mayflies are, Bartram writes, in "frame and organization ... equally wonderful, more delicate, and perhaps as complicated as ... the most perfect human being."[27] *Equally, more, as, the most.* Bartram's characterization, read properly, is subversive indeed: if the average mayfly is as complex as "the most perfect human being," doesn't this suggest, too, that the average human being is less complex than the average mayfly?

In the final paragraph of the mayflies episode, Bartram destroys whatever has remained of the lesson toward which he has dutifully gestured throughout this section. As should have been clear from the beginning, these little creatures are as different from us as can be. What indeed could we have in common with tiny organisms that spend the majority of their lives as an "ugly grub," buried in the mud, popping up only to snatch some food?[28] In Bartram's eye, such unpleasant details, included to make the reader take a step back from the scene, do not diminish these insects. Instead, they make the pleasure-loving mayfly's existence doubly remarkable: wonderful, mysterious, a brief flash of pleasure emanating from a dark, oozy background. If there's anything these tiny creatures *can* teach us, it's our failure to understand them properly. Elsewhere in *Travels* Bartram blames a deeply human tendency to feel superior to the world around us for the decline of the human species: if Indian tribes "make war against, kill, and destroy" each other, this is no different from what "all other nations of mankind" practice, namely "the ambition of exhibiting to their fellows a superior character of personal and national valour, and thereby immortalizing themselves, by transmitting their names with honour and lustre to posterity; or revenge of their enemy, for public or personal insults; or, lastly, to extend the borders and boundaries of their territories."[29] Behold the mayfly then, wonderfully formed, perfectly adapted to the world it inhabits, making no wars on anyone, living, as far as any observer who is not a mayfly can tell, for a brief moment of intense pleasure, but living that moment in "peace, love, and joy": a dream, no doubt, but one – again, as far as human observers can tell – preferable to the fret and constant worry of human existence.

***

William Bartram's *Travels* had a considerable influence on both literary and natural history. While his fantastical descriptions of lush southern landscapes and lagoons alive with shimmering fish and roaring alligators have inspired poets from Coleridge to W.S. Merwin, his lists of birds, the most complete inventory then available, jumpstarted American ornithology and inspired America's first professional observer of birds, Alexander Wilson (1766–1813), whom Bartram mentored. And even though Wilson's competitor and successor John James Audubon, the creator of the magnificent plates collected in *The Birds of America* (1827–1838), rejected both Bartram's "*flowery sayings*" and what he saw as Wilson's many inaccuracies, his own work would hardly have been possible without Bartram's efforts.[30]

In addition to the massive *The Birds of America* and the less ambitious sequel on mammals, *Viviparous Quadrupeds of North America* (1845–1848), finished by Audubon's sons and his friend John Bachman, Audubon père also produced more than 3,000 pages of essays, published as *Ornithological*

Biography (1831–1839), the most comprehensive account of American bird behavior ever attempted and soon to be one of the primary reference sources for Darwin's *The Descent of Man* (1871). Audubon's prose, revised into literary respectability by his collaborator, William McGillivray, is often hardly less flowery than Bartram's, and he further resembles his predecessor in the close attention he pays to the role of the human observer. Consider the following passage in his essay on the ruby-throated hummingbird, published in 1831. Unlike Bartram, Audubon does not offer the reader a ringside seat in his visual theater but invites her to recreate, in her imagination, what only he has seen directly:

> Could you, kind reader, cast a momentary glance on the nest of the Humming Bird, and see, as I have seen, the newly hatched pair of young, little larger than humble-bees, naked, blind, and so feeble as scarcely to be able to raise their little bill to receive food from the parents; and could you see those parents, full of anxiety and fear, passing and repassing within a few inches of your face, alighting on a twig not more than a yard from your body, waiting the result of your unwelcome visit in a state of the utmost despair, – you could not fail to be impressed with the deepest pangs which parental affection feels on the unexpected death of a cherished child. Then how pleasing it is, on your leaving the spot, to see the returning hope of the parents, when, after examining the nest, they find their nurslings untouched! You might then judge how pleasing it is to a mother of another kind, to hear the physician who has attended her sick child assure her that the crisis is over, and that her babe is saved.[31]

The visual drama involving author and reader begins as a hypothetical event: "could you . . . cast"; "[could you] see, as I have seen." And this is perhaps as it ought to be: Audubon is asking the reader to imagine, from the comfort of her home, something incomparably small (though not quite as small as Bartram's mayflies): freshly hatched hummingbird babies, coming from an egg the size of a jellybean, are barely larger than a thumbnail. As Audubon's adds behavioral detail (the fact that the young hummingbirds can scarcely lift their beaks high enough to eat) and measurements ("within a few inches of your face"; "a twig not more than a yard from your body"), the imagined event becomes real, as does the anxiety of the parents at this "unwelcome" interruption of their domestic life. Emily Dickinson called the hummingbird's flight "a route of evanescence," a spectacle that is over before we know it has passed us, but Audubon places these elusive birds right before us, at eye level.[32]

The second-person pronoun, the rhetorical form of address so often employed by Audubon, creates a terrific sense of intimacy between author and reader, and the measurements he includes, with their suggestion of closeness, further reduce the distance between the actual observer (the author) and the potential observer (the reader). The encounter is not a happy one – our presence causes the birds pain and anxiety, and, as we keep looking on, anticipated disaster appears to turn into tragic loss: we see the parents lamenting the "unexpected death of a cherished child." Note that Audubon represents this emotion not as something we recognize because it is familiar to us from our own experience, but as if we had come across it for the first time among the hummingbirds: our reference point is the experience of animals, not of humans. This is a fiction, of course, but – to use a phrase by Wallace Stevens, master of the defamiliar-izing point of view – it is a "necessary" one.[33] And it is one that Audubon would continue to enforce.

As we quickly end our disruptive visit, driven out by our guilt about damage we haven't even done yet, the birds' palpable relief helps us understand or "judge" the delight we might feel when it is our turn and a doctor gives *us* good news about our children. This is a small but not unimportant reversal: as Audubon puts it here, it is only after we have witnessed the pain felt by an animal mother that we will be able to understand the relief felt by us – or a human mother ("a mother of another kind") – in a situation where *our* offspring is in danger.[34]

Now Audubon *had* experienced such a danger twice (and with tragic outcomes). He had lost two very young daughters, Rose when she was still a baby and Lucy at the age of two. Given such likely resonances, it seems strange for Audubon to have framed his story of a visit to the humming-birds' nest as leading to some sort of a lesson the birds can teach *us* about *our* behavior, rather than the other way around. Anthropomorphism is a tool intended to reduce the distance between humans and animals, in order to take the latter's strangeness away. In this passage, Audubon's use of "ornithomorphism" (if the coinage is permitted) doesn't serve the purpose of making the nonhuman world more comfortably familiar to us human beings; instead, it defamiliarizes emotions we think we all know (grief, death, concern about family) and locates their origin elsewhere, among the animals. Read carefully, the primary purpose of comparing the human-inflicted pain of the hummingbird parents to the "pangs" felt by a human mother who might lose, or has already lost, her child, is not to get us closer to the birds but, quite bluntly, to make us, after a few stolen glances, leave them alone.

Audubon's plates in *The Birds of America* also feature a world in which birds are the primary residents. Like his texts, they shimmer with his appreciation for the birds' outlandish beauty. But Audubon cared about his backgrounds, too, employing other artists to help him place his birds in appropriate habitats. Remarkably, quite a few of Audubon's compositions contain evidence of human presence and activity, ranging from the small woodcutter's cabin in the plate showing a Swainson's hawk (*The Birds of America*, plate 372) to the elaborate view of Charleston, South Carolina, in the plate featuring two long-billed curlews (painted by Audubon's assistant, the landscape painter George Lehman; *The Birds of America*, plate 231). Similarly, in the plate depicting two canvasbacks, the birds in the foreground frame the view of Baltimore in the distance, as if Audubon wanted to invite us, mockingly, to go see Baltimore from a duck's point of view (*The Birds of America*, plate 301, Figure 1.1). Audubon's compositions, as art historian Alan Braddock has pointed out, thus disrupt the humanistic convention of landscape aesthetics in which the environment is seen from a human perspective only.[35]

In *The Birds of America* and *Viviparous Quadrupeds of North America*, Audubon's miniaturized representations of the human presence ask us to

Figure 1.1 Robert Havell, Jr. after John James Audubon, *Canvas backed Duck*. Aquatint Engraving. 1833. *The Birds of America*, plate 301. Detail. Courtesy, Lilly Library

imagine a world in which we are bit players only: not the owners of the landscape, but trespassers. The snowy egrets of South Carolina, for example, greet the human intruder with dismissive silence, as Audubon notes in the essay accompanying the plate: "they rise silently on the wing, alight on the trees near, and remain there until you depart."[36] In Audubon's watercolor, painted in the early spring of 1832, George Lehman included, at far right, a small plantation house and, closer to the bird and partially obscured by a ridge, the diminutive figure of a hunter in a tricornered hat who is clutching a matchstick-sized gun – an ironic contrast with the glorious, white-feathered beauty of the magnificent egret in the foreground (*The Birds of America*, plate 242).

If that hunter wasn't intended to represent Audubon, there can be little doubt about the tiny figure on the left in Audubon's 1833 watercolor of the golden eagle, now held by the New-York Historical Society. With a dead young eagle strapped to his back, Audubon has painted himself moving down a log that has been put across a deep chasm. As the hunter is laboriously descending, steadying himself with what looks like a small pickaxe, the real subject of the painting, an enormous female golden eagle, is ascending, a bleeding white hare in her talons. Not much ingenuity is required to figure out the story this painting sets out to tell: a mother's efforts to feed her baby have been thwarted by human intervention. The contrast between the godlike bird dominating the watercolor (some scholars think Audubon was inspired by Jacques-Louis David's painting *Napoleon Crossing the Alps*, 1801) and the small, cradle-robbing human might have been too blatant for Audubon's engraver Robert Havell, Jr. He removed the figure from the plate, leaving in place the empty log, which now, with no one straddling it, looks rather irrelevant.[37]

Audubon's final self-portrait came in one of the last compositions he was able to complete, and it's a truly strange one: in plate 78 of the *Viviparous Quadrupeds* we see an emaciated black-tailed doe (a mule deer), hurt by a small through-and-through bullet that was badly aimed, staggering away from a miniaturized hunter in the field on the left. Blood is staining the doe's lips and trickling from a small wound on her side. Unlike the hunter in the image of the snowy egret, the hunter's rifle is not pointed; indeed, he looks curiously dissociated from the damage he has wreaked, displaced by the spectacle of the dying animal in the foreground. A closer look reveals the similarities between the incompetent hunter's face and the features of the aging, toothless, sharp-faced Audubon, as captured in Mathew Brady's daguerreotype made in 1847/48 (Cincinnati Art Museum).

Audubon, to be sure, was an excellent marksman himself, a "two-legged monster, armed with a gun," as he wearily characterized himself.[38] But by the early 1830s, he had also realized that humans like him, with their logging, farming, trapping, and hunting, were actively diminishing bird populations across the continent. It is no coincidence that in his art the puniest things in nature are men holding guns.

***

Like Audubon, Susan Fenimore Cooper was partial to hummingbirds, spending several seasons watching them in order to determine which flowers they prefer over others. Leisurely nature observations form the core of Cooper's *Rural Hours*, a carefully crafted, often lyrical natural history journal she published in 1850, which served as the unacknowledged model for Thoreau's *Walden* (1854). Cooper was an avid reader of the natural history writings of her predecessors. But where Bartram and Audubon had ranged far, she stayed close to home, in the village of Cooperstown, New York, which her ancestors had founded. Like Audubon, Cooper cast a jaundiced look at her contemporaries, their propensity for exploiting and destroying an environment they had never bothered to get to know properly in the first place. Walking around her hometown in January, it occurred to her that where buffalo, foxes, wolves, and rabbits had once roamed the wintry landscape, their killers now traveled in comfortable coaches, wrapped in the very furs that they had taken from the animals.[39]

Rural Hours is first and foremost a tribute to the importance of local knowledge. Cooper's slow-moving book is an almost subversive gesture, a thinly veiled critique of the paternalistic spirit that helped create the very place she writes about. Unlike Audubon, Cooper does not want to list and describe what no one else is likely to have seen. Instead, she offers her readers a long, protracted look at what is familiar or perhaps only seems familiar. An education of the senses, *Rural Hours* encourages readers to look around, teaching them where to look, how to look, and, especially, how to look critically.

One of Cooper's favorite subjects is human wastefulness, a theme she inherited from her father, the novelist James Fenimore Cooper. Recall, for instance, the poignant scene in *The Pioneers* (1823), where Cooper's protagonist, Natty Bumppo or "Leatherstocking," a hunter subsisting on the edge of the wilderness, shoots a passenger pigeon on the wing, thundering "use, but don't waste," in the direction of his fellow citizens, who have just participated in a gigantic mass slaughter of these birds, covering the ground with more bird bodies than they will ever be able to consume.[40] As it turns out, decades later the daughter's little universe is under an even greater threat as animal species disappear, forests burn, and plants are displaced by invasive species. In *Rural Hours*, Cooper's critique of careless extraction is focused specifically on the damage her neighbors inflict on trees, whose charred remains and ragged stumps serve as a constant reminder of the high price the land pays when humans decide to grow roots and uproot the trees around them.[41]

Stories of white settlement in America follow a familiar pattern: an alleged wilderness is turned into a garden, and some of these gardens become cities, and so on. Success often depends on the erasure of the past, a process that is never complete, as occasional visits to Cooperstown of raggedy bands of Haudenosaunee remind her. Yet things are different in the nonhuman universe of the forest, where, as Cooper has observed, young and old, the present and the past, coexist in mutually sustaining relationships. One tree's death leads to another tree's new life, a cycle disturbed only by human interference. Trees are "incredibly slow," writes forester Peter Wohlleben, "their childhood and youth last ten times as long as ours."[42] If Bartram was intrigued by the minimal lifetime of his mayfly, Cooper is fascinated by the maximal lifespan of forest trees that go on living even after they have fallen down. As Cooper sees it, the dead and dying trees of America, "shivered and broken by the winds," are the country's truest ruins, surpassing the monuments that dot the landscapes of Europe.

> Broken limbs and dead bodies of great trees lie scattered through the forests; there are spots where the winds seem to have battled with the woods – at every step one treads on fallen trunks, stretched in giant length upon the earth, this still clad in its armor of bark, that bare and mouldering, stained by green mildew, one a crumbling mass of fragments, while others, again, lie shrouded in beautiful mosses, long green hillocks marking the grave of trees slowly turning to dust.[43]

Cooper seems to revel in the language of decay as she, hiding behind the mask of impersonality ("one treads"), gingerly traverses this jungle of fallen tree bodies.

Yet on closer inspection, nothing does in fact decay here. In the enchanted world of the forest, the boundaries between life and death are fluid. In the end of trees lies their beginning: old trees take a long time dying so that young ones may flourish. They are

> frequently found growing upon these forest ruins; if a giant pine or oak has been levelled by some storm, the mass of matted roots and earth will stand

upright for years in the same position into which it was raised by the falling trunk, and occasionally a good-sized hemlock, or pine, or beech, is seen growing from the summit of the mass, which in itself is perhaps ten or twelve feet high.[44]

Here the living hold the dying in loving, life-sustaining embrace:

> We have found a stout tree of perhaps twenty years' growth, which has sprung from a chance seed, sown by the winds on the prostrate trunk of a fallen pine or chestnut, growing until its roots have stretched down the side of the mouldering log, and reached the earth on both sides, thus holding the crumbling skeleton firmly in its young embrace.[45]

The phrase "young embrace" is particularly evocative – here death does no one part. Some trees, a familiar part of the landscape, remain standing for decades even as they die; prostrate pines preserve their sap for up to fifty years.[46] What distinguishes this wild community of trees is, precisely, that it is *not* like ours, a point reiterated a few years ago, in Wohlleben's bestselling *The Hidden Life of Trees*. We might attempt to describe that community, but compared to the natural world's webs of interdependence, any single human language – especially one that relies on familiar terms such as life and death or, for that matter, family and kinship, young and old – remains woefully inadequate.[47]

"In wildness is the preservation of the world," Thoreau wrote in his posthumously published essay "Walking."[48] Note that Thoreau, like Cooper a devotee of forest trees, isn't talking about the preservation of *wildness* but about the preservation of the *world*, to which wildness, he thinks, provides the one and only gateway. If he is right, and current research confirms it, the planet appears to be in its last throes today. The fallen log in Audubon's representation of the Golden Eagle might serve as a poignant symbol for what has been happening to the world's wild spaces. Areas untouched by human industry or agriculture are important buffers against the effects of human interference on the environment: they sequester twice as much carbon as degraded landscapes, offer refuges for threatened species, and help stabilize local weather patterns. Yet only just 23 percent of such wild landscapes remain today worldwide. In the last twenty years alone, close to 10 percent of global wilderness, an area twice the size of Alaska, has vanished. That puts additional pressure on the wild landscapes that remain, among them the forests of North America, which so fascinated William Bartram, John James Audubon, and Susan Fenimore Cooper.[49] As their example shows, the key to wilderness preservation lies not just in policy measures, as crucial as they are. What needs to come first is a shift in how we think about what being wild and being in the wild means. For Bartram, Audubon, and Cooper, it meant confronting "the world we did not make," a phrase I have borrowed from William Cronon's iconic essay "The Trouble with Wilderness."[50] The point of such lessons in humility or, in the terms of this essay, in productive self-diminishment, would be a change in the way we think about this planet as a whole, about the humble tree in our backyard (one of Cronon's examples) as well as what remains of the rockland pines of Miami-Dade County, where the endangered Bartram's scrub-hairstreak butterfly, named after Billy Bartram's botanist father, still holds on. Crucial to such an endeavor is, as Bartram, Audubon, and Cooper knew and as William Cronon has reiterated with even more urgency today, "critical self-consciousness," a deliberate effort to "withhold our power to dominate." A project that would seem near impossible were it not for environmentally minded writers in the American grain who, for quite some time, have shown us what such a shift in perception would look like.

CHAPTER 2

Slavery and the Anthropocene

Paul Outka

While the current scientific consensus about the dire reality of anthropogenic climate change is, of course, overwhelming, that dire reality is still only getting started. Wherever you are, and however bad the weather has been recently, it's going to get considerably worse. Even if humanity stopped burning fossil fuels tomorrow – and we're burning more, not less – the carbon dioxide, methane, and other greenhouse gasses we've already released into the atmosphere would continue to warm the planet significantly for many decades. Temperatures would still increase, because that's what happens to the inside of greenhouses when they are in sunlight; the storms will inevitably be stronger, the oceans will rise higher. However bad it is now, in other words, it's still only the beginning of the end of the world as we know it.

That sense of looming, but not fully arrived, apocalypse marks our moment. Despite the profoundly problematic ambiguity of the references of "our" and "moment" – and an exploration of that problematic ambiguity is at the heart of the chapter that follows – the grim generality that unites us all is an ever-increasing precarity, even though all of us will by no means suffer equally or simultaneously. The very generality of climate change is embedded in the term "Anthropocene," a name for the era in the planet's history where *Homo sapiens* became a geological force, when the collective impact of our numbers, our violence, our agriculture, our technology, remade "nature" itself on a global scale. We are early in the Anthropocene, in the time between the times as it were, at once at the peak of our species' collective power, wealth, and technological advancement, while also facing an impending existential threat to the basic survival of human and nonhuman animals alike. Such a profoundly and uniquely contradictory time presents similarly profound experiential challenges; it's unusually difficult to live in a present that is so fundamentally affected by a sense of what has been lost, and what even greater losses are to come. How do we "think," for example, about what it means that *half* of nonhuman species are predicted to be extinct by 2100 largely as a result of human activity, a death rate between 1,000 and 10,000 times faster than normal?[1] That humans cause the death of more than 3.3 billion birds every year in the US, contributing to a loss of a third of the avian population since 1970?[2] That 190–630 million people currently live below the projected high tide lines of 2100?[3] That a three-foot rise in sea levels would flood 20 percent of Bangladesh and displace 30 million people, most of them desperately poor by Western standards?[4] Where will these people go, in a world that already can't seem to welcome a tenth as many refugees from Syria, Yemen, or Guatemala? As Donna Haraway has recently noted, it is both difficult and essential in the early Anthropocene that we learn to "stay with the trouble" of our moment, and avoid the temptations of a retreat into a revanchist nostalgia for a lost nature, a techno-utopian future, or the passive despair of apocalypticism:

> In urgent times, many of us are tempted to address trouble in terms of making an imagined future safe, of stopping something from happening that looms in the future, of clearing away the present and the past in order to make futures for coming generations. Staying with the trouble does not require such a relationship to times called the future. In fact, staying with the trouble requires learning to be truly present, not as a vanishing pivot between awful or edenic pasts and apocalyptic or salvific futures.[5]

How to represent the Anthropocene and its definitional confusion of space and time – and how hard it is to stay with the trouble – is one of the many nearly intractable problems it poses, not because there's *a* true and false way to talk about it, but because there are so *many* different true ways to talk about it.[6] To borrow from Walt Whitman, it is large, it contains multitudes.

Global descriptions of the climate emergency, and their concomitant emphasis on the disjunctive and representationally challenging quality of the present and looming future, also risk a particular danger: these descriptions can all too easily erase how race, culture, gender, economics, and the like have marked which groups of people bear the greatest historical responsibility for the (very profitable) carbon emissions that are central to the problem, and which groups will suffer soonest and most.[7] While there certainly is a consensus among climatologists about the dire effects of increasing the concentration of atmospheric carbon dioxide beyond 450 parts per million, that deep decarbonization of electrical production, transportation, and agriculture is vital to preserving Earth's habitability, and so forth, the fact that such scientific descriptions of global climate change are "true" doesn't make other descriptions of the causes, victims, and solutions necessarily less so. But it does tend to make those causes, victims, and solutions much less visible. Put another way, to view the Anthropocene from the global, species level is to view it from the top, to see it as an impending crises starting to unfold into a terrifying future. If, however, we emphasize the anxiety, fear, helplessness, and sense of diminution that the collapse of the human and natural produces, viewing it from the bottom as it were, from the ground-level experiences of individuals, localities, and communities, the Anthropocene opens more radically into individual, local, regional, historical, racial, and not just "species" history. When we start from this ground-level view, we find the essential *experience* of anthropogenic anxiety and trauma isn't something that only happened recently as an accidental byproduct of a rapacious global capitalist system, or that necessarily has its authoritative meaning in the observations of climate scientists. If, for example, we view the Anthropocene through the lens of US chattel slavery, what emerges is not only how anthropocenic anxiety and trauma predate the term and the era itself, but also how slavery and the Anthropocene are in fact coextensive, in a symbiotic relationship that we risk missing when we read from a broader, top-down view.

This chapter will argue for putting US chattel slavery – including both the suffering of enslaved people and the role of the "master" – and not just the steam engine or measurements of spikes in atmospheric carbon dioxide concentrations, at the center of how we understand the Anthropocene. I do so, in part, as a corrective to a tendency in contemporary theoretical work on the Anthropocene to stress the apocalyptic novelty of the problem, a focus on the immediate present and emerging future that, however understandable, nevertheless risks obscuring the profound historical embeddedness of our environmental crises in white supremacy and racial oppression. As Axelle Karera writes, the "apocalyptic sensibilities which have significantly monopolized Anthropocenean discourses are powerful in disavowing and erasing racial antagonisms,"[8] a disavowal that has, indeed, led some recent commentators, including Haraway and Mendieta, to use the term "Plantationocene."[9] The history of those "racial antagonisms" is in fact inextricably part of the Anthropocene now and in the future. Particularly in the US, white enslavers, and the very institution of slavery itself, naturalized the absolute dominance of those considered fully human over whatever they considered natural, a hierarchy that has made racial and environmental politics inseparable.

The fact that they are inseparable in fact doesn't mean that race and nature aren't often – too often – discussed in isolation from each other.[10]

Part of this difficulty is inevitable, reflecting the formative division in ecocriticism between seeing nature as a construction, one used to reify just about any ideological position under our sun or moon (aka *culture*), and recognizing nature as always, also, referring to something outside of the merely human, an extra-textual but not transcendent living materiality that includes a very wide range of nonhuman creatures whose senses and mentation construct radically different versions of the world (aka the *wild*). Those two senses of the word "nature" – as human construction, and as actual Other – have, for most of human history, been distinct. One central feature of the experience of living in the Anthropocene, however, is the accelerating breakdown of the distinction between the two, resulting in a kind of (at best) degraded pastoral, a space neither untouched by the human nor simply our creation, but some shifting and inextricable entanglement of human and nonhuman that is everywhere, that has become the world itself. The fact that that global collective impact of our species has been, in general, the often unwitting byproduct of a myriad of local struggles to survive, flourish, or dominate means that we are now immersed in an environment at once artificial – our accidental creation – and as inescapable as any version of nature ever was. The Anthropocene, in other words, is a nature that is both made and found.

The Anthropocene's breakdown of the spatial distinction between wild/nonhuman/"found" nature and the environments our species deliberately makes has become fundamental to its definition. To understand how this breakdown links in critical ways to the imbrication of slavery and the Anthropocene – and perhaps more importantly, how the history of slavery might intervene on contemporary understandings of climate change – I want first to turn briefly to Dipesh Chakrabarty's foundational essay, "The Climate of History: Four Theses,"[11] published in 2009 in *Critical Inquiry*. The essay was one of the first to bring the Anthropocene to widespread critical attention in the humanities. Chakrabarty's first thesis is that "Anthropogenic Explanations of Climate Change Spell the Collapse of the Age-Old Humanist Distinction between Natural History and Human History."[12] In his analysis, until the Industrial Revolution produced the spike in atmospheric carbon, "humanists" saw nature (to the extent they saw it at all) as a sort of context or setting for human experience. The history of nonhuman nature was categorically different from the history of humanity's individual and collective activity, a categorical difference that has started to melt along with the ice caps, with the realization that, in Chakrabarty's words, "the climate, and hence the overall environment, can sometimes reach a tipping point at which this slow and apparently timeless backdrop for human actions transforms itself with a speed that can only spell disaster for human beings."[13] Anthropogenic climate change makes humans not just individual "biological agents" capable of acting upon the natural world locally, but "geological agents" who have now "reached numbers and invented technologies that are on a scale large enough to have an impact on the planet itself ... to attribute to us a force on the same scale as that released at other times when there has been a mass extinction of species."[14]

The ability to assume a separation between human and natural history hasn't, however, historically been a universal "human" experience. Rather, the ability to assume such distinctions has in fact served as a fundamental mark of racial privilege, a mark definitional to the structure of white supremacy. Whiteness has historically constructed itself in part by controlling the relation between the two categories, asserting at once its natural dominance and at the same time its categorical difference from nature. Such an assertion was coupled with, and depended on, its inverse: that people of color were naturally inferior because they were supposedly closer to nature. Nowhere is the collapse of those histories more visible, personal, or traumatically intimate than in chattel slavery.

Something Akin to Freedom: Anti-Nature Writing and the Slave Narrative

As I have argued elsewhere, nineteenth-century autobiographical narratives written by enslaved people might be thought of as "anti-nature writing." Rather than tracing the (white) nature writer's story of coming to associate their identity with some aspect of the nonhuman natural, the slave narrative records the author's hard-fought struggle to differentiate herself or himself from the domesticated animality that formed the fundamental conceit of and justification for slavery. Like a sort of Turing Test[15] of humanity set in the degraded landscape of the antebellum South, books such as Harriet Jacobs's *Incidents in the Life of a Slave Girl* and Frederick Douglass's three autobiographies functioned, among many other things, as intrinsic "proof" that Jacobs and Douglass were literary, and therefore human, and not as Jacobs wrote, "no more in the sign of their masters than the cotton they plant, or the horses they tend."[16] The existence of their books and the linguistic facility they manifested were "evidence" of their authors' transcendence of "mere" embodiment, their fundamentally immaterial value, their absolute difference from nature.

Unlike the conflation of indigenous people and the so-called wilderness that broadly obtained in the imagination of the European settlers in the colonial and antebellum periods, the nonhuman natural that enslaved people were conflated with, and that they sought to differentiate themselves from in their narratives, was the degraded pastoral of the South, a landscape neither wild nor urban, but some admixture of the two. While those European colonists could point to their labor to justify (at least to themselves) their often violent appropriation of the "new world," in the antebellum South, that pastoral landscape was not clear-cut and planted by white people per se, but largely through the forced labor of millions of enslaved African Americans. Rather than that labor making black people owners of the land, as it would in the traditional Lockean understanding of property, this labor instead seemed to make the enslaved coextensive with the landscape. By placing the enslaved in the same ontological category as the horses, dogs, pigs, cows, soil, cotton plants, and other elements that made the Southern pastoral landscape pastoral, white supremacy could in turn be two places at once, both natural and separate from nature, at once grounded in the land and possessing it. To be white within slavery was to be identified with the southern landscape in a carefully controlled and largely unidirectional way; the idealized pastoral landscape represented and instantiated whiteness and its supposed natural superiority, but not vice versa. Enslaved people, conversely, and crucially I will argue for how we should think about the Anthropocene today, were *only* natural, prevented by the brutally enforced metaphor of domesticated animality from the second term of separation and ownership. Put (perhaps too) simply, within the racist eco-ideology of slavery, the Southern pastoral landscape signified whiteness, while black people both signified and materially underwrote the Southern pastoral.

By putting chattel slavery at the origins of the Anthropocene, we can see how the early distinction between humanity and nature that Chakrabarty names in his first thesis was (a) not universally enjoyed but historically linked to whiteness, and (b) was maintained in part by the labor of enslaved people whose condition was predicated on and "justified by" the collapse of that distinction in the racist construction of their identities. The experience of the Anthropocene was always already an impacted trauma at the heart of the slave system: the suffering, anxiety, and degradation fundamental to the lives of enslaved people presaged in an even more intense and personal form the traumatic collapse of the boundaries between nature and the human that is central to contemporary accounts of the Anthropocene. We can see that trauma not only on the planetary scale of global climate change, but in the huge distance covered in the short walk between the Quarters and the Big House.

Take, for a literal example of this walk, Douglass's description in his second narrative, *My Bondage and My Freedom*, of the moment in his childhood when he transitioned from a relatively innocent and untroubled relationship between his natural and human experiences, to the moment when his identity as a slave transforms both those registers:

> Down in a little valley, not far from grandmammy's cabin, stood Mr. Lee's mill, where the people came often in large numbers to get their corn ground. It was a watermill; and I never shall be able to tell the many things thought and felt, while I sat on the bank and watched that mill, and the turning of that ponderous wheel. The mill-pond, too, had its charms; and with my pinhook, and thread line, I could get nibbles, if I could catch no fish. But, in all my sports and plays, and in spite of them, there would, occasionally, come the painful foreboding that I was not long to remain there, and that I must soon be called away to the home of old master.
>
> I was A SLAVE – born a slave and though the fact was incomprehensible to me, it conveyed to my mind a sense of my entire dependence on the will of somebody I had never seen; and, from some cause or other, I had been made to fear this somebody above all else on earth. Born for another's benefit, as the firstling of the cabin flock I was soon to be selected as a meet offering to the fearful and inexorable demigod, whose huge image on so many occasions haunted my childhood's imagination.[17]

Douglass begins by describing a view of nature as both different from him and yet one with which he is allied in a salutary way, a place of contemplation, freedom, and self-creation – in short, a relationship with nature that resembles the distinction between the human and nature of Chakrabarty's first thesis. What intrudes on this happy exchange, of course, is his transformation from a natural human boy to a domesticated animal, the "firstling of the cabin flock," a transformation that is synonymous with his identity as a slave, the threat of being taken from human history and thrust utterly into a commodified natural history.

He goes on to describe the actual walk he took from the relatively idyllic natural setting of his grandmother's cabin to the plantation:

> Releasing dear grandmamma from carrying me, did not make me altogether independent of her, when we happened to pass through portions of the somber woods which lay between Tuckahoe and Wye river. She often found me increasing the energy of my grip, and holding her clothing, lest something should come out of the woods and eat me up. Several old logs and stumps imposed upon me, and got themselves taken for wild beasts. I could see their legs, eyes, and ears, or I could see something like eyes, legs, and ears,

till I got close enough to them to see that the eyes were knots, washed white
with rain, and the legs were broken limbs, and the ears, only ears owing to
the point from which they were seen. Thus early I learned that the point
from which a thing is viewed is of some importance.[18]

The bitterly ironic resonance of "thing" in the final sentence is Douglass's
way of putting nature, mastery, and slavery into a system of relationality
that is determinative of reality itself. Just as Douglass is subjected to the
violent reconnection of his identity from human to animal, nature itself
transforms from monster to nature to the all-too-real monstrosity of his
final destination. It's the *master*, after all, who is both in and out of the
nature game, not just the humanist in general; to be able to assume
a categorical distinction in one's experience of natural and human history
was to be "white" in the antebellum South, a racial identity that didn't in
fact, as it claimed to do, represent a universal human experience, nor speak
exclusively for the "humanist tradition." It's the *master* who can claim the
plantation as a landscape that naturalizes and instantiates his dominant
identity, while at the same time having that landscape serve as a "mere"
backdrop for his individual and collective history. And, conversely, the
collapse of those two histories is at the heart of what I have called slavery's
fundamental conceit, its brutal, insistent, and pervasive conflation of the
enslaved person with a domesticated animal.

    However brutal, insistent, and pervasive, that conflation was inevitably
incomplete and unstable, requiring constant violence to maintain. It
needed that violence because, first and most obviously, the enslaved person
often fought back physically – when Douglass beats Covey, for example, or
when Jacobs hides for years in her grandmother's crawlspace – and psy-
chologically – when Douglass defies his owner Hugh Auld to teach himself
to read, or when Jacobs chooses the "something akin to freedom" in
deciding to sleep with Sands and defy Flint.[19] Reading these iconic
examples of resistance in Douglass and Jacobs in the context of the
Anthropocene reveals how they are not only profoundly courageous
moments of opposition to the master's tyranny in general, but in each
case a particular reinscription of the distinction between the enslaved
person's identity and the natural world. Douglass, for example, says that
before their fight, Covey's brutal treatment "succeeded in breaking" him,
"tam[ing]" him, "transform[ing]" him from a "man" into a "brute," but
the fight "revived within [him] a sense of [his] own manhood," and
produced a resolution that "however long [he] might remain a slave in
form, the day had passed forever when [he] could be a slave in fact."[20] The

"tamed brute" aka "a slave in fact" has his "manhood revived" and with that revival, is no longer coextensive with the natural world.

Similarly, Douglass's heroic effort to teach himself to read as a boy comes in response to Auld's statement that "learning would *spoil* the best n***** in the world ... if you teach [him] to read, there would be no keeping him. It would forever unfit him to be a slave. He would at once become unmanageable, and of no value to his master."[21] Douglass hopes that reading will make him "spoiled," "unfit," "unmanageable" and "of no value to his master" – all descriptions that would apply to an animal. That parallel, in an exquisitely painful irony, comes all too true when the young boy discovers that his literacy has awakened him to a fuller recognition of the naturalized degradation of his enslavement, a knowledge so terrible that it occasionally makes him want to merge fully with the natural world:

> As I read and contemplated the subject, behold! that very discontentment which Master Hugh had predicted would follow my learning to read had come, to torment and sting my soul to unutterable anguish. As I writhed under it, I would at times feel that learning to read had been a curse rather than a blessing. It had given me a view of my wretched condition, without the remedy. It opened my eyes to the horrible pit, but to no ladder upon which to get out. In moments of agony, I envied my fellow-slaves for their stupidity. I have often wished myself a beast. I preferred the condition of the meanest reptile to my own. Anything, no matter what, to get rid of thinking![22]

This tormented desire to reconstitute himself as wholly part of natural, rather than human, history, is more than (or perhaps less than) a desire to die. Instead, in his despair Douglass fantasizes about the possibility of enslavement actually accomplishing what is at once its enabling premise – that black people are "naturally" nonhuman animals – and its brutal *modus operandi* that does whatever it can to traumatize enslaved people into the indifferent bestial reptilian stupidity that Douglass (cruelly, himself) imagines as the condition of his fellow slaves. But Douglass, of course, by the very nature of being a *Homo sapien*, can't "get rid of thinking," however much his knowledge and his suffering are made coextensive by slavery. Here we see how the blurring of the humanity/nature distinction that is definitional to the Anthropocene is historically grounded in enslavement, how the rapacious capitalization of enslaved bodies and the natural landscape reinforced and justified each other by, in part, being collapsed into each other. The Anthropocene's partial breakdown between human and natural history can be seen not only in the distinction between master and slave on the plantation (where the master retains that distinction, and the latter suffers from the collapse of it) but within the enslaved persons themselves, in the endlessly recorded moments of resistance and despair that fill the narratives.

Moreover, despite Auld's insistence and Douglass's claim here, much of the enslaved person's value to the master lay in that conflation between human and nature being only partially and strategically accomplished – retaining the "usefulness" of the slave's human intelligence, sexual desirability, and so forth when it suited, while at the same time denying that humanity by thrusting the enslaved back into the nonhuman natural. As I have said elsewhere, ideology is what we think when we don't want to think something through. In this sense, the enslaved person's particular value lay in the master's *not* resolving the question of whether black people were a part of human or natural history, but in keeping both contradictory definitions available simultaneously.

We can see the "usefulness" of the irresolution of the status of the enslaved person in painful clarity in the figure of the so-called "fancy" or "fancy girl." This offensive term referred to light-complexioned women purchased for sexual enslavement. Their "value" for white supremacy consisted precisely in the fancy's forced embodiment of that contradictory identification between human and natural: her sexual desirability required her humanity, while her sexual availability required her animality. This forced contradiction is captured in the grotesque fact that women of color were in that period legally unrapable; their race was synonymous with their "consent," no matter what they said, or cried out, or fled from.[23] That fantasized categorical consent was importantly distinct from mere indifference to the question of consent (though certainly many men were indifferent); prohibitions against bestiality were typically grounded in concerns about what it did to the human, not whether or not the animal wanted to have sex. There were no such prohibitions on sex with black women since desire was supposedly intrinsic to their "nature." None of this is meant to excuse white men from the crime of rape; they undoubtedly knew better. White supremacy provided a threadbare excuse for sexual violence and exploitation, a sort of ideological plausible deniability intended for an audience of other complicit white people, and that allowed those men to do what they wanted – force women to have sex with them – without having to name themselves explicitly as rapists with the unpleasant personal and social consequences that owning that action would presumably have entailed.

The way white supremacy viewed the fancy as human when the question was whether or not a white man wanted to have sex with her, but animal in the sense that whether she wanted to have sex was never a question for white supremacy – should make us ask how privilege functions in the contemporary wavering between human and natural histories that supposedly marks the Anthropocene. In this context, the strategic pivot between human and natural that the fancy embodied was structurally similar (though by no means morally comparable) to a broader strategic pivot between environmental affinity and exploitation that obtains to this day, especially though not exclusively for white people in the US, the sort of behavior that, for example, allows people to love their anthropomorphized pets deeply while being untroubled by the gruesome cruelty of factory farming, or to identify themselves with wild nature while supporting ecocidal lifestyles and politics. One central task for critics is to point out the histories in which we are embedded and the fantasies of innocence that such histories enabled, to call attention to the structures which privilege and mastery deploy to inoculate themselves against a recognition of their otherwise obvious culpability. The so-called "fancy's" forced exemplification of contradictory attitudes toward nature – as simultaneously a mirror of human status and yet utterly exploitable – demonstrates the profound linkages among racial, sexual, and environmental violence, and the strategies used to keep them hidden. The fantasy, in every case, is of attachment without responsibility, of an intimate relationship that can somehow coincide with one party having no agency or rights and the other imagining its rights are limitless.

Anthropocene/ Enslavement

The fact that the master/slave relation so precisely parallels the human/ nonhuman natural relationship is hardly coincidental. As a wide range of commentators have pointed out, almost all forms of systematic dehumanization involve comparing some group of humans to the nonhuman world – "they" are vermin, monkeys, insects, disease, sheep, dogs, whatever – and certainly American slavery's conceit of domesticated animality was emblematic in this. Such comparisons are premised on an abjected view of the nonhuman natural, in comparison with the master/human who is the entity defined as that-which-can-do-whatever-it-wants to the natural. This relationship makes racial and environmental violence part of a larger internally reinforcing system, one in which racism depends on a preexisting view of nonhuman nature as subservient and degraded, a view of the natural that is in turn reinforced by its association with racism.

I am not claiming that contemporary anxiety about the Anthropocene and its collapse of human and natural history is "like" being an enslaved person in a way that "helps us understand what it was like," or that we're all becoming slaves too, or some similarly crude formulation. The fact that there are some disturbing structural parallels between slavery and the contemporary Anthropocene does not make their traumas fungible; position matters radically, always. Nor am I saying that slavery somehow caused the Anthropocene directly – indeed in a cruel irony, it is likely that a reliance on the labor of enslaved people reduced the carbon footprint of the South by retarding the turn to the carbon-intensive industrialization that the North made more quickly and that likely gave the Union a decisive edge in the War. I want to close this chapter by moving away from a focus on individual experience, and from the poles of, on the one hand, a former time when there seemed to be (for some) a separation between human and natural history, and when we hadn't yet come to see ourselves a geologic force as a species, and on the other, an apocalyptic time to come when human history will have been subsumed by natural history. Instead, I want to end by asking what sort of power and violence comes from straddling those two histories. How do privilege and abjection function as positions within the unstable and violent hybridity that marks our Anthropocenic moment? How might the history of slavery and white supremacy provide some vitally important contexts for how we think about our modernity, about a past that isn't past, no matter how urgently we use this crisis to imagine that the past is irrelevant to the present?

These questions resonate powerfully with Latour's view of what he calls the "modern constitution," a series of nature/culture hybrids whose power comes in part from the contradictory insistence that, despite that hybridity, nature and culture are fundamentally different things.[24] For Latour, the modern state makes "Nature intervene at every point in the fabrication of . . . societ[y]," while at the same time "attributing to Nature its radical transcendence," a combination that allows the "moderns" to "become the only actors in their own political destiny, while they go right on making their society hold together by mobilizing Nature."[25] Latour's thesis not only reinforces how profoundly unsettling the Anthropocene's collapse of nature and culture is to the modern order, but implicitly suggests a deeper and even more disturbing parallel between that order and the slave plantation under white supremacy. The master-as-white-man was supposedly free, agential, the "only actor in his political destiny," in contradistinction to "his" slaves, a group of people whose forced association with nature not only stripped them of agency, but were precisely the labor that made the master's "society hold together." In this context, the culture/nature distinction supposedly at the heart of the time-before-the-Anthropocene in general was quite literally embodied – rooted – in the plantation landscape and the people who lived there.[26] To the extent Latour's influential thesis is correct, modernity and the plantation are inextricable.

Perhaps more important, the breakdown of that distinction was one that African Americans had been negotiating with, often as a matter of physical and psychological survival, since the first enslaved people arrived on this continent in 1619. If the collapse between human and natural history is fundamental to the definition of the Anthropocene, then the millions of human beings held in chattel slavery experienced a much more extreme version of the Anthropocene a long time before Chakrabarty's "humanists" did, one that imbricates the historical brutality of racism and the slow-motion ecocide that is unfolding before us. Looking to writers such as Douglass to understand this profoundly fraught negotiation between natural and human identity reminds us – or should remind us – of two critically important contexts for our contemporary understanding of the Anthropocene.

First, Douglass's exemplary anguish in being unable to either "become a beast," or endure his all-too-human knowledge should make us considerably less sanguine that a deeper identification between human and natural will *necessarily* lead to salutary results for either group. Of course such an identification in our current moment does and will unfold differently, but keeping the pernicious racist history of how a human/natural collapse justified the exploitation of people and land by making them coextensive could help us better think through the way forward. It is all too easy for (white, especially) ecocritics and environmentalists to assume, in an implicitly ahistorical way, that humans "should" embrace the natural world, learn to live in "harmony" with nature, celebrate "our" connection with nonhuman animals, reject the anthropocentric assumptions at the heart of a rigid nature–culture distinction. While doing so might avoid some of the horrors of the master's position, and the racial and environmental violence it instantiated, any rejection of anthropocentrism must first acknowledge and then engage with the historical consequences of such a rejection for powerless enslaved people such as Douglass and Jacobs. Viewed in that context, the enslaved person's involuntary "closeness" to nature and the degradation, humiliation, and subjection that connection occasioned, should provide a powerful check on the too-easy assertions that greater connections between human and nonhuman will automatically be good for both, and that anyone who finds that connection difficult, if not traumatic, is, at best, unenlightened. Put another way, the partial breakdown between human and natural history that the Anthropocene names forecloses the possibility of a "right" or morally pure position outside of it that we might occupy, and in doing so relieve ourselves from the messy burden of living in a semi-broken world. Neither a separation between human and natural, nor a collapse of the two, nor an uncertainty in their relation, offer some intrinsic way of being that frees us from taking ongoing responsibility for our collective actions. There can all too easily be a moral narcissism in the search for individual innocence or guilt, as if the "real" question is how to manage one's own personal implication in the Anthropocene. If, instead, we start with the inevitability of such an implication we might be better at focusing on the historically saturated world we actually inhabit, rather than trying to find a place outside of it where our individual guilt or innocence is what matters.

Second, taking responsibility for our implicated position within the Anthropocene means not only making the traumatic history of naturalized degradation suffered by enslaved people central to how we understand climate change, but recognizing how the figure of the master is often the part of that history many of us most share. Human authority over nature – our authority – is intimately tied to racial mastery; to be ignorant of that connection is, somewhat paradoxically, most fully to participate in it. Just as contemporary white identity in its most powerful form is transparent to itself, a supposedly normative and ahistorical individuality that is (culpably) unaware of the racial history and context in which it is embedded, so too is the privilege of Chakrabarty's "humanist," marked precisely by the humanist's ability to blithely assume the universality of the separation between human and natural history he enjoys. Both figures have long occupied a position both in and out of the twinned game of race and nature, perhaps expressing grave "concern" about the "issue," but never with the same (literal) skin in the game as those human and nonhuman animals whose abjection depended on those realms being indistinct.

It is no accident that one of the only places "master" is still used conversationally (outside of educational degrees or formal titles) is in the human/pet relationship, a conjunction that again underscores the profound imbrication of white supremacy and the sort of authority humans assume over the nonhuman natural. Granting subjectivity, interiority, rights, etc. to the nonhuman natural would "spoil the best n***** in the world," where the stars might replace "a-t-u-r-e," as easily as the word Master Auld deploys, a word that, regardless, to him means much the same thing. This second form of responsibility refuses to see either racial or environmental mastery as originary; slavery was neither merely an extension of environmental dominance, nor its root cause or ultimate explanation. Rather than trying to parse the chronological order of each register of dominance or collapsing one into the other, racism and ecological violence were always amalgamating, reflexively influencing the other, oscillating between collapse and distinction to suit the desires of the master to maximize his/our authority and minimize responsibility. That history of authority without responsibility is at the core of our contemporary environmental crises because of the history it shares with white supremacy. Acknowledging and resisting the long history of mastery over race/nature is where any adequate approach to the problem of climate change must begin, because that history is in fact the history of the Anthropocene itself.

CHAPTER 3

(In)conceivable Futures: Henry David Thoreau and Reproduction's Queer Ecology

Sarah Ensor

In the late winter of 2016, twinned meditations on the plight of reproduction in an era of environmental crisis appeared in major periodicals. The first, Madeline Ostrander's "How Do You Decide to Have a Baby When Climate Change Is Remaking Life on Earth?" published in *The Nation*, introduces readers to a group called Conceivable Future, which predicates its work on the premise that "the climate crisis is a reproductive crisis" and thus encourages conversations about how global climate change affects reproductive decision-making.[1] A few days later, there appeared in *The Guardian* a shorter op-ed, Dave Bry's "Does Climate Change Make It Immoral to Have Kids?" which meditates on its titular question before ultimately "com[ing] down on the side of advocating reproduction."[2]

For those of us attuned to the discourses of contemporary environmentalism, such first-person accounts may seem to be just more of the same. From the pervasive rhetoric of "future generations" that dominates sustainability logics to Sierra Club advertisements that depict pregnant bellies as toxic sponges in order to provoke onlookers to environmental action, few things have come to feel more inevitable – or, dare I say, more natural – than the aligning of environmentalism's necessary(?) orientation toward the future with reproductive paradigms. Indeed, the discourse of reproduction looms large in environmental discourse for (at least) two distinct reasons: first, because environmentalism as a political movement invests in a future that it often identifies with the figure of the Child[3] and, second, because the continuance of human life – and of the planet – as we know it is understood to be predicated on biological reproduction. Environmentalist rhetoric tends to collapse these two paradigms, and consequently often conflates the process of biological reproduction with the (social reproduction of the) nuclear family form. Thus in talking about the future (or continuance) of the planet, environmentalists frequently end up talking about families: about parents and children, about proprietary forms of investment and privatized models of care, about a future that resembles the present like the biological child resembles the biological parent, about a model of "sustainability" predicated on intergenerational continuity across time.

Such a logical collapse is exemplified by the work of environmental writer Roy Scranton. In an essay titled "Raising a Daughter in a Doomed World," Scranton, pondering much the same question as Bry, insists that while "nobody *needs* to have children[, i]t just happens to be the strongest drive humans have, the fundamental organizing principle of every human culture, and the *sine qua non* of a meaningful human world, since it alone makes possible the persistence of human meaning through time."[4] As he goes on to reflect, "I chose to have a child with my partner because I believe in life, because I want the wheel of life to keep turning."[5] Scranton's account of his daughter's birth – especially insofar as it appears in the context of a piece pondering environmental futurity – manages simultaneously to naturalize the nuclear family form (itself a product of specific historical conditions) and to render parenting the privileged path to socio-environmental care.

This conflation, far from being a mere rhetorical quirk, is at least partially responsible for many of the most exclusionary and politically regressive tendencies of the mainstream environmental movement. For in consciously and unconsciously yoking the continuation of the planet/species to the persistence of the nuclear family, environmental discourse tends to offer a model of care that is not only unnecessarily narrow (familiar, familial) but also hyper-personalized. As many thinkers before me have pointed out, such personalization both obscures the extent to which environmental activism involves investing in strangers (distant from us in space, time, and experience) and risks diminishing the extent to which our current planetary situation requires change at the structural, not personal, level. Relatedly, the logic of the articles with which I began, and of Scranton's essay as well, tightly binds environmental stewardship to questions of individual (reproductive) choice – a tactic that not only replicates the problematic emphasis on individual consumer choice foundational to capitalist techniques of "greenwashing" but also falsely universalizes the authors' (specifically classed and racialized) relationship to reproductive futurity – and reproductive decision-making – itself.[6] As Christina Sharpe, among many others, reminds us, and as other chapters in this volume trace in more depth, not all children are born into innocence or futurity, and reproduction, far from being a simple matter of individual choice, has long been a tool of state power.[7] Relatedly, whereas environmental continuance is commonly yoked to the reproduction of the white nuclear family, non-white reproduction, as Andil Gosine has demonstrated, often has been deemed an ecological threat or even an "act against nature."[8]

In response to such exclusionary and falsely universalizing paradigms, many queer theorists have critiqued the extent to which biological reproduction conditions our privileged models of time, community, and care, with some going so far as to encourage the abandonment or refusal of political projects (such as environmentalism) predicated on "reproductive futurism." Queer ecocritics, unwilling either to give up on continuance or to embrace environmentalism's normative, familiar, and familial understanding of it, have traced alternate possibilities for where a non-reproductive future might be thought to lie, ranging from my own theorization of a "spinster ecology" invested in intransitive or avuncular futurity to Nicole Seymour's hope that queer theoretical approaches "could inspire environmentalist agendas that seek to achieve positive ends without resorting to heterosexist, homophobic, or *pro-reproductive ideologies*."[9]

However, these engagements with biological reproduction – which urge us binarily to take it or leave it, embrace it or refuse it – often fail either to interrogate the foundational term in their debate, or to sufficiently disentangle reproduction from the normative family paradigms with which it is so often collapsed. Queer ecocritics thus miss the possibility of challenging from *within* the familiar, and too often naturalized, model of reproduction that, in privileging the kind of futurity focused on maintaining the ("sustainable") status quo, makes another kind of futurity unimaginable: namely, one in which things happen differently than they do in the present, in which we're able to imagine and inhabit the world otherwise. In other words, while queer theorists have creatively and consistently rejected reproductive futurism, they have been so quick to dispense with its normative trappings that they may have (pun intended) thrown the baby out with the bathwater. For once we stop reifying a model of reproduction identified with replication and sameness, and with a future made valuable through our familial (or otherwise proprietary) claims to it, we may free ourselves to acknowledge that biological reproduction, if reconceived, can itself be the ground of socioenvironmental change rather than a barrier to it.

Where the group that hosts house parties to talk about the reproductive crisis engendered by climate change deems itself "Conceivable Future," this chapter asks how our conventional understanding of reproduction has made possibilities within both the present and the future *inconceivable.* If we want to conceive of a future importantly different from (or discontinuous with) the present, then we must think about how and why and what and when we reproduce. Indeed, we might be well served to embrace the idea that "the climate crisis is a reproductive crisis" – if by that we mean a crisis *for* reproduction, and an occasion to rethink its contours.

* * *

Rather than take a side in the extant debates between mainstream environmentalists and queer theorists, then, I want to examine the extent to which biological reproduction may itself already be queerer – less familiar *and* less familial – than we think. In order to develop the terms of such a claim, I look to a perhaps unexpected figure: Henry David Thoreau, for whom reproductive paradigms are consistently sites of curiosity and relational possibility. In Thoreau's explorations of insect and plant life, reproduction becomes a way of thinking relation *ecologically*, of avoiding the reification of the nuclear family or directed, linear, proprietary paths of transmission and instead emphasizing indirect and often collateral modes of care. By lingering with Thoreau's work, we can see how much his understanding of reproduction has to teach both the ecoparents who embrace the ideology of reproductive futurism and the queer theorists who staunchly refute it.

For Thoreau, studies of nurse species (including insects and trees and the earth itself) became an occasion not only to query normative paradigms of reproduction and succession but also to link such studies – via his characteristic rhetorical forms of analogic and sideways movement – to the (oft-impugned) experience of childless human subjects, himself included. In attending to such figures, Thoreau dislocates reproduction in both space and time, urging us to attend to a broader range of participants – and a broader range of contributing actions – in our account of the reproductive process. What emerges is a queer understanding of reproduction that dispenses with normative futurity in favor of modes of suspension and delay, decenters biological parents (insisting instead on the importance of collateral participants and forms of surrogation), and replaces a preoccupation with reproductive products or ends with an emphasis on the ecological conditions of reproduction's very (im)possibility.

The terms of such a reconceptualization first become clear in an 1851 journal entry, where Thoreau, indirectly responding to critiques of his own bachelorhood and non-(re)productivity, analogically links the neuter insect species discussed in Louis Agassiz and A.A. Gould's recently published *Principles of Zoology* to the condition of those "maiden aunts & bachelor uncles" whom society so frequently misunderstands:

> Down the R R. before sun rise A freight train in the Deep Cut. the sun rising over the woods. – When the vapor from the engine rose above the woods the level rays of the rising sun fell on it it presented the same redness – morning red – inclining to saffron which the clouds in the eastern horizon do.
>
> There was but little wind this morning yet I heard the telegraph harp – it does not require a strong wind to wake its strings – it depends more on its direction & the tension of the wire apparently – a gentle but steady breeze will often call forth its finest strains when a strong but unsteady gale – blowing at the wrong angle withal fails to elicit any melodious sound.
>
> In the psychological world there are phenomena analogous to what zoologists call *alternate reproduction* in which it requires several generations unlike each other to produce the perfect animal – Some men's lives are but an aspiration – a yearning toward a higher state – and they are wholly misapprehended – until they are referred to or traced through all their metamorphoses. We cannot pronounce upon a man's intellectual & moral state until we foresee what metamorphosis it is preparing him for.
>
> It is said that "the working bees – are barren females. The attributes of their sex – seem to consist only in their solicitude for the welfare of the next generation, of which they are the natural guardians, but not the parents." Agassiz & Gould. This phenomenon is paralleled in man by maiden aunts & bachelor uncles who perform a similar function.[10]

Before I engage the question of reproduction itself, let me address the rhetorical and argumentative logics of this entry. For what are we to make of the seemingly incongruous juxtaposition of the morning's atmospherics and insect reproduction? We might note that these seemingly disparate topics are linked by Thoreau's interest in reading nominally linear, directed, instrumental materialities (the telegraph wire, biological reproduction) in terms of their lateral spread and their medial conditions of possibility. The "gentle but steady" wind athwart the "strings" wakes the harp in the wire, turning a technology designed to transmit a message into an accidental musical instrument; likewise, the discussion of biological reproduction makes room for the avuncular or slantwise presence of "aunts ... & uncles," just as man's "yearning toward a higher state," which itself echoes the morning sky's red "inclining to saffron," makes room for multiple "metamorphoses," which must be circuitously "traced." Indeed, as the structure of my own sentence already begins to suggest, the analogic of the entry – which links vapor to cloud and telegraph wire to harp and alternate reproduction to human yearning before, finally, linking working bees to "maiden aunts & bachelor uncles" – prioritizes lateral over forward movement, a topic to which I will return. And, of course, it seems important to point out that Thoreau's own linking of (animal) biological reproduction to (human) social function anticipates contemporary environmentalism's collapse of biological reproduction and the nuclear family social form – with two key differences. First, as will become clearer as we proceed, Thoreau's privileged reproductive unit is less the family than it is the community or the *socius*. Second, rather than *collapsing* social relation and biological reproduction, Thoreau *analogizes* them, thus leaving space for new understandings of reproduction's sociability to emerge.

The specific terms of Thoreau's expansion of reproductivity become much clearer when we turn from his allusive journal entry to its source. Of particular interest to Thoreau was the "Alternate and Equivocal Reproduction" section of Agassiz and Gould's chapter "Peculiar Modes of Reproduction." The section focuses on the cercaria, one developmental stage of a parasitic flatworm, and opens with a lengthy discussion of how its embryo develops within the body of another stage of the worm, "which seemingly has no other office than to protect and forward the development of the young Cercaria" and, "on this account, . . . has been called the *nurse*." This relationship, however, turns out to be multiply embedded, as the nurse itself has been nursed in the body of yet another host. The members of this generation – the nurses of the nurse – are thereby deemed *grand-nurses*. After this nesting-doll pattern of hosting has been established, Agassiz and Gould continue:

> 343. Supposing these grand-nurses to be the immediate offspring of the Distoma, . . . as is probable, we have thus a quadruple series of generation. Four generations and one metamorphosis are required to evolve the perfect animal; in other words, the parent finds no resemblance to himself in any of his progeny, until he comes down to the great-grandson.
>
> 344. Among the Aphides, or the plant-lice, the number of generations is still greater. . . . [I]t is sometimes the eighth or ninth generation before the perfect animals appear as males and females, the sexes being then for the first time distinct, and the males provided with wings. The females lay eggs, which are hatched the following year, to repeat the same succession. Each generation is an additional step towards the perfect state; and, as each member of the succession is an incomplete animal, we cannot better explain their office, than by considering them analogous to the larvae of the Cercaria, that is, as nurses.*

> * There is a certain analogy between the larvae of the plant-louse (Aphis) and the neuters or working ants and bees. This analogy has given rise to

various speculations, and, among others, to the following theory, which is not without interest. The end and aim of all alternate generation, it is said, is to favor the development of the species in its progress towards the perfect state. Among the plant-lice, as among all the nurses, this end is accomplished by means of the body of the nurse. Now, a similar end is accomplished by the working ants and bees, only, instead of being performed as an organic function, it is turned into an outward activity, which makes them instinctively watch over the new generation, nurse and take care of it. It is no longer the body of the nurse, but its own instincts, which become the instrument of the development. This seems to receive confirmation from the fact that the working bees, like the plant-lice, are barren females. The attributes of their sex, in both, seem to consist only in their solicitude for the welfare of the new generation, of which they are the natural guardians, but not the parents. The task of bringing forth young is confided to other individuals, to the queen among the bees, and to the female of the last generation among the plant-lice. Thus the barrenness of the working bees, which seems an anomaly as long as we consider them complete animals, receives a very natural explanation so soon as we look upon them merely as nurses.[11]

To eyes accustomed to the paradigms of reproductive futurity omnipresent in our current environmental(ist) discussions, Agassiz and Gould's treatment of insect reproduction may seem radically disorienting. Gone is the assumption that reproduction is initiated by a single act and completed within a single gestation period. The timeframe of successful reproduction is not one generation but instead multiple generations – sometimes as many as nine. Reproduction, in other words, may not be the purview of individual beings or even individual generations; what we typically understand as intergenerational paradigms are, for Agassiz and Gould, a single process, part of a single being's trajectory toward its "perfect state." And equally important to this lengthening of the timetable is what happens within the protraction or delay. Unlike the reproductive futurists' fixation on the child-as-future, in which the future resembles the present as the child resembles the parent (in a way that impedes the potential for true political change), the aphids' reproductive paradigms are predicated on forms of *non-resemblance*: "the parent finds no resemblance to himself in any of his progeny, until he comes down to the great-grandson." While this may simply be read as differently teleological, what seems important to a reading of Thoreau is not the ultimate arrival of that end, but the capaciousness and experience of the "until" itself. Suspension, non-fruition, and incompletion become *part* of the reproductive process rather than being understood as barriers to or signs of failure within it.

Alienation, difference, and non-identity, likewise, become as meaningful a set of relational traits as resemblance and identity. Perhaps most importantly, an individual being's contribution to the reproductive process cannot be understood unless we expand both the temporal scale of our attention (the *when* of reproduction) and our very definition of contribution (reproduction's *what*). For in the logic by which Agassiz and Gould's lengthy footnote proceeds, "[i]t is no longer the body of the nurse, but its own instincts, which become the instrument of the development." The barrenness of the working bees does not impede or foreclose the reproductive process but instead indirectly facilitates it. Just as reproduction is no longer contained within the timeframe of a single gestation period or single being's lifespan, neither is it contained solely within the bodies and practices of those most directly involved in procreation.

It is a long way, it seems, from aphides or cerceriae to "maiden aunts & bachelor uncles." Yet within the context of Thoreau's own writing, where indirection is a methodology and an object of attention alike, that distance seems to be part of the point. For the aim of thinking uncles and insects together is to cast them not as identical but rather as analogical: as similar with a difference, as similar in precisely such a way as to preserve that difference. Indeed, Thoreau's claim about "maiden aunts & bachelor uncles" is multiply or even recursively analogical; it is as embedded in a single pattern of thought as Agassiz and Gould's young cercaria are in the bodies of their ever-developing nurse-hosts. The very reproductive paradigm to which Thoreau draws his analogy – that of the neuter or working bee – is itself already two analogical steps removed from the zoologists' initial treatment of the cerceriae. Agassiz and Gould first "cannot better explain [the aphids' intermediary generations'] office, than by considering them analogous to the larvae of the Cercaria, that is, as nurses"; immediately thereafter, in their footnote, they turn to the possibility that "There is a certain analogy between the larvae of the plant-louse (Aphis) and the neuters or working ants and bees." By the time Thoreau, using less technical language, suggests that the practices of the neuter insects are "paralleled in man by maiden aunts & bachelor uncles who perform a similar function," the appearance of the avuncular being is deeply embroiled in analogical, rather than (re)duplicative, relations.[12]

Another way to understand this point might be to say that the "argument" of both this section of *Principles of Zoology* and of Thoreau's journal entry resembles the very paradigms of reproduction in which they are invested. Both texts (like the mode of perception able to perceive the "telegraph harp") move forward precisely by moving sideways,[13] and seem to make a point not through linear argumentation but through associative logic (or analogic) and concatenated claims, by a willingness to reach an unpredicted end. Argumentative fruition is suspended in favor of an accretive mode of analysis as invested in adding dimensionality to individual ideas as it is in propelling these claims forward toward an irrefutable claim.

Furthermore, whereas our typical environmentalist engagement with reproduction fixates on the reproductive product or end, Thoreau instead emphasizes the *conditions* for the success of the reproductive process. In an address to the Middlesex Agricultural Society nine years after he read *Principles of Zoology*, for instance, Thoreau sought to account for "how it happened that when a pine wood was cut down an oak one commonly sprang up, and *vice versa*" – in other words, for the fact that the succession of forest trees sometimes confounds our expectation of direct propagation or resemblance between successive "generations."[14] His answer – that animals transplant seeds from one region of the forest to another, that pine forests become the ideal shield for hardwood saplings – is, today at least, hardly surprising. What remains striking, however, is the terminology that he applies to the relationship between the tree species; successful planters "have simply rediscovered the value of pines as nurses for oaks. The English experimenters seem, early and generally, to have found out the importance of using trees of some kind as nurse-plants for the young oaks."[15] If the pines here are not themselves non-reproductive in the same way as neuter nurse insects, then neither are they participating simply in a linear paradigm of intergenerational reproduction. Instead, these nurse trees yield the condition – the literal ground – for another species to seed itself and successfully reproduce.

This emphasis on the role of surrogate or collateral participants in the reproductive and parenting process appears in yet another entry from Thoreau's journal concerned with gestation, where the nurse title applies not to a category of insect or to a species of tree but, more broadly and provocatively, to the earth itself:

> Sept 9th (1854)
> this morn I find a little hole ¾ of an inch over my small tortoise eggs — & find a young tortoise coming out (ap. In the rainy night) just beneath — ... Only one as yet. I buried them in the garden June 15th — I am affected by the thought that the earth nurses these eggs — They are planted in the earth — & the earth takes care of them — she is genial to them & does not kill them. It suggests a certain vitality & intelligence in the earth — which I had not realized. This mother is not merely inanimate — & inorganic — Though the immediate mother turtle abandons her offspring — the earth & sun are kind to them — The old turtle on which the earth rests takes care of them while the other waddles off — Earth was not made poisonous & deadly to them. The

earth has some virtue in it — when seeds are put into it they germinate —
when turtles' eggs they hatch, in due time — Though the mother turtle
remained and brooded them — it would still nevertheless be the universal
world turtle which through her cared for them as now — Thus the earth is the
mother of all creatures —[16]

On first glance, this account seems to risk simply reifying the normative
notions that this chapter has sought to complicate. The earth is "the mother
of all creatures"; she is "kind" and "genial" and "vital[]" and "virtu[ous]."
And yet the passage quite quickly becomes queerer than it initially seems:
from its mixed metaphors of fertility (eggs planted like seeds) to its inhabit-
ation of the delicate line between materiality and figuration (literal turtle
eggs meeting the mytheme of the World Turtle), from its conjoining of
images of birth with images of death (those eggs buried in the ground, the
claim that the earth has demonstrated its benevolence largely by not being
deadly to the eggs) to its intertwining of claims to the natural with the
performance of human intervention, Thoreau's entry is hardly
a straightforward account of the naturalness or inevitability of biological
reproduction. And still more remarkable is the way in which surrogation –
this paradigm omnipresent throughout Thoreau's engagement with nurse
species – becomes the prevailing way of understanding gestation and reproduction alike; if the earth (and, indeed, Thoreau) here gets involved in the
incubation process only when "the immediate mother turtle abandons her
off spring," then we are also informed that the mother herself is best
understood as a kind of surrogate. For even were she to remain and do
what we typically conceive of as her "own" or "proper" work, she would still
best be understood as a conduit for a broader, more impersonal paradigm of
care; it would be "*through her*" that the "universal world turtle . . . cared for
[her offspring]." In his account, in other words, reproduction is fundamentally indirect and collateral; none of us – including biological parents deeply
invested in their own children and their own families – has as direct or
straightforward relationship to reproduction as we are wont to believe.

Such an understanding of earth-as-nurse thus also complicates the
proprietary gestures common to narratives of reproduction (beginning
with the familiar phrasing of "having" a child); for the language of ownership here is attached not only to the mother turtle ("her off spring" – a
claiming gesture made only, interestingly enough, when describing her
abandonment of the eggs) but also, importantly, to Thoreau himself ("my
small tortoise eggs"). What Thoreau's engagement with nurse species,
broadly conceived, achieves, then, is a transformation of our narrowly

proprietary paradigms of reproduction into more broadly social models of care. Whereas we often think of Thoreau as a philosopher of sufficiency, his major contribution to our project here may be his implicit insistence upon insufficiency: upon the fact that biological parents, no matter how careful and attentive, are insufficient to maintain the health of their children or to guarantee the success of the reproductive process both narrowly and broadly conceived.

And so, to bring the conversation back to where it began, rather than asking familiar questions about reproduction in a new guise, we might instead ask: in an era of environmental degradation, what can be seen as "central to the gestational process"?[17] For if, via Thoreau, we understand the viability of the reproductive process – now imagined at a transpersonal and transgenerational scale rather than as belonging to/within the dyadic couple of the nuclear family – to depend upon keeping the earth from being "made poisonous & deadly to" those who gestate and develop and grow within it, then we must acknowledge that reproductive questions – and their concomitant paradigms of stewardship and care – necessarily implicate us all. And in so doing, we might also acknowledge that, while it perhaps requires the environmental crisis to alert us to this fact, human reproduction is itself a fundamentally ecological phenomenon, relying upon a range of participants variously proximate to (or distant from) the meeting of ovum and sperm, and variously aware of (or interested in) their possible implication within the reproductive process.

It is worth noting that, even in Thoreau's examples, it takes a kind of crisis or puzzle to encourage us to rethink reproduction. It takes a mother turtle who has abandoned her eggs. It takes a forest where something seems out of place, where succession proceeds otherwise than we might predict. It takes the neuter insects whose capacity to flourish was the locus of crisis in Darwin's account of reproductive fitness. And so, moving from 1854 to 2022, it seems necessary for all environmentalists – both those invested in the existing terms of reproductive futurity and those invested in resisting them – to engage thinkers who inhabit a capacious notion of reproductive care. We might look to Emily Rapp's narrative of raising a terminally ill baby, an experience that detaches her from a proprietary investment in her son's future and instead forces her to parent "for the humanity implicit in the act itself."[18] We might look to Belle Boggs, whose ecological account of her own infertility once again helps us to rethink the naturalness of heterosexual reproduction.[19] We might look to Dr. Mona Hanna-Attisha, the Flint pediatrician who helped to expose the city's complicity in the lead poisoning of its residents, who has "worked hard to help her own two children adjust to . . . her role as pseudo-mother to thousands of children she knows are counting on her to find help for their futures."[20] We might look to Rachel Carson, famously dismissed for being childless, who wrote not only *Silent Spring*, the book indirectly responsible for the founding of the Environmental Protection Agency (EPA), but also *The Sense of Wonder*, beloved as one of the most powerful descriptions of parenting environmentally. Too often we characterize these accounts as exceptional, when in fact they may be exemplary.

And so too might we – *must* we – engage those activists who work to collectivize reproduction, and who demonstrate that questions of reproductive and environmental justice are inseparable. We might look to the emerging collaborations between BLM activists and reproductive justice organizations, and their coalitional response to the threat that racial violence – including environmental injustice – poses to "the right to breathe, the right to exist."[21] We might look to the work of Indigenous women such as Katsi Cook, the Mohawk midwife who coined the term "environmental reproductive justice," thereby not only insisting that the process of "reproduction" itself involves humans' intimate relationship to (the reproductivity of) the land, and not only "mov[ing] the debate [over reproductive justice] from individual bodies to cultural collectives," but also demonstrating the possibility of "reclaim[ing] reproduction in decolonized terms."[22] We might look to Sophie Lewis, whose manifesto *Full Surrogacy Now: Feminism Against Family* calls for a "gestational commune," insisting that we might "explode notions of hereditary parentage" and "build a care commune based on comradeship, a world sustained by kith and kind more than by kin."[23]

These writers and activists demonstrate the oversimplifications in, and the ethicopolitical problems of, the way in which reproductivity is widely understood in mainstream environmental(ist) conversations. In so doing, they also alert us to an understanding of reproduction that, through its attention to indirect and collateral effects, its embrace of surrogate participants, its refusal to reify the future, its emphasis on conditions over products, its inhabiting of suspended and sideways and prolonged temporalities, and its reckoning with forms of temporal and spatial interconnection, is both more *social* and more *ecological*. Such accounts of reproduction thus begin to relieve the shadow that the white nuclear family, the figure of the Child, and privatized models of care cast over contemporary environmental discourse. With their help, we can better understand how and why we *reproduce* the norms that continue to govern mainstream environmental politics – and thus can better imagine the world, and our collective practices within it, otherwise.

CHAPTER 4

Narrating Animal Extinction from the Pleistocene to the Anthropocene

Timothy Sweet

Two pulses of colonization have radically reshaped North America's bio-diversity. The first human colonization during the late Pleistocene Epoch, some 15,000 to 20,000 years ago or perhaps earlier, resulted in the extinction of the megafauna: large herbivores such as mammoths, mastodons, musk oxen, and giant ground sloths, and large carnivores such as the saber-toothed cat that preyed on the herbivores. While hunting was the primary cause of this decimation, new disease pathogens brought by the migrants may have played a role. Rapidly fluctuating climate during this epoch may also have been a contributing factor.[1] As the Pleistocene migrants established a more or less stable baseline of human–animal relations, they became the indigenous Americans that Europeans encountered in 1492. These peoples' oral traditions may preserve Pleistocene Epoch memories, however altered through millennia of transmission.[2] Indigenous stories of the extinction of the mammoth, for example, in dialogue with European natural history beginning in the eighteenth century, raised this question of primal memory and sometimes commented on the colonial encounter.

The European colonial encounter or conquest caused a new wave of extinctions and endangerments that continues today as part of the global decimation of biodiversity often termed the Sixth Extinction.[3] In addition to the direct exploitation of animals, such as the hunting of bison to near-extinction, the conquest continues to destroy critical habitats and, as part of the global carbon economy, contributes to the geophysical changes, such as human-caused global warming, that have characterized the Anthropocene.[4] Through the Enlightenment era, many European settler-colonists observed local extinctions – animals denominated vermin, such as wolves, were often targeted for extirpation – but the idea of global species extinction was not generally accepted until the nineteenth century, well after French paleontologist Georges Cuvier established extinction as a fact of the fossil record.[5] Although acceptance came late, after the loss of many species such as the passenger pigeon, the fact of extinction ushered in a new emotional register of mourning and memorialization, and a new politics concerning the protection of endangered species.[6]

Whereas Enlightenment thought separated nature from culture so as to enable the human domination of nature, in the Anthropocene we now confront the entanglement of nature and culture in global phenomena such as human-caused climate change. Humankind as a species has set into play geophysical forces that human individuals feel powerless to alter.[7] One response to this situation is to concede, as eco-philosopher Timothy Morton does, that "Nonhuman beings are responsible for the next moment of human history."[8] Morton's concession leads him to advise reflection and "rest" in practices of "mindfulness, awareness, simple let-ting-be."[9] Other responses have been more active and suggest possibilities for species survivance and ecological futurity.[10]

This chapter will reflect on the two waves of North American extinctions correlating with the Pleistocene and post-Columbian colonizations, with brief case studies of narratives of the mammoth and the passenger pigeon respectively. The chapter will then turn toward the present Anthropocene context and look toward the future through narratives of a threatened species, the monarch butterfly. These three cases show that our current concern with animal extinction has a long North American history and that extinction is not linked only to one technology, politics, or national configuration. A brief conclusion will put the history of North American extinctions in global context.

Mammoth

The mammoth was a key exhibit in Thomas Jefferson's refutation of George-Louis Leclerc, Comte de Buffon's claim that American nature was degenerate because its climate was colder and wetter than the Old World's.[11] According to Buffon's view of environmental determinism, the American climate "diminished all the quadrupeds" and favored the pro-duction of "insects, reptiles, and all the animals which wallow in the mire, whose blood is watery, and which multiply in corruption, are larger and more numerous in the low, moist, and marshy lands of the New Continent."[12] Against Buffon's claim, Jefferson, in his 1785 *Notes on the State of Virginia*, marshalled as evidence the size and number of American quadrupeds, beginning with the mammoth, an elephant-like creature whose remains had been discovered in the mid-eighteenth century at Big Bone Lick, a salt spring on the Ohio River near present-day Cincinnati.[13]

The mammoth is the first entry in the *Notes*' comparative table of American and European quadrupeds; the bison (which within a century would face its own anthropogenic extinction crisis) is second. No European quadruped comes close in bulk.[14]

The quarrel with Buffon was not the only reason Jefferson hoped the mammoth still existed, however. For Jefferson, a species' ultimate fate was determined not by human action, but by a superhuman actor – God or nature. The indigenous Americans from whom Jefferson attempted to gain information on the mammoth evidently held the same view. According to a Lenape story of the fossil remains at Big Bone Lick, told to Jefferson in 1781 and transcribed in the *Notes*, the mammoth or "big buffalo" arrived at Big Bone Lick a long time ago and "began an universal destruction of the bear, deer, elks, buffaloes, and other animals, which had been created for the use of the Indians." The "Great Man Above" perceiving this threat to the people's wellbeing, became "so enraged that he seized his lightning, descended on the earth, . . . and hurled his bolts among them till the whole were slaughtered" except for one large bull who escaped and "bounded over the Ohio, over the Wabash, the Illinois, and finally over the great lakes, where he is living at this day."[15] Spirit power, according to the Lenape story, directly intervened to encourage human flourishing by eradicating another species. Other versions of the story by Shawnee and Haudenosaunee narrators are similarly anthropocentric in their accounts of environmental relations. In all these accounts, humans occupy the ecosystem's point of privilege.

While Jefferson recognized that species could be locally eradicated, he did not want to accept the possibility of global extinction. He asserted that "such is the oeconomy [*sic*] of nature that no instance can be produced of her having permitted any one race of her animals to become extinct; of her having formed any link in her great work so weak as to be broken."[16] He hoped that the Lewis and Clark extinction would furnish proof that the mammoth was not extinct but still roamed the American West, as the Lenape story seemed to suggest.[17] In a scientific paper on the fossil remains of another giant animal he named the megalonyx (great claw), he reiterated this position: "For if one link in nature's chain might be lost, another and another might be lost, till this whole system of things should evanish [*sic*] by piece-meal; a conclusion not warranted by the local disappearance of one or two species of animals."[18] In this refusal to accept the possibility of extinction, Jefferson anticipated the modern, elegiac response to biodiversity loss and species extinction, "this whole system of things" meaning the interlinkage of all creatures including humankind. If one of these vanished, unprotected by a governing creator, so might we. Extinction would violate the world's wholeness; it would seem unjust.[19] Jefferson later came to accept the fact of extinction, but only if it were regulated by a superintending deity.[20]

A century after Jefferson recorded the Lenape story, Penobscot historian Joseph Nicolar returned to this story in his *Life and Traditions of the Red Man*, in order to position the mammoth as an anti-colonial object lesson in ecological relations. Throughout the nineteenth century, Euro-Americans had associated species extinction with the cultural or even genetic extinction of indigenous Americans – and indigenous Americans were aware of this association. A Pawnee Chief from the Missouri territory delegation to President Monroe in 1822, for example, arguing against pressure for land cessions, acculturation, and reservation life, asserted that "we have plenty of buffalo, beaver, deer and other wild animals" and "we have plenty of land, if you will keep your people off it." The colonizers, however, "have caused such a destruction to our game" as to endanger the Plains peoples' livelihood. The Pawnee chief thus envisioned cultural extinction: "we wish you to permit us to enjoy the chase until the game in our country is exhausted – until the wild animals become extinct. Let us exhaust our present resources before you make us toil and interrupt our happiness." With the extinction of the game, "subsistence ... may become so precarious as to need and embrace the assistance" of the United States.[21] With the game animals' extinction, the ecology of indigenous life would change. By mid-century, in response, Euro-American writers such as George Catlin and Henry David Thoreau were imagining the creation of reservations that would preserve indigenous hunting cultures and the game populations that supported them – spaces where, as Thoreau put it, "the bear and the panther, and even some of the hunter race, may still exist, and not be 'civilized off the face of the earth.'"[22]

In Nicolar's account, the mammoth behaved in effect like a settler-colonist, taking up too much of the world, and was therefore punished with extinction. Nicolar retained key motifs from the Lenape Big Bone Lick narrative, such as a spirit power wielding lightning bolts, but with one major difference. Where the Lenape story has one mammoth escaping, in Nicolar's version extinction is permanent. The mammoth brings extinction upon himself during the early times when creation is still being set in order. In those times, all the animals were large and threatening to the people. The first man, Klose-kur-beh, a culture-bearer who receives instruction from the Great Spirit, sets out "to clean the earth of all obstacles" and "to subdue the animals and beasts, so that man will not have much trouble in conquering them afterwards."[23] Klose-kur-beh asks the animals one by one to become smaller. All the animals agree (some such as squirrel need persuading) except for mammoth, who believes he is invincible, saying, "Their weapons I do not fear, because my skin is so thick and hard even hair will not grow out of it; and my flesh is so deep that it covers my life, there can nothing reach that life which can be brought against it by your children; therefore I will repeat and say no." "Woe unto you," warns Klose-kur-beh, "your pride will fall with your body."[24] Taking the obedient animals with him, Klose-kur-beh departs as "the clouds began to roar very loud all over the heavens and the lightning shooting in every direction, and the howling of the animal was heard no more."[25] The mammoth's pride and power prefigure the European colonizers' pride and power, for like the mammoth, the colonizers take up too much of the world. Nicolar prophesies that when "the substance of the water, air and earth have been drawn out and used for comfort sake, and all these things have been left like the empty hornet's nest," then the Great Spirit will extinguish the colonizers along with those indigenous peoples who have followed the colonizers' overconsuming ways.[26] Only those who follow the Great Spirit's ecological teaching will survive this mass human extinction event.

In the late twentieth century, in response to evidence for the anthropogenic extinction of the mammoth and other Pleistocene megafauna, Quaternary Period expert Paul Martin formulated a response to Jefferson's hope that the mammoth was still alive in the North American West. He proposed a rewilding project that would set aside large tracts of land, eradicate modern European species such as burros, and introduce the nearest phylogenetic heirs of Pleistocene Epoch species or their ecologically functional equivalents. Extending the project to Central or South America would enable the establishment of the mammoth's nearest living relative, the Asian elephant. Such a project, as Martin put it, would recover "nature's intentions for the New World."[27] These "intentions," according to Martin's logic, had been violated by the Pleistocene colonists – the ancient ancestors of the Lenape storyteller and Joseph Nicolar.

Passenger Pigeon

The Pleistocene megafaunal extinctions may have helped to create the ecosystem in which the passenger pigeon flourished.[28] The pigeon's abundance, in any case, made it one of the more visible extinctions caused by European colonization. To these colonists, the passenger pigeon was a wonder, a source of food, and a pest – their multitudes constituting a "biological storm" that "roared up, down, and across the continent, sucking up the laden fruits of the forest and prairie, burning them in a traveling blast of life," as Aldo Leopold put it.[29] One of the earliest accounts was given by Massachusetts colonial magistrate Thomas Dudley (father of the poet Anne Dudley Bradstreet), who wrote in 1631 that he had observed a flight of "so many flocks of doves each containing many thousands, and some so many, that they obscured the light, that it passeth credit, if but the truth should be written." The event evidently disconcerted Dudley, for he ended by remarking in good Puritan fashion, "what it portends I know not."[30] That the wonder of a pigeon flight "passeth credit" became a common trope, although the interpretation of flights as portents dropped away.[31] For example, John James Audubon remarked before reporting on a flight he encountered in 1813 near Hardinsburg, Kentucky: "Indeed, after having viewed them so often, and under so many circumstances, even now I feel inclined to pause, and assure myself that what I am going to relate is fact."[32] When he got to Louisville, fifty-five miles away, "the Pigeons were still passing in undiminished numbers, and continued to do so for three days in succession."[33] The trope of wonder remained in memory as the pigeon faced extinction, as Potawatomi Chief Simon Pogakon reflected in 1895: "I have stood by the grandest waterfall of America and regarded the descending torrents in wonder and astonishment, yet never have my astonishment, wonder, and admiration been so stirred as when I have witnessed these birds drop from their course like meteors from heaven."[34]

Much as eighteenth-century indigenous American accounts regarded the mammoth as harmful to human flourishing, and thus best eradicated, European American farmers regarded the pigeons as pests. A notable instance is the account of the pigeon shoot in James Fenimore Cooper's 1823 novel *The Pioneers*, which was based on his father William Cooper's founding of Cooperstown. In the novel, passenger pigeon migration is described (incorrectly) as a regular seasonal event, flocks descending every spring to eat the grain that the settlers have just planted and then again to "overrun our wheat-fields, when they come back in the fall."[35] When the spring flight arrives, the settlers muster all their firearms, including a small cannon left from the Seven Years' War, in a massive assault on the birds. This assault turns the flight away from the valley, but not before the destruction of thousands of birds. Judge Temple, William Cooper's avatar in the novel, declares a bounty, "sixpence a hundred for pigeon's heads only," and his cousin the Sheriff remarks that "every old woman in the village may have a pot-pie for the asking."[36] Yet Cooper writes with some ambivalence.[37] Knowing nothing of the species' extinction a hundred years hence, he shows Judge Temple's regret on "discover[ing], after the excitement of the moment has passed, that he has purchased pleasure at the price of misery to others."[38] Cooper's iconic woodsman Natty Bumppo does not necessarily share Judge Temple's cross-species sympathy – he makes his living as a hunter, after all – but rather criticizes the pigeon shoot as one of the settlers' "wasty ways." "Use, but don't waste" is Natty's motto.[39] Even so, while Natty scolds that "it's wicked to be shooting into flocks in this wastey manner," he cannot resist when one of the settlers challenges him to "a single shot."[40] In a brilliant display of marksmanship, Natty kills one bird in flight.

Conservationists blamed market hunting, enabled by railroad transport, for the rapid population decline in the third quarter of the nineteenth century and lobbied for regulation and protection.[41] Yet ornithologists and hunters alike insisted that the population would persist as long as there was sufficient habitat. Audubon, having witnessed a massively destructive hunt, said that the species could easily survive such "dreadful havoc. . . . [N]othing but the gradual diminution of our forests can accomplish their decrease."[42] This idea was echoed by a veteran pigeon-hunter who responded in 1878 (the year of the last large nesting) to calls for stricter game laws: "The pigeon will never be exterminated so long as forests large enough for their nestings and mast enough for their food remain." If these conditions were met, "the pigeon . . . can care for itself."[43] Although individual pigeons were vulnerable to predation, the pigeon persisted as a species by reproducing profusely, satiating its predators, including humans, with overwhelming numbers. As Pokagon remembered, in the old days "whole tribes would wigwam in the brooding places" and kill them "by thousands." Yet "under our manner of securing them, they continued to increase."[44]

The passenger pigeon became an object of elegy long before the Sixth Extinction crisis was recognized. Writing in 1925, Gene Stratton-Porter used its extinction as a synecdoche for the decimation of the natural environment that she had described in loving detail in popular novels such as *Girl of the Limberlost* (1909). She imagined the last male searching for a mate and mimicked its distinctive call to develop a plaintive, Whitmanesque cadence: "See? See? See what you have done to me! See what you have done to your beautiful land! Where are your great stretches of forest? Where are the fish-thronged rivers your father enjoyed? . . . Why have you not saved the woods and the water and the wildflowers and the rustle of bird wings and the note of their song?"[45] The last wild pigeon, killed in 1902, was memorialized by a statue erected in 1947 in Wyalusing State Park in Wisconsin. Subsequent memorials include the Passenger Pigeon Memorial Hut at the Cincinnati Zoo, roadside markers in Pennsylvania, Indiana, Michigan, and Wisconsin, and a mural commissioned on the hundredth anniversary of the death of the last pigeon, named Martha, in the Cincinnati Zoo.[46] The hundredth anniversary also saw the publication of several commemorative books.[47]

Of such memorials, Leopold observed that "for one species to mourn the death of another is a new thing under the sun. The Cro-Magnon who slew the last mammoth thought only of steaks ... But we, who have lost the pigeons, mourn the loss. Had the funeral been ours, the pigeons would hardly have mourned us."[48] Such elegiac response has become general, functioning for example as the organizing genre of Maya Lin's multimedia project *What Is Missing?*[49] The project began with a bronze and wood sculpture, *Listening Cone*, and has since expanded into a website.[50] Billed as "Creating a Global Memorial to the Planet," the website enables users to locate species extinctions spatially or temporally from 2000 BCE forward and asks them to "share a memory about something you, or your parents or grandparents, have personally witnessed diminish or disappear from the natural world."[51]

Monarch Butterfly

While European settler-colonization continues to threaten extinctions through ongoing habitat destruction, the introduction of invasive species, and other factors, human-caused climate change threatens another wave of extinction. In this context, North American extinctions index global forces. In a sense, climate-driven extinctions return us to the position of Nicolar and the Lenape storyteller, who understood extinctive agency as superhuman power – but now with the difference that extinctions are no longer perceived to shape the world for human flourishing as the extinction of the mammoth had done. Probably because of such shifts in the understanding of world-shaping agency, imaginative literature has not yet successfully engaged the problem of climate-driven extinction. In the futures imagined in cli-fi novels such as Paolo Bacigalupi's *The Windup Girl* or Kim Stanley Robinson's *2312* – like earlier sci-fi novels such as Philip K. Dick's *Do Androids Dream of Electric Sheep?* – major extinctions have already happened. There is little sense of process and experience.

Conventional narrative chronology is not adapted to the scale of climate change.[52]

Two narratives centered on a threatened American species, the monarch butterfly, are suggestive in this context: Barbara Kingsolver's bestselling novel *Flight Behavior* and Donna Haraway's recent venture into speculative fiction, "The Camille Stories."[53] Critics have praised Kingsolver for raising consciousness about climate change.[54] The means by which she accomplishes this, however, are problematic. The climate scenario in *Flight Behavior* concerns the fall migration of the eastern population of monarchs, which have congregated not in their usual roosting locations in Mexico but rather massively at one site in eastern Tennessee, in the midst of climate-change-denying rural America.[55] The cause of the mismigration is unclear. A scientist who comes to study the roost hypothesizes that perhaps the Mexican sites have become too warm, or perhaps a parasite infestation has weakened the butterflies so they are unable to complete the journey, but in any case "a biological system is falling apart along its seams" because of "global warming."[56] Yet according to a leading expert on monarchs, "the behavior of monarchs that was the basis of [Kingsolver's] story is very unlikely."[57] In the novel, the roosting monarchs survive through a mild Tennessee winter until a February storm brings killing cold. The scientist leaves, "pack[ing] up his lab with the mood of closing a house after the death of a family."[58] The novel ends, however, with the butterflies' miraculous resurrection, "masses of pooled, streaky color, like the sheen of floating oil, like lava flow. That many ... Maybe a million. The shards of a wrecked generation had rested alive like a heartbeat in the trees, snow covered, charged with resistance. Now the sun blinked open on a long impossible time, and here was the exodus."[59] It seems Kingsolver has devised a scientifically implausible catastrophic event that renders the whole eastern monarch population vulnerable – and uses the event to rehearse the (overly reified) conflict on climate between rural Americans and the scientific establishment – because the more plausible scenario of the monarch's potential decline over a long period due to habitat loss and pesticide mortality would be difficult to narrate in novelistic time.[60] This more plausible scenario, moreover, would not be available for the analogy Kingsolver develops between the monarchs' flight behavior at the end of the novel and the behavior of the protagonist, who finally leaves a failing marriage to attend college. Thus the conventions of scientific reportage and literary narrative remain at odds.

Haraway by contrast brackets the problem of climate as she attempts to integrate scientific and literary discourse in "The Camille Stories." The outcome is a radical innovation of the familiar elegiac response to extinction. This innovation follows from the creation of human-animal "symbionts" through gene splicing and the introduction of "microorganisms from the symbiont animal."[61] Thus equipped, the human symbiont is tasked with "learning how to live in symbiosis so as to nurture the animal symbiont" into the anthropogenically damaged future.[62] Although Haraway emphasizes the work of nurturing, the eventual outcome in many such cases is a new form of elegy, for if the animal symbiont becomes extinct, the human symbiont becomes a living memorial. Haraway chooses monarch butterflies as her sample case, sketching the lives of five generations of symbionts named Camille over four hundred years. Camille 1 receives in utero "a suite of pattern-forming genes" that color "per" [*sic*] skin like a monarch's wings, genes enabling "per" to taste milkweed and nectar sources on the wind, genes and gut microbes enabling "per" to process the milkweed's toxic alkaloids, and other such enhancements that make present to the human the butterfly's experience of the world.[63] Subsequent generations may choose further enhancements, such as the butterfly-antennae chin implants chosen by Camille 2, who migrates to do decolonial work with habitat restoration in the monarch's overwintering sites in Mexico. Despite such nurturing, the monarch inevitably succumbs to extinction circa 2300 during the life of Camille 4. After the animal's extinction, the human symbiont's role shifts. Camille 5 becomes a "Speaker for the Dead" who "teach[es] practices of remembering and mourning" the monarch.[64] Unlike Kingsolver, Haraway does not attempt to address climate change. Nor does she imagine the restoration of a pre-human American wilderness, as Paul Martin fantasizes. Rather, she sets her story in the toxic, debris-ridden aftermath of mountain-top-removal coal mining, where she imagines nurturing human–animal interaction. The future of such interaction after extinction becomes a more active form of elegy than that invited by prominent modern extinctions such as the passenger pigeon and embodied in Maya Lin's *What Is Missing?* If "The Camille Stories" do not directly engage the relation between modern and Pleistocene-era colonizations, as do the cases of the mammoth and passenger pigeon, they do open that possibility with Camille 2's decolonization work in Mexico.

North American Extinctions in Global Context

The correlation of animal extinction with human colonization is not unique to North America. Notable cases attributable to modern settler-colonization include the extirpation of the Irish elk (Ireland), the dodo

(Mauritius), the great auk (North Atlantic coasts and islands), the Ezo wolf (Hokkaido), the Cape lion (southern Africa), and the thylacine (Tasmania). The Maori's extermination of the moa from New Zealand some 600 years ago, long before the arrival of Europeans, is similarly a result of settler colonialism.[65] Yet as the case of the mammoth indicates, the correlation with human colonization precedes these modern extinctions by millennia. Scientific research has found a strong correlation between megafaunal extinction events and the arrival of humans in Australia (some 80,000 to 40,000 years ago), Europe (50,000), and the Americas (15,000 to 20,000 or earlier) but only a weak correlation between extinction events and climate changes.[66] In the Anthropocene, climate change – overall global warming and locally more extreme weather events – puts additional, human-caused stress on many species. Even in the global context specified by the Anthropocene, however, North America remains a critical theater for understanding extinctions, as some of the cases examined in this chapter suggest, not least because here we often find narratives from two pulses of colonization in dialogue.

CHAPTER 5

Pastoral Reborn in the Anthropocene: Henry David Thoreau to Kyle Powys Whyte

Wai Chee Dimock

This chapter is an attempt to bring together two looming prospects of non-survival: the possible non-survival of the humanities, and the already demonstrated, already tangible non-survival of many plant and animal species. Using this shared danger as the beginning of a thought experiment, I'd like to argue that by linking the fate of the humanities self-consciously to the fate of the planet, we can face up to the worst-case scenario as a possible outcome with a good chance of becoming real, one that, at the very least, should have the effect of galvanizing us into action.[1] What might the humanities look like articulated through a future none of us would like to see? Can a discipline self-recognized as weak, perhaps already set on a path to extinction, adapt in time to reclaim its place in the world, producing along the way a new synthesis of the arts and sciences, and a new engagement with our shared crisis, designed to survive through the twenty-first century and beyond?

Eclogues in Extremis

In what follows, I'd like to explore one such heuristically "weak" synthesis, acting out of its less than secure claim on life and improvising out of dire necessity. Who are some of the partners we might reach out to, which archives might we consult, and which genres might we reanimate?

I begin with William Empson's famously counterintuitive argument that pastoral is a poetry of desperation, driven by the crises of its time rather than by bucolic fantasies, and that all "proletarian" literature is for that reason pastoral.[2] Dreaming of peace and harmony while contending with "human waste and limitation," this genre locates itself at a point just before catastrophe is final and irreversible, putting what could have been and what might yet be back into the picture. It turns these conjectural outcomes into "double plots," "tragi-comedy" pulling in opposite directions, never clearly telling the reader (or making up its own mind about) whether the comic or the tragic is dominant.[3]

Tracing these double plots back to antiquity, Raymond Williams argues that the classical form (e.g. Virgil's *Eclogues*) has always been double-edged, driven by "living tensions."[4] Pastoral goes hand in hand with counter-pastoral, giving it an alternating rhythm: the idyllic yoked with its imminent collapse; "summer with winter; pleasure with loss;" the quotidian life of the farmer with the impersonal "observation of the scientist."[5] This alternating rhythm resurfaced in the seventeenth century as contrary intuitions: "the enjoyment of what seems a natural bounty, a feeling of paradise in the garden, is exposed to another kind of wit: the easy consumption goes before the fall."[6]

Equally struck by the inevitability of the fall, Paul Alpers argues that the version of pastoral that is most elegiac also "sum[s] up the whole genre."[7] Pastoralism in general, like "pastoral elegy" in particular, takes "human life to be inherently a matter of common plights," an idyll that confronts us at every turn with "the question of how the world continues after a loss."[8] Asking the most common and most inconsolable of questions, pastoral is "less a genre than a mode," Leo Marx says, deriving "its character not from its formal properties, as a genre does, but rather from a special perspective on human experience."[9] It is a "cultural equipment that western thought has for more than two millennia been unable to do without," Lawrence Buell observes.[10]

That longevity surely has something to do with its recurring sense of urgency, its habit, as Kenneth Hiltner says, of always granting an endangered world "its belated emergence into appearance even as it disappears."[11] Pastoral owes its "staying power" to its long-running "covenant with life and the times," Seamus Heaney tells us, a covenant that, under "extreme conditions," turns it into an "eclogue *in extremis*."[12] This is certainly the case with Andrew Marvell's "Upon Appleton House," an eclogue in extremis for the seventeenth century updated now for the twenty-first, singing a dirge for nonhuman species as urgent today as it was back then:

> Unhappy Birds! what does it boot
> To build below the Grasses Root;
> When Lowness is unsafe as Hight,
> And Chance o'ertakes what 'scapeth spight?
> And now your Orphan Parents Call
> Sounds your untimely Funeral
> Death-Trumpets creak in such a Note,
> And 'tis the *Sourdine* in their Throat.

That dirge is a call to action as much as an act of mourning. "The very survival of our species depends upon" hearing it anew, claims Terry Gifford.[13]

Hound, Bay Horse, and Turtle Dove

Thoreau's *Walden* doesn't go quite as far. Still, it is an eclogue in extremis of sorts, not least when it is pastoral in what seems a naively idyllic sense, waxing sentimental in a bucolic setting:

> I long ago lost a hound, a bay horse, and a turtle dove, and am still on their trail. Many are the travellers I have spoken concerning them, describing their tracks and what calls they answered to. I have met one or two who had heard the hound, and the tramp of the horse, and even seen the dove disappear behind a cloud, and they seemed as anxious to recover them as if they had lost them themselves.[14]

What exactly is the occasion for this? It seems at once over-motivated and under-explained, which is probably why its sense of loss seems prolonged and tenacious, not easy to dispel. Thoreau himself is unable to take leave of it. On April 26, 1857, ten years after the publication of *Walden*, he would come back to it in a letter to B.B. Wiley, but glossing it in such a way as to leave what is unspecified still unspecified:

> If others have their losses, which they are busy repairing, so have I *mine*, & their hound & horse may perhaps be the symbols of some of them. But also I have lost, or am in danger of losing, a far finer & more ethereal treasure, which commonly no loss of which they are conscious will symbolize – this I answer hastily and with some hesitation, according as I now understand my own words.[15]

What is it that Thoreau has just lost, or is in danger of losing? The uncertainty here seems part of a larger pattern of uncertainty. The problem isn't just Thoreau's, because the English language itself seems to be at a loss when it comes to the phenomenon in question. What seems clear, though, is that something is in the air, a change is afoot, of a magnitude unlike anything we have seen. And Thoreau seemed to have some inkling of this, some glimpse into a future that is quite unlike the world we have grown used to, a non-affirmation and non-recuperation of the present. How was it that he already managed to have some understanding of this phenomenon, some sense that a large-scale, and for the most part irreversible, process was just around the corner? Quite aside from his immersion in Virgil, what other genres might have contributed to this eclogue in extremis?

Old Testament Against Darwin

Stanley Cavell, in *The Senses of Walden*, suggests one source for this intuition. Of all the genres readily encountered in nineteenth-century America, the one most serviceable to Thoreau, closest to his temperament, might turn out to be the fiery lamentations of the Old Testament prophets, especially Jeremiah and Ezekiel.[16] These are voices crying in the wilderness, speaking in tongues, seeing a calamity in the near future and providing the language, the rhetorical structure, and above all the emotional fervor to mourn large-scale devastations already upon us or just ahead of us. Here is Jeremiah: "For the mountains will I take up a weeping and wailing, and for the habitations of the wilderness a lamentation, because they are burned up, so that none can pass through them; neither can men hear the voice of the cattle; both the fowl of the heavens and the beast are fled; they are gone."[17]

Jeremiah only talks about all these species being "gone"; he does not use the word "extinction." He couldn't have – the word first appeared in the sixteenth century.[18] But the conceptual universe in which he operated was one in which that word would have meaning, one fully aware that the world was no longer what it used to be, and would never again be what it used to be. This sense of a process already well underway, unstoppable and non-benign, is particularly striking if we compare it with the rhetoric of "extinction" that would later gain currency in the mid-nineteenth century.

"Extinction" was a word that loomed large in *The Origin of Species*, especially the pivotal Chapter 4, "Natural Selection." True to Darwin's faith in a continually self-regenerating world, it was not a word that caused alarm. On the contrary, Darwin was reassured by this phenomenon, glad that there was this longstanding and always-reliable mechanism that would allow the world to update its inventory, getting rid of what is obsolete and ill-adapted. Natural selection would have been impossible without extinction, since this is the very means by which inferior species are eliminated to make way for superior ones: "The extinction of species and of whole groups of species, which has played so conspicuous a part in the history of the organic world, almost inevitably follows on the principle of natural selection, for old forms will be supplanted by new and improved forms."[19] We shouldn't be unduly sentimental about species that die out, because it is to the benefit of all that "new and improved varieties will inevitably supplant and exterminate the older, less improved and intermediate varieties."[20]

Thoreau was an admirer of Darwin. He had read *The Voyage of the Beagle* when its New York edition appeared in 1846, taking plenty of notes.

When *The Origin of Species* was published in late 1859, Thoreau was among the first to read and comment on it. And yet, on one subject – the extinction of species – he was much less sanguine, much less convinced that it was a good thing, indeed much closer to the lamenting spirit of the Old Testament prophets. On March 23, 1856, he wrote in his journal:

> Is it not a maimed and imperfect nature that I am conversant with? As if I were to study a tribe of Indians that had lost all its warriors. Many of those animal migrations and other phenomena by which the Indians marked the season, are no longer to be observed. My ancestors have torn out many of the first leaves and grandest passages, and mutilated it in many places . . .. All the great trees and beasts, fishes and fowl are gone; the streams perchance are somewhat shrunk.[21]

Endangered Humans

By the mid-nineteenth century, the world already seemed like a damaged place, with vital parts of it gone and never to be recovered. Quite apart from the Old Testament prophets, where else did Thoreau get this idea: that there are losses that are not compensated for, and not folded into a story of progress, of creation through destruction? The two references here to Native Americans – that the world that was once fully there for them is no longer there for us, and that these depletions in nature are related to depletions among these native tribes – seem especially significant. After all, the fate of these indigenous populations was plain for all to see. Survival was not something they could count on, nor the survival of the habitat in which they had been naturalized, in which they could flourish.

That much was clear. The question, though, was how to interpret this fact. Were Native Americans stand-alone casualties, an exception and an anomaly, dying out for reasons peculiar to themselves? Their long histories in the Americas, begun since time immemorial, could also make them necessary casualties at this point. They are no longer meant for this world precisely because they once had a self-evident relation to it.

Thoreau did occasionally embrace this line of thinking. *The Maine Woods*, in fact, opens with a strangely cavalier remark about the "extinction" of Native Americans, taking it for granted. "The ferry here took us past the Indian Island. As I left the shore, I observed a short, shabby, washerwoman-looking Indian – they commonly have the woebegone look of the girl that cried over spilt milk . . .. This picture will do to put before us the Indian's history, that is, the history of his extinction."[22]

The word "extinction" stands out starkly, even though it is in fact encountered relatively infrequently in Thoreau. His preferred term was narrower in scope and policy-specific – "extermination" rather than "extinction" – the outcome of a military campaign, rather than an impersonal natural process. His casual usage here seems not to register the gravity of the term, though this was hardly uncharacteristic of the mid-nineteenth century. It is helpful here to turn briefly to Washington Irving and Herman Melville to gain a broader and contrasting sense of the assumed cause and prospect of extinction, and the extent to which it was localized, indigenized, and taken for granted.

Irving and Melville

Irving was by far the most outspoken on the subject, not mincing words on where the responsibility fell. White society, he writes in *The Sketch Book*, has advanced upon native populations "like one of those withering airs that will sometimes breed desolation over a whole region of fertility."[23] He is especially outraged by the 1637 Mystic Massacre, the burning down of the wigwams of the Pequots and the "indiscriminate butchery" that ensued. Entering the swamps where the Pequot warriors had taken refuge with women and children, the troops "discharged their pieces, laden with ten or twelve pistol bullets at a time, putting the muzzles of the pieces under the boughs, within a few yards of them," so that all were "despatched and ended in the course of an hour."[24]

New World pastoral, for Irving, was indeed a history of mass extinction – accomplished not by the benign hand of natural selection but the trigger-happy hand of war. It was atrocious, but it was also *fait accompli*. That *fait accompli* calls for a form of elegy limited to just one function: mourning. Native Americans "will vanish like a vapor from the face of the earth; their very history will be lost in forgetfulness."[25] Irving ends with the lamentation of an old Pequot warrior: "our hatchets are broken, our bows are snapped, our fires are nearly extinguished: a little longer and the white man will cease to persecute us – for we shall cease to exist!"[26]

That path to non-existence seems to be taken for granted as well in *Moby-Dick*, though more offhandedly, in the form of a reminder about Ahab's oddly named ship: "the *Pequod*, you will no doubt remember, was the name of a celebrated tribe of Massachusetts Indians, now as extinct as the Medes."[27] The fate mourned by Irving as a crying shame seems here to be no more than a casual aside. But that casual aside turns out to be premature (or deliberately misleading on Melville's part), for as we soon find out, the supposedly extinct are never at any point absent from the narrative. Beginning with the "old squaw, Tistig, at Gay-Head," who issues the veiled warning that "the name [Ahab] would somehow prove prophetic," a surprisingly robust Native presence runs through the past, present, and future of *Moby-Dick*, a web of tangled kinship ensnaring everyone, irrespective of race.[28]

In Chapter 61, the first time a whale is killed, as the blood comes pouring out, the "slanting sun playing upon the crimson pond in the sea, sent back its reflection into every face, so that they all glowed to each other like red men."[29] *Like red men*: the relation between whites and Indians is no longer one of contrast, but one of resemblance. Stubb and his crew in the whale boat are doing what seafaring Native Americans – the original Nantucketers – have done for eternity. That resemblance is dramatized by the reflected red glow on their skin. Could this shared livelihood – and shared skin color – be the index to a future equally shared? The ending of *Moby-Dick* seems to suggest as much. In the final scene, as the concentric circles of the deadly vortex carry "the smallest chip of the *Pequod* out of sight," the disappearance of that prophetically named ship is accompanied by the most forceful reference yet to Native Americans, on hand until the bitter end:

> But as the last whelmings intermixingly poured themselves over the sunken head of the Indian at the main-mast, leaving a few inches of the erect spar yet visible, together with long streaming yards of the flag, which calmly undulated, with ironical coincidings, over the destroying billows they almost touched; – at that moment, a red arm and a hammer hovered backwardly uplifted in the open air, in the act of nailing the flag faster and yet faster to the subsiding spar. A sky-hawk that tauntingly had followed the maintruck downwards from its natural home among the stars, pecking at the flag, and incommoding Tashtego there; this bird now chanced to intercept its broad fluttering wing between the hammer and the wood; and simultaneously feeling the ethereal thrill, the submerged savage beneath, in his death-gasp, kept his hammer frozen there; and so the bird of heaven, with archangelic shrieks, and his imperial beak thrust upwards, and his whole captive form folded in the flag of Ahab, went down with his ship.[30]

Characteristically turning verbs into adverbs and nouns, Melville's idiosyncratic lexicon here seems to serve one specific purpose. Words like "whelmings," "intermixingly," and "coincidings" mix together different parts of speech, a blurring of grammatical distinction that seems to play out as well on the level of narrative logic: in the end, everyone becomes mixed together, a watery death unites all. Ahab's flag and the imperial eagle and the red arm and hammer all go down as one. *Moby-Dick*, in this sense, handily inverts the lamented but localized demise of Native Americans assumed by Irving. Mass destruction in Melville is not race-specific; it is indiscriminate and across the board. With the exception of Ishmael (whose survival is mentioned only in the Epilogue belatedly added to the American edition), there is no way out of that vortex.[31] Fatality for one is fatality for all.

Nontragic Pastoral

Here then is a version of pastoral pushed to its tragic limits: austere, inexorable, and non-negotiable in its casualty list and its fated catastrophe. Thoreau's approach is different. Equally fatalistic about Native Americans, he concentrates nonetheless not on the sublime drama of the predestined end but the day-to-day task of preserving what is still existing. Starting in 1847, during his stay at Walden Pond, he systematically compiled notes on indigenous peoples both in North America and elsewhere, eventually ending up with eleven volumes, containing "2,800 handwritten pages or over 500,000 words," Richard Fleck tells us. These "Indian Books," written "in English, French, Italian, Latin, and occasionally Hebrew," now housed in the Morgan Library, make up the single largest Native American archive in the nineteenth century.[32] In 1853, filling out the questionnaire and membership invitation from the Association for the Advancement of Science that asked about the "Branches of Science in which especial interest is felt," Thoreau gave this response: "The Manners and Customs of the Indians of the Algonquin Group previous to contact with the white men."[33] Native American languages, along with material artifacts, creation myths, and animal fables were constantly on his mind for the last fifteen years of his life.

These scientific inquiries suggest that another thought must have occurred to Thoreau, a sense that Native Americans might not be an anomaly at all, but rather an advance warning to the rest of us, giving us a glimpse of our collective future in their present condition, a preview we ignore at our own peril. This extraordinary passage, also from *Maine Woods*, shows a world with the tables turned and the axis of survival and non-survival reversed. Suddenly finding himself in a flourishing pre-Columbian sonic habitat entirely without meaning for him, Thoreau intuits for the first time that perhaps it isn't the Native Americans but he himself who is the alien and misfit:

It was a purely wild and primitive American sound, as much as the barking of a chickadee, and I could not understand a word of it . . . .. These Abenakis gossiped, laughed, and jested, in the language in which Eliot's Indian Bible is written, the language which has been spoken in New England who shall say how long? These were the sounds that issued from the wigwams of this country before Columbus was born; they have not yet died away.[34]

Listening to the sounds of the Abenaki language, Thoreau has a kind of negative epiphany: these sounds belong to these woods, and he does not. Native Americans, of course, were the ones usually made to feel that way. It says something about Thoreau that he is able momentarily to switch places with them, and subject himself to that surreal sense of involuntary non-belonging. Doing so, he makes default vulnerability a baseline human condition, the most persistent and most widely shared common denominator for our species. Listening to Native Americans in that light, he hears them for what they are: veterans of survival and prophets in the wilderness, speaking in tongues that have "not yet died away" and perhaps will never die away, tongues whose vital import is just becoming apparent.

Climate Resilience

Here then is a resilient form for the twenty-first century: an indigenous pastoral, not a hide-bound genre but a crisis-responsive mode, intimate with the forces of catastrophe and able to project hope out of the company it keeps. The soundtracks of now legendary names – Charley Patton, Jimi Hendrix, Mildred Bailey, Robbie Robertson, Link Wray, and Redbone – featured in Catherine Bainbridge's award-winning film *Rumble: Indians Who Rock the World*, make up one strand of this new pastoral.[35] The live performances in the National Museum of the American Indian make up another strand.[36] A record number of Native Americans winning congressional and state legislative seats in 2018 add a third.[37] The growing number of indigenous languages programs – from the two-year Master's program at MIT;[38] to the eight-language offerings at Yale;[39] to the pioneering American Indian Studies Research Institute at Indiana University, which uses digital tools and online "talking dictionaries" to offer instruction in Arikara, Assiniboine, and Pawnee to elementary schools, high schools, and community colleges – add yet another.[40] And the NEH-funded Standing Rock Lakota/Dakota Language Project at Sitting Bull College, which brings together the last generation of fluent speakers to transcribe indigenous texts and make live recordings to inspire new speakers, suggests that the volume might be far from its limits.[41]

Kyle Powys Whyte, Potawatomi philosopher, author, and activist, is especially helpful in linking these resurgent sounds to time-tested strategies of adapting honed through long practice. The massive disruptions that we now associate with climate change – ecosystem collapse, species loss, involuntary relocation, and pandemics – had always been part and parcel of New World colonialism, in play since the sixteenth century. Newly seen as apocalyptic in the twenty-first century, they seem far less so to Native peoples who have long suffered under them and lived through them, emerging with a different relation to the nonhuman world, and to ancestors and descendants both. "Climate adaptation" has always been key to indigenous communities, Whyte argues, a form of knowledge that makes them veterans and pioneers in a "forward-looking framework of justice." Honoring "systems of responsibilities" ranging from "webs of interspecies relationships to government-to-government partnerships," Native Americans are now on the front lines of climate activism, setting into motion a "green print" for the future, to which the rest of us are just beginning to rally.[42]

Native American reservations, taking up only 2 percent of the land in the US, hold 20 percent of the nation's fossil fuel reserves, including coal, oil, and gas, worth some $1.5 trillion. Rather than privatizing and profiting from these reserves, Native Americans are among the most vocal opponents of a carbon-based economy. Deb Haaland, Congresswoman from New Mexico, is committed to 100 percent renewable energy. "The fight for Native American rights is also a fight for climate justice," she said.[43] Sheila Watt-Cloutier, Chair for the Inuit Circumpolar Council and nominated for the Nobel Peace Prize in 2007, has likewise made energy the key issue in global governance, working with Earthjustice and the Center for International Environmental Law to petition the Inter-American Commission to conduct hearings on the relation between climate change and human rights.[44]

This climate activism takes center stage in the Standing Rock Sioux Tribe's vigilance over the Dakota Access Pipeline, in play ever since the proposed plan was first announced in 2014.[45] Even though the pipeline was approved by the Trump Administration, this activism remains undiminished as indigenous protestors monitor the oil leaks,[46] while scoring a major legal victory in March 2020, when a federal judge ordered a new, full-scale environmental review of the Dakota Access Pipeline.[47] They are also gearing up for a new fight against yet another proposal, known by the innocuous name "Line 3." *The Guardian* reports:

Winona LaDuke, a veteran Native American activist and remarkable orator, has led a series of horseback rides along the pipeline route. Last year a group of Native youth organized a 250-mile "Paddle to Protect" canoe protest along the Mississippi River, which will be crossed twice by Line 3.

If you want to hear what the resistance sounds like, "No Line 3" by Native rapper Thomas X is a good place to start; if you want to get a literal taste of it, Native women have routinely brought traditional breakfasts like frybread with blueberry sauce to the various public hearings over the project, sharing the food with everyone right down to the pipeline lawyers. (If you'd like you can also order some wild rice from LaDuke's Honor the Earth, one of the premier indigenous environmental organizations on the continent.)[48]

Here then are the sights, sounds, and tastes of pastoral reborn. Energized as never before, indigenous in its full glory, it challenges the rest of us to be similarly resilient, to improvise in ways that will fend off extinction, push it further and further into the distant future.

PART II

Environmental Genres and Media

CHAPTER 6

The Heat of Modernity: The Great Gatsby *as Petrofiction*

Harilaos Stecopoulos

"I read somewhere that the sun's getting hotter ever year."
Tom Buchanan, *The Great Gatsby*[1]

What would it mean to read *The Great Gatsby* as petrofiction? To set aside the Roaring Twenties vision of the novel and read the text as a rich response to the gasoline age? In certain respects, *Gatsby* and oil are likely bedfellows. A work preoccupied with driving and automobiles, this classic novel regularly references petroculture. Tom Buchanan buys a puppy from a man who resembles oil magnate John D. Rockefeller; a drunk driver at Gatsby's party wonders "where there's a gas'line station?"; Nick jokingly asks Daisy if gasoline affects her chauffeur's nose; and Gatsby warns Tom Buchanan that his car doesn't have "much gas."[2] Oil is as indispensable to Fitzgerald as it is to any writer chronicling "the constant flicker of men and women and machines" typical of propulsive modernity.[3] Like Upton Sinclair, Vladimir Nabokov, Jack Kerouac, and countless other novelists, Fitzgerald can't write America without engaging with gasoline.[4]

Not that all oil texts are equal. Most modern novels represent petroleum in what Joshua Schuster rightly calls "indirect forms," descriptions of "cars, speed, consumption, and energy expenditure."[5] And when those texts do engage more explicitly with oil culture, they usually offer generic depictions of filling stations or predictable accounts of stopping for gas that do little more than testify to the ubiquity of this resource. Twentieth- and twenty-first-century fiction often reminds us of how we have been "living in oil," to borrow Stephanie LeMenager's resonant phrase, but it rarely repays analysis of how resource capitalism can incite an aesthetic vision, let alone a social critique.[6] Thin descriptions of cars and fuel render most literature symptomatic not diagnostic of petroculture.

The Great Gatsby is different. The novel doesn't offer readers sustained examination of the petroleum industry as Upton Sinclair's *Oil!* would one year later. There are no lurid tableaux of oozing crude or well fires in Fitzgerald's text. Instead, this classic novel examines how "oil [defines] so much of being in modernity" by engaging with petroculture at the level of character.[7] Oil and its infrastructure provide Nick with a discourse with which he can represent the more doomed figures of his narrative. For "the careless" Tom, Daisy, and Jordan, oil is so thoroughly mediated that it barely registers. They take this resource for granted. But for George, Myrtle, and Gatsby, the three characters outside the charmed circle of established privilege, fuel represents dreams of modernity. Little wonder, then, that they live near oil or work with oil, whether in the upper echelons of business as does Gatsby or in the trenches of the service station like Myrtle and George. Petroleum energy is for those fated characters closely linked to social energy, to the drive needed to climb and succeed. Gasoline is more than a throwaway detail in the novel; it is fundamental to how Nick Carraway attempts to comprehend the characters' relationship to the possibilities and dangers of twentieth-century life.

In what follows, I put the gas back in *Gatsby*. I begin by looking at a major historical source for Fitzgerald's critical approach to oil: the Teapot Dome Scandal (1921–1923) that first highlighted the new dangers of federal and corporate corruption in resource management. I then turn to how oil discourse informs Nick's relationship to the narrative's three aspirant characters, Gatsby, Myrtle, and George. Nick links each of those figures to the promise and failure of petromodernity. What Nick dubs "the savage violence" of resource capitalism shapes the novel, particularly the homicides central to the denouement.[8] If gas evinces rich emancipatory potential in this narrative, it signifies most palpably through a plot in which energy ends up having little relationship to modern freedom and possibility. Instead, the promise of petroculture seems to require terrible bloodletting and the sacrifice of the novel's most vulnerable characters. Oil ontology and precarity inform one another in *The Great Gatsby*. The chapter concludes with some speculations about how Fitzgerald's novel might offer us a new perspective on oil and modernism.

***

Ever since Patricia Yaeger coined the term "the energy unconscious" in 2011, scholars have reread literature with an eye to teasing out its relationship to a particular resource.[9] This has been a largely historical project as academics typically link a literary text to a specific Western fuel system, whether whale oil in Jamie Jones's important work on *Moby-Dick* or coal in Heidi Scott's insightful reading of *Wuthering Heights*.[10] *The Great Gatsby* invites a similar historicist approach. Literary critics rarely interpret the post–World War I period in terms of oil but this era of flappers, sheiks, and bathtub gin was also a time in which the nation first embraced a new type of fuel and the vehicles that depended upon it.[11] Many of the most famous texts of the era – *Cane* (1923), *The Great Gatsby* (1925), *The Professor's House* (1925), *Manhattan Transfer* (1925), *A Farewell to Arms* (1929) – evince significant interest in oil. Their repeated references to cars, ambulances, roads, gasoline, pumps, and garages testify to modernism's imbrication with the gasoline economy and supportive infrastructure. Some of those literary works don't probe deeply into the oil imaginary, but others find in gasoline a new way of pondering the meaning of modern American life. As Peter Hitchcock puts it, "The Great American Oil Novel is contemporaneous with the emergence of oil in American history."[12]

The furor over the Teapot Dome Scandal demonstrates how contemporary events encouraged a fascination with oil.[13] Arguably the most important example of resource corruption in the twentieth century, this scandal loomed large in the post–World War I era as a case of greed and manipulation more notorious than the fixing of the 1919 World Series cited in the novel.[14] In 1921, President Warren Harding shifted control of the naval oil reserves at Teapot Dome, Wyoming, and at Buena Vista and Elk Hills in California to the Department of the Interior. Following the transfer, Albert Hall, then Secretary of the Interior, secretly leased the Wyoming reserves at a low rate to Harry Sinclair of the Mammoth Oil Company, and the California reserves to Edward Doheny of the Pan Am Petroleum and Transport Company. In return for an opportunity to engage in illegal drilling on what were federally owned lands, Sinclair invested in Hall's New Mexico ranch while Doheny paid the Secretary $100,000 outright. Illicit resource extraction paid substantial dividends.

The fallout from Teapot Dome would implicate those three men as well as President Harding. Hall would eventually be convicted for taking bribes from Sinclair and Doheny, and, prior to his untimely death in 1923, Harding would endure the shame of having endorsed the transfer of the oil reserves, and generally turning a blind eye to the corruption that permeated his administration. Sinclair and Doheny would escape punishment and reassert themselves as resource oligarchs but Teapot Dome soon become synonymous with Big Oil's corrupt business practices. As Montana Senator Thomas J. Walsh (D) put it, the scandal was "the most stupendous piece of thievery known to our annals."[15] If the 1920s marked the beginning of a full-fledged petroculture, it did so in a manner that highlighted the backroom dealings and outright criminality that would characterize the oil era. Enormous profits could be made through the illegal privatization of publicly owned natural resources.

Set in 1922, the year journalists first broke the story of Secretary Hall's chicanery, *The Great Gatsby* recognizes oil as both alluring and dangerous. Fitzgerald makes the threateningly seductive aspects of petroleum evident by linking the resource to expressions of wealth and power. The "hulking" plutocrat Tom Buchanan suggests as much when he informs Nick early on that his extravagant East Egg estate with "a half acre of . . . roses" "once belonged to Demaine, the oil man."[16] What drives this point home, however, is Fitzgerald's insistence that the reader should understand the nascent petroleum industry and, indeed, all resource extraction, as a lucrative criminal practice. He does so most visibly by portraying Dan Cody, the tycoon who mentored the young Jay Gatz, as something of a gentrified thug, if one who made his money in copper instead of loan-sharking and gambling. Remembering the portrait of Cody on Gatsby's wall, Nick describes the copper magnate as a "pioneer debauchee, who . . . brought back to the Eastern seaboard the savage violence of the frontier brothel and salon."[17] Cody, Gatsby's father-figure, embodies the close relationship between mining and the physical terror of the West. And the connection between resources and violence persists into the modern era represented in the novel. As Tom Buchanan implies toward the end of the narrative, the criminals who sell illegal alcohol under the counter at Prohibition-era drugstores might very well also sell "gas."[18] In Fitzgerald's view, we may speculate, Westerners such as Dan Cody or Mammoth Oil's Harry Sinclair have more in common with Wolfsheim and other urban gangsters than their different regional contexts might suggest.

Writing in the wake of the Teapot Dome Scandal, Fitzgerald recognized the larcenous nature of those public figures who attempted to control oil, but he also understood a more subtle home truth: the degree to which the new fuel regime could exert power over ordinary American lives. In 1920, Scott and Zelda drove their Marmon Speedster from Westport, Connecticut to Montgomery, Alabama, a largely comic experience chronicled in the novelist's essay "The Cruise of the Rolling Junk" (1924). Replete with pot-holed highways and cranky mechanics, the piece delights in the couple's misadventures on the road. At the same time, "The Cruise of the Rolling Junk" also calls attention to how an incipient petroculture reduced the Fitzgeralds' values and expectations to an all-consuming need for fuel. In one notable scene, the celebrity couple realize they are almost out of gas while driving through rural Virginia, and they devolve into a state of panic and desperation. The world now signifies solely in terms of oil. As they approach a small town, Fitzgerald rejects civil society in the name of petroleum. "Let it lack churches and schools and chambers of commerce," he proclaims, "but let it not lack gasoline!"[19] For this modernist, American life depends far more on fuel and energy than it does on the institutions usually thought to comprise civilization. When "the oil register showed zero," Fitzgerald later states, "We became very sad . . . the game was up."[20] Without oil, Fitzgerald implies, contemporary American existence is difficult if not futile.

As this biographical anecdote should suggest, Fitzgerald understood, however inchoately, that the alluring potential of petroculture coexisted with the unsettling limitations of oil dependency.[21] *The Great Gatsby* makes the dangerous seductiveness of this fuel even more palpable by dramatizing through the titular character how petroleum suggests untold possibilities. It is customary to understand Gatsby in terms of his enormous cream-colored automobile and the luxurious lifestyle it represents.[22] His Jazz Age is very much an era of speed, of "fenders spread like wings" and "cars going up and down."[23] But Nick also links Gatsby to gasoline in different ways, and the mysterious figure is in many respects as emblematic of a new type of energy as he is of a new type of transportation. This connection to petroleum redounds to Gatsby's criminal reputation as "a bootlegger" "who has killed a man."[24] By informing Daisy that he used to be in the "the oil business," the mysterious man of affluence claims a tie to an industry that signified as an example of corrupt if not illegal dealings.[25]

More importantly, Nick ascribes to Gatsby what LeMenager dubs "the charisma of energy" – a captivating and almost magical capacity to affect the world.[26] When the two characters witness an immigrant funeral procession upon entering Manhattan, for example, Nick draws attention to the titular character's oil-fueled glamour by saying "I was glad that the sight of Gatsby's splendid car was included in their somber holiday."[27] For the narrator, this object of petromodernity provides uplift for the unfortunate mourners because it is at once gorgeous and mobile, a fabulous instantiation of the social movement to which they aspire. The "splendid car" is from this perspective both the glittering jewel of a capitalist American dream *and* a physical reminder of the fossil fuel subtending new socio-economic possibilities. Oil isn't only a sign of illicit wealth gained through corrupt means; it is also emblematic of a desire to find in resource extraction all that modernity has promised.

Nick's attempt to explore the mystery of Gatsby draws on a welter of social and cultural discourses, from nativism to popular jazz to sartorial style. Initially, gasoline doesn't seem to enter the picture. But petroleum informs Nick's account of the titular character and his vision of modernity, and it emerges in geological cum infrastructural representations of Gatsby's charismatic self-creation. Those images begin early in the novel when Nick informs the reader that Gatsby's "heightened sensitivity to the promises of life" rendered him akin to "one of those intricate machines that register earthquakes ten thousand miles away."[28] Nick refers here to the seismograph, first invented in 1880 but improved over the early twentieth century, in part because of its military value in identifying World War I artillery locations by registering tremors. By the early 1920s, use of the seismograph had become more widespread and the expanding petroleum industry began using those "intricate machines" to identify new sources of fossil fuel through a refraction process that measured ground disturbance.[29] Some of Fitzgerald's contemporaries would have understood the seismograph as linked to oil extraction, particularly after the use of seismic refraction led to the discovery of oil in Orchard Dome, Texas in 1924.[30] In linking Gatsby to a new form of geoexploration, the narrator inadvertently connects him to an incipient petroculture.

Nick invokes this connection not to comment directly on earthquakes let alone oil drilling, but rather to celebrate Gatsby's "heightened sensitivity to the promises of life." The titular character's capacity to express himself through style, fashion, parties, and romance first emerges through the narrator's geological language. And Nick persists in using such rhetoric to demonstrate that, as Dipesh Chakrabarty might argue, Gatsby's "mansion of modern freedoms stands on an ever-expanding base of fossil fuel use."[31] In recounting the experiences of the young James Gatz later in the narrative, for example, Nick turns, tellingly, to another metaphor that suggests subterranean potential. For the riotous-hearted Gatz, our narrator explains, wild "reveries" of future success depend on the belief that "the rock of the world was founded securely on a fairy's wing" – that beneath the rock existed something extraordinary.[32] Gatsby has the capacity to register earthquakes, but he also has the ability to identify magic below the soil, and it is the latter talent that seems integral to his self-creation. Like Ryszard Kapuscinski, Nick suggests that "oil creates the illusion of a completely changed life."[33] The ability of James Gatz to become Jay Gatsby and recover the dream of Daisy Buchanan depends on an era enabled by petroleum. *Gatsby* is a novel about the dream of repeating the past; but it is also a novel about how a culture of fossil fuel claims to turn the (material) past into a bright future.[34]

The sense that Gatsby's charismatic qualities depend on – and are connected to – petromodernity grows more manifest still when Nick links Gatsby to oil infrastructure. Describing his drive home from the Buchanans, the narrator rhapsodizes on the quotidian sights he witnesses during the short journey: "Already it was deep summer on roadhouse roofs and in front of wayside garages, where new red gas-pumps sat out in pools of light." Moving dynamically from an aerial ("on roadhouse roofs") to an earth-bound perspective ("in front of"), Nick fixates on the "new red gas-pumps" that sit "out in pools of light." More than any aspect of the roadside tableau, the pumps demand Nick's attention and he responds in kind, depicting them as alluring objects that warrant their own nimbi. For Nick, those pieces of petroleum infrastructure seem as sacred, even totemic, as they are modern and "new."[35]

Gatsby elicits from Nick a comparably rapturous description a few lines later. Upon returning to his home, the narrator notices he is "not alone – fifty feet away a figure has emerged from the shadow of my neighbor's mansion and was standing with his hands in his pockets . . .. Something in his leisurely movement and the secure position of his feet upon the lawn suggested that it was Mr. Gatsby."[36] Thanks to his proprietary physical presence ("the secure position of his feet upon the lawn"), Gatsby stands out from the dark surroundings. Like the new red pumps, he attracts the eye, lit not by electricity but by the "loud, bright night."[37] Gatsby manifests an exceptional quality that distinguishes him from everything and everyone around him. But Fitzgerald also gestures subtly at a Dan Cody-like connection between those pumps and his hero when in the midst of Nick's lyrical tribute, there emerges a telling hint of the possessive. In musing on why Gatsby has stepped into the night air, Nick imagines that the mysterious figure is there "to determine what share was his of our local heavens."[38] However lyrically rendered, Nick's description doesn't paint Gatsby as the romantic figure pining after his lost love – the fabled green light will make its first appearance in the next paragraph – but instead renders him a speculator eager to identify the extent of his claim. The magic promise of oil draws from, and helps reflect, its pecuniary allure.

By highlighting Gatsby's proprietary qualities, Nick reminds us that he rarely neglects the bottom line. For all his romantic yearning and extravagant expenditure, Gatsby is a successful businessman who shares certain mercantile qualities with the other wealthy characters of the novel. The fact that he works with Walter Chase, one of Tom Buchanan's friends, on an unnamed illicit deal makes this even more apparent.[39] Those connections only go so far, however, particularly when it comes to oil and speed. Nick takes pains to emphasize that the Buchanans and Jordan Baker stand apart from Gatsby in their relationship to petromodernity. Tom, Jordan, and Daisy's capacity to "[smash] up things and creatures," as Nick puts it, reflects a sense of energy entitlement that reaffirms the status quo and denies the social possibility Gatsby seems to embody.[40] As Patricia Yaeger might put it, Tom, Daisy, and Jordan exist "in a system of mythic abundance not available to the energy worker who lives in carnal exhaustion."[41] The power made possible by oil is, for the plutocrats, a new way of dominating the world. Nick seems to recognize this. In an era when the media tended to demonize African American and immigrant drivers, it is telling that Fitzgerald depicts the wealthy as particularly dangerous behind the wheel. Tom has crashed a car in southern California, breaking the arm of his date, a chambermaid from the Santa Barbara hotel; Jordan barely misses a workman, clipping a button on his clothes; and Daisy kills Myrtle in an act of vehicular homicide.[42] The automobile is, in their hands, tantamount to a weapon against those who seek in petromodernity the possibility of personal and social uplift.[43]

Energy has no relationship to work for Tom, Daisy, and Jordan, and this hard fact opposes them not only to Gatsby, for whom energy signifies as a kind of imaginative and speculative labor, but also to Myrtle and George who physically exert themselves to make petromodernity a reality. The latter's ravaged portion of Queens makes palpable a visceral relationship to the ugly realities of resource capitalism. Described as a "desolate area of land" "bounded by a small foul river," "the valley of ashes" exudes toxicity due to the many garbage and coal fires that characterize the area.[44] The ecological devastation suggested by the area also recalls the fuel sold at the couple's garage. For all its status as a valued commodity, gasoline exists on an incendiary continuum with the burning industrial waste that defines this metropolitan periphery.

George Wilson's garage is equally unprepossessing. The "dim," "unprosperous and bare" building resembles the "dumping ground" around it.[45] But as Nick points out, there is more here than first meets the eye. "It had occurred to me," he states upon entering the Wilsons' business, "that this shadow of a garage must be a blind."[46] Nick imagines "that sumptuous and romantic apartments were concealed overhead" but he soon discovers another secret at the filling station: the novel's main site of oil consumption is also its locus of desire and violence.[47] This garage figures prominently in the most unsettling parts of the narrative: first, in Chapter 2, when Tom and Nick disembark from the train to meet Myrtle Wilson; second, in Chapter 7, when Tom, Nick, and Jordan stop at the station for gas and Myrtle mistakes Jordan for Daisy; third, in Chapter 7, when Daisy accidentally kills Myrtle while driving Gatsby's car; fourth, and finally, when George Wilson locates Gatsby and murders him before committing suicide. If George Wilson's garage is a repository of fuel, it is also a site that makes manifest petroleum's intimate relationship to the violence of modern life. The latter point has a narrative correlative. By linking the garage to betrayal and bloodletting, Fitzgerald implies that oil and its infrastructure are the catalysts needed to propel the plot. Much like the characters who stop at Wilson's to fill their tanks, the novel finds in this gas station a valuable source of energy. Without the garage, it's hard to imagine *Gatsby* fulfilling its narrative arc.[48]

Importantly, that arc comes at great cost to Myrtle and George, the two lower-middle-class characters who depend on petroleum for their livelihood, and who, like Gatsby, are linked to oil infrastructure in the novel. Myrtle may seem to affirm the romantic vision of hidden apartments given her capacity to transcend through libidinal power the dismal surroundings. Her "thickish figure" and "surplus flesh" project a heat that seems to escape the valley of ashes.[49] "There was an immediately perceptible vitality about her," Nick informs us upon meeting Tom's mistress, "as if the nerves of her body were continually smouldering."[50] This description colludes with Tom's treatment of Myrtle by defining her solely in terms of an irrepressible physicality. But Nick's account of Myrtle is as we shall see also a commentary, inadvertent or otherwise, on the newly emerging energy regime of the 1920s. Excessive and combustible, Myrtle evinces the promise and fatality of living oil.

Nick implies at several points that Myrtle's relationship with fossil fuel exceeds economic imperatives let alone dusty garages; the energy represented by oil is at some level inseparable from her powerful life force. The narrator suggests as much when he spies Myrtle while driving with Gatsby toward Manhattan. "I had a glimpse of Mrs. Wilson straining at the garage pump with panting vitality," he tells us.[51] To be sure, in depicting Mrs. Wilson "straining" and "panting" at the "pump," Nick shifts into an eroticized discourse unusual for the novel. But his excessive language in this brief moment may attest as much to his interest in oil and labor as it does his fascination with Myrtle's sexuality. Nick's description inadvertently reminds us that the word "pump" at this moment in petromodernity functioned as both noun and verb far more than it does in twenty-first-century America. And with good reason. In the 1920s, one pumped gasoline by cranking a handle that raised the oil to the level where it could drain into the automobile.[52] Petroleum's promise of easy energy paradoxically involved exertion, mostly by working- and lower-middle-class workers.[53] For all its sexual meaning, Myrtle's "straining" at the pump also highlights the intimate relationship of labor to fuel. Her "panting vitality" isn't so much opposed as connected to the filling station.

That Nick understands Myrtle in terms of petroleum and its infrastructure grows more manifest in his postmortem depiction of her. Repeating his association of Myrtle's body and energy, he describes her corpse as a reservoir that has failed: "The mouth was wide open and ripped at the corners as though she had choked a little in giving up the tremendous vitality she had stored so long."[54] Myrtle's death seems more the result of an explosion from within than an automotive crash from without. In this scene, vitality doesn't seem an ineffable quality or characteristic. Instead, vitality assumes material properties as if it were a substance that Myrtle retained but couldn't dispense without fatal consequences. She assumes the properties of a conduit or a tube uncontrollably releasing a substance from internal storage. Torn open by what seems to be a high-pressure surge, Myrtle seems to have died from the equivalent of a gusher, a phenomenon Upton Sinclair would describe in equally explosive terms: "The inside of the earth seemed to burst through that hole; a roaring and rushing."[55] Myrtle's intimate connection to oil has made her the victim, not the agent, of petromodernity.

Myrtle's husband manifests an equally unsettling connection to petroleum and modern energy more broadly. As *Time Magazine*'s book reviewer reminded readers in 1925, George is "an accessory in oil-smeared dungarees" and the garage owner is often linked to the pumping of gasoline.[56] "Let's have some oil." Tom Buchanan demands of George at one point, emphasizing that this character has no identity outside the fuel he provides.[57] But unlike Myrtle, the gas station owner manifests no visceral connection to oil. Stressing his lack of physical presence, Nick describes George as "spiritless" and "anaemic," a "ghost" of a man barely distinguishable from "the cement color of the walls" in his office.[58] This invisibility signifies most tellingly in terms of an energy deficiency. As George tells Tom at one point, "I'm all run down."[59] The garage owner has no life force; he suggests little more than enervation and impending stasis. "He was one of these worn-out men," thinks Michaelis, George's neighbor.[60]

The irony is palpable. The man who sells fuel has barely any energy at all. Fitzgerald emphasizes this point by having George provide other drivers with fuel but never allowing him to have any interaction with an automobile as either a mechanic or a driver. When George does attempt to purchase a car, he turns to the wealthy Tom Buchanan, only to repeatedly come up empty-handed. "When are you going to sell me that car?" George asks his wealthy interlocutor.[61] Several chapters later, George queries Tom again, "I need money pretty bad, and I was wondering what you were going to do with your old car."[62] George has no chance of gaining access to this or indeed any automobile in a world dominated by plutocrats. The garage owner only signifies as, in Tom's mock caption, "George B. Wilson at the Gasoline Pump"[63] – a lower-middle-class man forever providing oil to those who benefit from the freedom and possibility it affords them. George may always be "at the pump" but unlike the Buchanans and indeed, the Fitzgeralds themselves, he can never claim the prerogatives of petroculture.

There is one seeming exception to the garage owner's lack of energy: his successful tracking and murder of Gatsby, the character to whom Fitzgerald ascribes the possibility and potential of living oil. Tellingly, George's hunt is, at least initially, for a car – the "death car" that struck and killed Myrtle.[64] But he also makes his broadly uneasy relationship to automobiles palpable by staring "oddly" at "motorists" "from the side of the road."[65] Indeed, George's relationship to cars is so overdetermined that the police assume he spent the better part of the day "going from garage to garage . . . inquiring for a yellow car."[66] If the immigrant funeral procession enjoyed Gatsby's "splendid" automobile as a sign of potential social uplift, George views the same vehicle as a sign of how the elite destroyed his life.

But Fitzgerald doesn't allow the enervated garage owner to signify solely as an example of how the new petroleum regime reflects the prevailing social order, with the rich accessing the power of petroculture and the more marginal standing in vexed relation to oil's possibilities. Instead, the novelist uses the lower-middle-class purveyor of gasoline to demonstrate that even those arrivistes who, like Gatsby, seem capable of embodying the freedom of oil, are in the end doomed by the corrupting power of the resource they exploit. As Nick later confirms, George did not visit countless Long Island garages in his quest for Gatsby. On the contrary, he located Tom Buchanan and learned Gatsby's name and address, tracking down the titular hero and killing him.[67] If petromodernity had offered Gatsby the magic of energy, the capacity to go, to drive – to always see a green light urging him on – resource capitalism created his antithesis in George, the man whose evisceration by oil renders him an inadvertent weapon of the ruling class. The magic of fossil fuel, its promise as an emancipatory force for modernity, vanishes in a murder-suicide that eliminates both challenges to the narrative's reigning capitalist. Tom Buchanan absorbs modernity's new energy to oppress those precarious characters who attempt to find in the new fuel the basis for a new social reality. In his hands, oil "proves to be . . . the instrument of [their] undoing."[68]

***

In *Culture and Imperialism*, Edward Said famously argued that modernism responded to "the external pressures on culture from the imperium" by instantiating in formal and thematic terms the metropole's uneasy relationship to the colonies from which it drew resources, labor, culture, and profit.[69] Conrad, Forster, Malraux, and other writers took "narrative from the triumphalist experience of imperialism into the extremes of self-consciousness, discontinuity, self-referentiality, and corrosive irony." *The Great Gatsby* reminds us that some US modernists – Fitzgerald, Sinclair, Faulkner, Hurston, Steinbeck – exhibited a similarly "extreme, unsettling anxiety" about resource capitalism and its integral role in the making of modernity.[70] This was due in part to the connection linking modernism's generative engagement with empire to its rich awareness of energy resources. Modern writers sensitive to colonial dynamics understood that the national and global peripheries provided coffee, sugar, tobacco, and others forms of stimulation for metropolitan bodies. But energy modernists also diverged from their counterparts in attending to the speed and destruction endemic to petromodernity. Responding to the contemporary cult of "adrenaline aesthetics" evident in everything from Futurism to stock market speculation, those writers expressed unease with their culture's newfound dependence on fossil fuel, recognizing, however fitfully, that new forms of resource capitalism demanded the sacrifice of people and places.[71] For them, we might say, modernism's obsession with speed incited a concomitant turn to an incipient energy politics sensitive to both the marginal *and* the subterranean, the precarious *and* the planetary.[72] *Gatsby* evinces this trend not by providing realistic representation of oil and its infrastructure but by relying on metaphors that capture the high cost of petro-exploitation. However indirectly, Fitzgerald's account of bodies as gushers, seismic machines, and depleted energy fields dramatizes how vulnerable Americans would suffer for the dream of extracting magic ("a fairy's wing") from beneath the rock.[73] And he suggests that the earth pays a price as well. The end of this modernist classic leaves the reader with a self-conscious warning about the resource capitalism that subtends the freedom and expressiveness of the Jazz Age. For all its allure, for all its potential, the energy produced from oil leads to a "holocaust," whether in the violent deaths of a gas station owner and his victim or in the devastation of a "green . . . world" fast becoming a "valley of ashes."[74] Fitzgerald careens through the glamour of petromodernity only to arrive at a sobering ecological conclusion.

CHAPTER 7

Children in Transit / Children in Peril: The Contemporary US Novel in a Time of Climate Crisis

Min Hyoung Song

In September 2015, the photograph of a lifeless three-year old Syrian boy lying face down on a beach was inescapable, as it appeared in every conceivable news venue around the world and became a constant presence on social media. Alan Kurdi had died alongside his five-year-old brother and his mother when the boat they were on capsized in the Mediterranean. The image of his body was part of a larger story about a growing migration crisis, stemming not only from Syria but from all over the Middle East (or West Asia), Africa, and Central America, which is itself part of an even larger – but muted – story about the role of climate change in pushing large numbers of people into motion. What arrested attention on this particular image, as opposed to the many others that were widely available, was the fact that the refugee who died was so young. In the photograph, Kurdi's body is tiny. He looks more asleep than dead. Maybe the viewer could reach over, give him a hug, and stir him awake.[1]

This image conjures the connection childhood has to race, migration, and the environment, which many American writers have been exploring through speculative fiction. Childhood itself is, of course, conventionally associated with an innocence that requires guarding and that figures a future of exciting possibilities. As Lee Edelman explained over a decade and a half ago:

> That Child remains the perpetual horizon of every acknowledged politics, the fantasmatic beneficiary of every political intervention. Even proponents of abortion rights, while promoting the freedom of women to control their own bodies through reproductive choice, recurrently frame their political struggle, mirroring their anti-abortion foes, as a "fight for our children – for our daughters and sons," and thus as a fight for the future.[2]

There is in this still compelling assessment of the role of the Child, "not to be confused with the lived experiences of any historical children,"

93

a coercive equation of children with the future because they are thought of as being at the very start of their lives, innocent yet to what awaits them.[3] The children *are* our future, which means the future is defined by children, but only so long as they remain in – or alternatively are allowed to inhabit in the first place – a childlike state of innocence. The Child, deliberately capitalized to signal the difference between symbol and "lived experiences," cannot grow up, for this would mean to arrive at a future that remains future precisely because it can never be reached. To grow up is to be no longer innocent. By definition, then, Edelman insists, the future is what lies ahead in time, an abstraction of something impossible that, as it becomes synonymous with the figure of the Child, excuses any abuse, any injustice, any negligence in the present.

And yet, as persuasive as Edelman's argument is, much of it rides on the disclaimer, "not to be confused with the lived experiences of any historical children," for not all children are valued equally. As Natalia Cecire points out, blackness and whiteness in the United States mark the extremes of the racial divide between other and self, and between experience and innocence: "The just-so story of blackness – as if requiring explanation – takes whiteness as an originary state and blackness as somehow acquired by experience – thus antithetical, in that sense, to innocence."[4] Christina Sharpe puts this point more succinctly: "the meaning of *child*, as it abuts blackness, falls . . . apart."[5]

As we can see in the case of Kurdi, however, race works a little differently for children who are neither black nor white. As someone from Syria, Kurdi is not firmly fixed in a black-and-white binary, and as a result it was easier for him to be held up as a symbol of innocence deprived. Then again, three short years after his photograph was taken, the US would be embroiled in a divisive debate about what to do with the children, some of whom were infants and toddlers, separated at its Southwest border from their parents. The parents of these children thought of themselves as asylum seekers, but those in power in the US wanted to classify them as illegal immigrants and as criminals. Jacqueline Bhabha observes, "the approach to 'otherness' in our societies is ambivalent – caught between an identification of the other as 'human like me' and a hostility or indifference toward the other as separate or threatening. This is particularly so for migrant children, where perceptions of vulnerability ('poor and innocent children') and otherness ('not *really* like *our* children') coalesce."[6]

This observation leads to the consideration of one more term's connection to the Child – the environment. For what the refugees from Syria have in common with asylum seekers from the Northern Triangle (the countries of Honduras, El Salvador, and Guatemala) is that both places have notably been experiencing the effects of climate change. As the climate scientists Colin Kelley et al., observe, "Before the Syrian uprising that begin in 2011, the greater Fertile Crescent experienced the most severe drought in the instrumental record. For Syria, a country marked by poor governance and unsustainable agricultural and environmental policies, the drought had a catalytic effect, contributing to political unrest."[7] Similarly, the western highlands of Guatemala have been hit hard by wild weather. A 2014 scientific report warned that this region "was the most vulnerable area in the country to climate change," including three hurricanes that struck its coastlines in the years before the report and "wide fluctuations in temperature – unexpected surges in heat followed by morning frosts – and unpredictable rainfall" that have since marked its seasons.[8]

When we try to make sense of how climate change affects migration in either of these cases, we are brought back to the Child. As Rebecca Evans notes: "Highly visible activist figures such as James Hansen and Naomi Klein frequently refer to their own children and grandchildren to structure their emotional calls for climate action, while John Kerry made headlines for signing the landmark Paris Agreement on climate change while holding his young granddaughter."[9] The use of children in this way is almost inevitable, as Rebekah Sheldon suggests:

> For all the heavy weather of global climate change and all the suffering born of industrialism – extinctions, droughts, melting ice caps, rising sea levels, oil spills, poor air quality, and ocean acidification, to name a few – much of the horror of ecological disaster comes from the projected harm to the future these things portend. And the future is the provenance of the child.[10]

If the future is the child's provenance, is it possible to imagine the future without the aid of the Child? Who gets to be a Child, and who is excluded from its dense coding of meaning? What happens to children when they are forced to be on the move? These are the kinds of questions many American writers have had to contend with as they turn their attention to climate change and environmental disruptions of various kinds. In novels such as Cormac McCarthy's *The Road*, Cherie Dimaline's *The Marrow Thieves*, Chang-rae Lee's *On Such a Full Sea*, Omar El Akkid's *American War*, Ruth Ozeki's *A Tale for the Time Being*, and Octavia Butler's *Parable of the Sower*, young characters in particular are forced to endure the unfolding of environmental catastrophes of various kinds by being in motion.

They can't be said to be refugees, asylum seekers, or internally displaced persons, for nation-states themselves are under such duress in these novels that distinctions between those who cross national borders and those who roam within borders don't hold up very well. What matters more is that their young characters are in motion and in peril as the world around them grows ever more dangerous. These novels speak to the struggle to make such connections – between the Child (itself always a contested category), the imagination of the future, migration, and environmental crises – more sensible, more often than not by projecting their narratives into the near future where climatic upheavals have become extremely pronounced. Despite this commonality, they also differ in their approach to race. *The Road*, for instance, eschews all discussion of race while *The Marrow Thieves* makes race central to the drama that unfolds around the child migrant beset by ecological turmoil.

Into the Raceless Future

The Road offers an unrelenting portrayal of a future landscape marked by environmental catastrophe and of how such a landscape forces a child to be on the move and in constant danger, which foregrounds the environmental concerns that have been in the background in discussions about the Syrian Civil War and the dangers migrants like Kurdi face. Even if the cause of catastrophe in the novel is never explained, the effects are pronounced. The sky is perpetually cloudy, refusing to let any sunlight shine through. Trees everywhere are dead, their lifeless husks failing around the novel's main characters. There is no food, so the people whom the two central characters – an unnamed man and his son – encounter often see them as potential sustenance, cannibalism now a common occurrence. Environmental catastrophe is thus imagined as the transformation of the natural world to the point where it can no longer sustain life of any kind.

The story is exclusively focused on the father and son, and the fact that they are unnamed and given very little physical description contributes to strong reader identification with the father in particular. The novelist Michael Chabon offers one example of how powerful this identification can be when he writes in a review about how the novel embodies "a parent's greatest fears." "And, above all," Chabon stresses, "the fear of knowing – as every parent fears – that you have left your children a world more damaged, more poisoned, more base and violent and cheerless and toxic, more doomed, than the one you inherited."[11] *The Road* succeeds in stripping away the details of a populated landscape, like animals, colors, foliage, and so forth, so as to center the drama on characters who may seem as a result archetypal. The father could be any father; the son any son. Or, perhaps, it's more accurate to say, both the father and son are idealizations, the former ever watchful and protective, and the latter ever compliant and grateful. In either case, what's notable about Chabon's response to the novel is how identification is unmarked by racial difference: any reader can feel the way Chabon felt (although, of course, not all readers will).

This effect may be a luxury exclusive to print fiction, for the film adaptation of the novel makes explicit what in retrospect might seem implicit all along: the father and son are white.[12] How much, then, does the universality of the characters depend on the default race of unnamed characters being understood to be white? So long as race is never specified, we can read with the assumption that such characters are white without having to think about this assumption. The boy in particular could be viewed as innocent in the way Cecire describes, drawing on the work of James Kincaid and Robin Bernstein: "Precisely because of its negative definition, innocence is constituted as temporally *prior*, whether to knowledge, or experience, or to culpable action."[13] The film, on the other hand, injects race into this story, especially at a crucial emotional moment. Near the end, when they have made their way to the sea, in the hopes that it might offer them some succor (it doesn't), their meager belongings are almost stolen. In the film's rendering of this scene, the thief – who is only ever referred to in the novel as "the thief" – is black, the only non-white character in the film.[14] Even in the apocalypse, it seems, black men can't avoid being typecast as a thief – "thief" becoming, at least in the minds of the filmmakers, a synonym for black.

It's difficult, however, to say whether the film brings out something implicit in the novel; I reread this scene in *The Road* several times and I find only some inconclusive indication that the thief is black. His physical description could be of any race: "Standing there raw and naked, filthy, starving. Covering himself with his hand. He was already shivering."[15] He does have a tendency, however, to say "man" a lot in the few occasions in which he speaks, but it's not clear if it means anything specific or if he's addressing the father, who is usually referred to in the novel as "the man." He also tends to speak more colloquially than the father and his son, in a way perhaps that could be interpreted as an African American way of speaking: "Come on, man. I done what you said. Listen to the boy."[16] It's possible to read racial difference into this speech, especially in the "I done what you said," but it's far from irrefutable. And this inability to place the race of this character seems relevant, for the novel encourages its readers not to think of race at all, but rather to focus attention on the starkness of the environmental collapse it depicts and the ways in which this collapse makes its characters migrants in search of the essentials (food, water, shelter) necessary for survival. Identification, then, depends on the negation of racial difference, something the film cannot reproduce given the visual nature of its medium.

Just as important, identification centers on the father, who idealizes his child as needing protection. Perhaps no other moment heightens this possibility more than when father and son discover an underground bunker full of clean water and nourishing canned food. They can take a bath, sleep in comfortable cots, and be sheltered from the cold and rain. But because the bunker is in the middle of a field, there is always the danger that other survivors will come along and discover them. They are unsafe, so the father reluctantly decides they must leave and keep moving. In this brief moment of respite, the father finds time to reflect on the world as seen through his son's eyes: "He turned and looked at the boy. Maybe he understood for the first time that to the boy he was himself an alien. A being from a planet that no longer existed. The tales of which were suspect."[17] The father has seen the world before the collapse; the son knows only the world they can barely inhabit in the present, so that the word "alien" in this passage acts as a moment of free indirect discourse that thrusts the reader, momentarily, into the boy's subject position. Such a sharp shift of perspective suggests how differently the father and the son see the world around them.

Concerns about migration or environmental collapse, then, are filtered through a focus on generational difference and how it affects the relationship between father and son. If so, I may have to rethink my claim about the son as innocent, for he has been born into a world that affords innocence to no one and is therefore foreclosed to him. The boy might be, according to Cecire's logic, already an Other to the man, in that the boy cannot represent a future in a world where the future itself no longer seems to have any place for the human. What happens to the Child when there is no future is that the Child can no longer exist. There is no possibility for a blank slate upon which the future of humanity is supposed to be written. The man might continue to view his son in this way, but as this passage suggests, the boy does not understand himself as a figure of innocence or promise.

The Child in Danger

Nearly as dire as the world *The Road* depicts, Cherie Dimaline's *The Marrow Thieves* portrays a landscape marred by climate change, when the North American coasts have largely been flooded, the Arctic melted, and a war has broken out over ownership of fresh water supplies. And yet its characters find a way to inhabit this landscape, and to sustain a sense of community and common purpose that is lacking in McCarthy's world. Don't look to the future, *The Marrow Thieves* seems to instruct its readers despite being set in the future, but look to the present, and value the social bonds that survive despite the depravities of contemporary extractive industries. The point Dimaline's novel thus makes is that the struggle its non-white children face isn't somehow to find a way to be fitted into the stories told about white children, as never-aging symbols of an always deferrable future (which don't work that well anyway as environment crises foreclose the imagination of desirable futures), but rather to find meaning in the connections they make with others in the present.

What takes center stage in this world, then, are the kinds of connections its characters are able to forge with each other. While Dimaline herself is Canadian and Indigenous, and the novel set north of what remains of Toronto, it's also the case that current national boundaries have little meaning in this world as they've been replaced by a different political ordering. This is why I decided to focus on this literary work – because it calls attention to how the very idea of a "US novel" itself becomes complicated by the imagination of environmental catastrophe and the ways in which such catastrophes are often accompanied by mass migration and loss of state protections. What matters most in this novel is not the nation, but the relationship between settlers and Natives. As Miigwan, the only adult male character in a band of migrants running away from captors, tells his young charges, highlighting how, because of environmental degradation and the relentless pursuit of extraction, the distinction between the US and Canada fell apart:

> America reached up and started sipping on our lakes with a great metal straw. And where were the freshest lakes and the cleanest rivers? On our lands, of course. Anishnaabe were always the canary in the mine for the rest of them. ... The Great Lakes were polluted to muck. It took some doing, but right around the time California was swallowed back by the ocean, they were fenced off, too poisonous for us.[18]

The borderless future in this novel is a familiar one. All the predicted worst outcomes of a business-as-usual representative climate pathway, also known as RCP 8.5, have been realized.

At the same time, this is a story told from the perspective of Indigenous characters, which leads the novel to explore what this future might mean specifically for these characters. They aren't refugees, in the sense that they once belonged to a nation-state and can now no longer stay there without risking great harm, and so they become stuck in some politically limbo place petitioning for refuge from a host nation. Nor are they asylum seekers, who are in the process of appealing to a host nation they have somehow already physically gained admission to for security. Nor are they internally displaced persons, who because of natural disaster are forced to move to some other part of their own nation. The dissolution of the very idea of the nation has made such terms meaningless. They are, instead, a natural resource, their bodies containing an essential chemical that the extractive economy of the other surviving humans requires – a role that might not be a dramatic departure from the way Native Americans have long been treated. Moving from the race-blind world of *The Road* to one where race is centrally and explicitly a part of the story is also accompanied by a specific kind of catastrophe: not the unnamed one that produces McCarthy's imagined world, but the very specific one produced by the emission of fossil fuels.

Here is the twist to the fears familiar to readers about impending environmental catastrophes that *The Marrow Thieves* offers: as these fears become realized, people lose their ability to dream. Many are going insane, and killing themselves and others. Yet the one group that hasn't lost this ability are Indigenous people, and they are now being hunted so as to drain from their bodies whatever essence allows them to dream. The hunters call themselves Recruiters and the centers where the fluid is extracted schools (explicitly reminiscent of Indian boarding schools and a strong reminder of how the racism these characters are experiencing in the present of the novel is a continuation of the racism they faced in the past). The novel is told entirely from the perspective of a single young character, Frenchie, who has spent most of his life on the run and separated from his family, a climate migrant in a world that cannot offer him any refuge because it views him only as an essential commodity.

The novel is careful, as it slowly reveals the details of its imagined world, to understand why the settlers are preying on them and to connect dreaming with the power of story. When Miigwan talks about the Recruiters and the schools, he observes, "We are actually both motivated by the same thing: survival." The others challenge him on this point, thinking it collapses important moral distinctions between them and their persecutors, to which he asks, "What would you do to save us?"[19] Dreams are thus given an enormous importance in this story, as survival depends on being able to have them, and the dreams themselves are wrapped up in the nightmare that has been the lives of the novel's central characters. Throughout the first half of the novel, we hear their "coming-to stories," and each is as horrific as the next. The telling itself takes place at specific times in the evening, and the very young are not allowed to listen because of how the stories might affect them. When one of the characters tells her story, the girl RiRi overhears and is distraught. More distraught is Wab, the teenage character telling the story: "Wab was mortified, holding her hand over her mouth. She slumped down on the couch, shaking her head, eyes closed now."[20] At another important moment in the novel, nearly marking the end of the first half and the start of a quick moving plot, Miigwan tells Frenchie: "Sometimes, you have to not bring things into the open, put them aside so that people have the hope to put one foot in front of the other."[21] Dreams and stories, so like each other, have enormous importance in this novel – important enough to kill for in a systematic way – as they recall the past, allow escape in the present, and project a path into the future.

In the novels mentioned at the start of this chapter, what readers find are children, or at least childlike characters, who inhabit worlds that environmental collapse or proliferating environmental catastrophes have made perilous. These children are necessarily on the move, trying to make a life for themselves under impossible circumstances. The presence of such children encourages the reader to feel for them a strong protective sense of obligation. As Chabon's remarks on *The Road* emphasize, they encode the failure of the parental figures in their lives to protect them. Strong reader identification with the adults who are supposed to protect the Child reveals the adults' failures. For *The Road*, travel becomes monotonous and meaningless as much as it remains dangerous, since there's no hope of actually finding a better place. The boy thus figures a future that might still exist despite all evidence to the contrary. At the end of *The Road*, the man dies and the boy is adopted by a family, comprised of a mother and a father and two children, that has been following them all along. Among the man's last words to his son is this destiny foretold: "But you'll be okay. You're going to be lucky. I know you are."[22] If children are our future, *The Road*, alongside many other like-minded novels, suggests what the futures are that might be waiting for the children when they grow up, which is, predictably, nothing to look forward to. The knowingness of the boy, in turn, "turns parental care back on itself," as Adeline Johns-Putra observes,[23] such as when he offers to share the Coke they discover or when he says he's the "one" who has to "worry about everything," not his father.[24]

So it is that in these novels, one of the most significant challenges their authors face is in depicting child characters who can pull the reader into a greater investment in the troubled worlds of their imagination, while allowing them to become more than mere figures of the Child who gesture toward a future we feel nothing but anxiety about. *The Road* has a mixed relationship with these aspirations, focused as it so often is on the father's sense of responsibility to his son and the future the son represents, while *The Marrow Thieves* comes closer to allowing its young characters to exist independent of the meanings encoded by the Child. The latter's central young adult character seeks to hold together a non-familial community together in the midst of an environmental crisis, and thinks explicitly about how stories can bind them together in the pursuit of common survival even as they can tear individuals apart because of the horrors they recall. It's noteworthy that all the children in *The Marrow Thieves* have lost their parents, and, even when Frenchie finds his father late in the novel, this is a less important relationship than the ones he's made with his travel companions. The Indigenous child must turn to community for parenting, while the racially unmarked child has a father and eventually a nuclear family to protect him.

Even when it must hinge on a phenomenon without any scientific basis (no one, as far as I know, is afraid that climate change will make people lose their ability to dream in a literal way), the future Dimaline imagines seems all too possible. The characters in her novel are engaging and, most importantly, in portraying its child characters as it does, the novel self-consciously resists the tendency to make children into symbols of the future. Indeed, the end of *The Marrow Thieves* explicitly signals its refusal to connect the idea of the future to reproduction, which the Child cements, by culminating in the reunion of a gay man with his lover, who was thought to have died in the first wave of attacks on the Indigenous:

> Miig opened his mouth. The movement unhinged his legs and he fell to his knees, knocking down the grass like so much chaff. He held his hands out, palms turning upwards in a slow ballet of bone, marrow intact after all this time, under the crowded sky, against the broken ground. "Isaac?"[25]

This is a big moment, toward which the novel has been slowly and subtly building. As gay men, Miigwan and Isaac figure a queer togetherness in the face of climate catastrophe and the unraveling of the environment's ecological balances that short-circuits an earlier focus on a young heterosexual couple. What matters for the closing of the novel, and the hope it seems to want to give its readers, is focused on community and bonds of love in the here and now. If there is a future waiting for these characters, it's because of this focus.

That *The Marrow Thieves* is marketed as a young adult novel is apt, since it seems to provide a perspective (embodied by its young narrator and characters) lost to authors who can only look at children with pity when they think of either mass migration or environmental crises. From the perspective of the young characters, what matters most is not the future they embody but rather the relationships they have cultivated in the present. Every member of the group who dies in their travels is viscerally painful for Frenchie, leading him eventually to rescue an old woman who has been traveling with them. Her life is as valuable as everyone else's, even though she can't contribute much to their survival and may even slow them down. After she is taken away by the Recruiters, the others decide they will continue to travel north, in search of the faint promise of refuge, but Frenchie says no: "The rest of my little family looked at me with curiosity. Something had changed. . . . But there was no more north in my heart."[26]

Coda: Vermiculate Imaginaries

It doesn't feel good simply to praise Dimaline's novel at the expense of McCarthy's. While the contrast works well to highlight how one provides its readers with the importance of focusing on the present, rather than always seeking out some faint, elusive promise of a future, and the ways in which bonds with a community can make such a focus on the present possible, it's also the case that McCarthy's novel might end with an image that beacons beyond both the present and the conventional future figured by the Child. The final paragraph of *The Road* contains a description of brook trout that "once" existed. It's unclear whether the trout are being described as they lived in the past or as they exist in the present of this paragraph – dead, desiccated, a notional trace. There's an intentional temporal ambiguity, as if the paragraph is straining to conjure a mood that is somehow felt outside of our ordinary notions of time.

A sense of being out of time, or of time being somehow out of joint, is buttressed by description of the trout's form. Their remains are imagined as having backs of "vermiculate patterns that were maps of the world in its becoming."[27] The word vermiculate comes from *vermiculus*, the diminutive of *vermis* or worm (OED). A vermiculate pattern, then, suggests something worm-eaten, tunnel-like in shape in the way worms might move through organic matter but also old, in the sense of something that has for a long time been inhabited by worms. The ambiguity of the meaning does not try to capture into place what might be there, before our eyes. Rather, it takes what we can easily imagine, trout swimming in a stream, and renders it a mystery. The rarity of the word itself, like so much of McCarthy's much celebrated prose, conjures something other-worldly and out of time, a diction appropriate more to an ancient sacred text than to a contemporary novel that is specifically working within the confines of a conventional genre narrative – in this case, the post-apocalyptic thriller.

So we might say, when we look closely at this passage, that there is a tension between McCarthy's rarified language and the genre elements that are the center of *The Road*'s narrative (the roving cannibals, the desolate landscape, desperate but resourceful survivors, the explicit language of "good guys" and "bad guys"). The vermiculate mystery of the trout's remains offer an intimation of a deep time that no child can ever figure. Finite beings in an infinite universe must find the meaning of their existence elsewhere, McCarthy seems to suggest, not in a future when we will inevitably all have been dead for a very long time but rather in a now with all the other beings with whom we share this moment, no matter how fraught the moment is or becomes. Perhaps it's this emphasis on a shared present that *The Marrow Thieves* inherits from its predecessor. After all, one of its epigraphs is a quotation from *The Road*: "When you've nothing else, construct ceremonies out of the air and breath upon them."[28]

CHAPTER 8

Meta-Critical Climate Change Fiction: Claire Vaye Watkins's Gold Fame Citrus

Rick Crownshaw

Like much climate change fiction, Claire Vaye Watkins's novel *Gold Fame Citrus* (2015) speculates on the near future, in this case a drought-ravaged California, where the climate-changed environment has intensified desertification to such an extent that the state, and indeed much of the American Southwest, is being engulfed by the Amargosa, a gigantic moving dune sea. So, typical of literary speculations on the environmental future, this novel imagines a more fully realized Anthropocene, our new geological epoch in which the human species has, collectively, become the primary geophysical agency in (catastrophically) shaping the planet's chemistry. The plot focuses on the plight of Luz Dunn and Ray and the child they name "Ig," whom they rescue from, we presume, traffickers, and their flight from California and through the Amargosa. The journey of Luz, Ray, and Ig affords an exploration of a speculative Anthropocenic landscape of the near future, as the narrator follows their progress but also ranges more widely to focalize the experiences and perceptions of other characters and their communities in the face of radical environmental change, as well as popular opinions and widely held cultural beliefs. In exploring the social, cultural, and physical contours of this landscape, these narrative itineraries emplot some well-trodden themes, settings, and motifs of climate change fiction that have to some extent characterized the Anthropocene and the literary genre itself: aside from desertification and extreme weather, toxic landscapes, uncontrollable environments, socio-economic and ecological collapse, the disposability of life, the prospect of extinction, and an imperiled future.

These tropes of the Anthropocene have also been well theorized in ecocritical discourses. Reading Watkins's novel, then, evokes theoretical paradigms deployed in the literary criticism of climate change fiction and in the analysis of representations of the Anthropocene more generally. More than that, the novel's narration of climate change and the

Anthropocene reads as theoretically informed, and, as such, anticipates (indeed provokes) its own paradigmatic theorization. This self-reflexivity affords opportunities to reflect critically on the limits and possibilities of the theory and practice of climate change fiction, constituting a form of meta-critical fiction.

Particularly prominent in *Gold Fame Citrus* are themes of "reproductive futurism," nonhuman agency, and scale: all enunciated issues in ecocriticism. Tracking these themes, this chapter will perambulate across the settings of the novel's multiply focalized and digressive narrative, weaving, like Watkins's narration itself, in and out of various experiences of the Anthropocene. Discussed at length elsewhere in this collection, reproductive futurism will be discussed in this chapter as way of introducing the idea of nonhuman agency. Reproductive futurism, which in this novel describes the survival of the human species in near-extinction scenarios, is a mainstay of much post-apocalyptic climate change fiction, and is often figured by the Child. However, the desire to survive and protect the future so figured can reproduce pre-apocalyptic, normative sexual, gender, racial, and national identity scripts, along with unquestioned melancholic attachments to extractive capitalist regimes of the past (our present).[1] What reproductive futurism in Watkins's novel struggles to reproduce is the idea of a pristine humanity not disastrously entangled with the more-than-human world and not bearing the imprint of an environment lent agency by catastrophically repercussive human actions. The problem with theories of nonhuman agency, though, is the potential for agency to extend as far as any thing, because any thing in an assemblage with humans, has, theoretically, the potential to effect material change. For Andreas Malm, this is an unwelcome universalization of agency, the logic of which, pushed to an extreme, blurs the anthropogenesis of environmental catastrophe.[2] Malm's homogenization of (new) materialist theories notwithstanding, he raises important questions about whose or what agency matters – questions that Watkins's novel provokes. Those entanglements also call into question the residual humanisms of the theory and practice of literature. These are evident in the novel genre's typical events, plots, dramas, and senses of time and space, which are scaled to all-too-human horizons and purviews, and in the humanist enclosures of theory that fail to apprehend the imbrications of the human and more-than-human across the multiple scales of the Anthropocene.[3] However, the scaling up of the literary and theoretical imagination, to meet the representational challenges posed by the multiple and intersecting, often inhuman, temporal and spatial scales and materials through which the Anthropocene unfolds, risks overlooking the specificity of the human histories driving and mediated by the Anthropocene. Put another way, the conceptual flexions of space, time, and matter can empty them of historical specificity, which Watkins's novel restores.

This chapter begins, though, with the leitmotif of the safeguarding, rescue, and survival of a child in climate change fiction – Cormac McCarthy's *The Road* (2006) is one of the most canonical examples[4] – that normally signifies what Lee Edelman has described in other cultural contexts as "reproductive futurism."[5] To put it simply, for Edelman the Child signifies "futurity": the maintenance and reproduction of a meaningful, extant, normative social order.[6] In scenarios of environmental catastrophe and consequent ecological collapse, and the possibility of the extinction of the human species, the figure of the Child is particularly resonant.

Watkins's novel appears to stage just this kind of reproductive futurism. For example, as an infant, Luz Dunn is the poster child of California's environmentalist hopes for the future in a climate-changed, drought-ridden present. She was adopted by the "Bureau of Conservation" as an image of an embodied future to come, which she and the rest of the human species (or at least Californians) might live to see and thrive in, as long as the state's hydrological engineering efforts were successful. Growing up, however, "Baby Dunn" marks instead ecological and socio-economic collapse as California's water supply dwindles, its aquifers, reservoirs, rivers, and lakes dry up, along with its agriculture, and its inhabitants (human and nonhuman) face the prospect of dying of thirst if they do not evacuate.[7] Abandoned by her father in her adolescence, Baby Dunn grew up to be a sexually preyed-upon model (before the collapse of the Southwest). In the novel's present, Luz is twenty-five and living through anthropogenic environmental catastrophe that could not be mitigated by geoengineering.

The novel's representation of Luz (her body discursively and materially exhausted by what it has been made to signify and to do) is still oriented toward the reproduction of the future of a sexualized, extractivist capitalism. J. Heather Hicks argues that Watkins configures Luz in the guise of the *femme fatale* because the figure's "historic association with toxicity, materialism, and proliferating destruction make her an especially effective conduit through which contemporary apocalyptic environmental fears can be projected onto women."[8] Her configuration as such demonstrates not just the cultural displacement of the materialism that drives the Anthropocene, but also the fact that her materialist attitudes are an extension of the extractive capitalism that has consumed organic and inorganic resources with abandon, including her own body. Those attitudes, argues Hicks, can be found in

Luz's compulsive mimicry of the starlet in whose mansion she and Ray now squat; it can be found in her nostalgia for the more "charismatic fauna" that once populated the surrounding hills (and the nation and planet) but which have since migrated or become extinct (a fetishization of the loss of some species that occludes wider losses and ecosystemic interspecies intimacies); and it can be found in Luz's fascination with the lives and biographies of John Wesley Powell, Meriwether Lewis and William Clark, Sacajewea, William Mulholland, and John Muir.[9] Lewis and Clark navigated the Western half of the continent in 1804–1806 to establish an American presence primarily for political, military, trading, and economic purposes, enlisting the aid of Shoshone Sacajewea; Unionist Civil War veteran and sometime director of the US Geological Survey, Powell led numerous expeditions exploring the American West in the postbellum era; Mulholland designed and built the Los Angeles Aqueduct, siphoning water from the Owens Valley to the San Fernando Valley, enabling the growth of Los Angeles; Muir was a geologist, conservationist, and national parks advocate in the late nineteenth century, primarily in California.[10] As these sketches suggest, Luz is drawn to the life stories of those who mostly paved the way for the settlement of the American West and Southwest (even if Muir tried to conserve those regional environments), and whose frontier-crossing trajectories she and Ray find themselves enacting.[11] Even though their intended destination is the Southeast,[12] they find themselves having to navigate the Amargosa, which from its origins in the West has been effectively pushing back settler society and ploughing up a new frontier in its path, this time moving in an easterly direction.

Not only aligned with the terraforming of the Southwest, Luz is also aligned with the terra that has been re-formed – an alignment implied by the way Luz's own body has been consumed in the past.[13] As such, Luz's body represents a configuration of the American continent, operational since colonialism, as a female, penetrable, exploitable resource, and which is now, the narrator notes, seen as completely exhausted, despite geoengineering efforts:

> Nature had refused to offer herself to them. . . . had been denied them so long that with each day, each project, it became more and more impossible to conceive of a time when it had not been denied them. The prospect of Mother Nature opening her legs and inviting Los Angeles back into her ripeness was, like the disks of water shimmering in the last foothill reservoirs patrolled by the National Guard, evaporating daily.[14]

While Hicks reads such configurations by historicizing them, this chapter is more interested in what they say about the future.

Just as Luz as Baby Dunn had failed to signify a secure future, she continues that failure in her and Ray's rescue of Ig. Rescuing and escaping with Ig drives the plot of *Gold Fame Citrus*, but the narrative itself is built on illegible foundations. More specifically, it is Ig who remains an illegible symbol. She is frequently characterized as inhuman and unknowable in her appearance and behavior: "her strange skin, her amphibian eyes, her haunting moans."[15] This is not just because of the nature of signification itself (always falling short of referent and signified) but because of the very ecological grounds for the figure of the Child. The figure of the Child, argues Rebekah Sheldon, has been burdened with the future hopes of the species since at least the nineteenth century, when as a mode of "timekeeping" it represented the embodiment of the evolution of the species, the advances of which supposedly coincided with the racial and national identity of the imperial subject. Fostered appropriately, the Child would one day become and reproduce this subject.[16] Taking shape through the Industrial Revolution – one possible inception point of the Anthropocene – and its disturbance of the more-than-human world, the configuration of the Child emblematizes a form of (biopolitical) governance that becomes increasingly urgent.

In the face of the catastrophe of the Anthropocene, the Child fundamentality figures the futurity of the human species (well, at least ostensibly, as some racialized lives come to matter more than others).[17] However, in the context of the Anthropocene, this figure becomes less legible because of the "resurgent materialism" of the more-than-human world that has been activated by humanity and which is now intimate with the human. As Sheldon puts it, the Anthropocene reveals the impossibility of keeping "the agential subject conceptually distinct," as the inextricability of the more-than-human and human is revealed but in ever more catastrophic terms. The Child's configuration now attempts to contain the irrepressible environment with which the Child finds itself intimate and so "stands in the place of complex systems at work in ecological materiality."[18] Kath Weston might describe this in terms of animacy: "In this sense animisms literally reconceive humans as the products of an 'environment' that has itself taken shape through embodied human action" in historically specific scenarios of intimacy with the more-than-human.[19] It is no surprise that in its cultural reiteration, the figure of the Child has become an unruly signifier of uncertain futures, and therefore as illegible as Ig. The fixation on Ig in Watkins's novel, and more generally the continued configuration of the Child in speculative fiction, marks a compulsive return to the future in an attempt to police the increasingly blurred boundaries of the (more-than-)

human in the face of "insurgent," uncertain futures driven by "resurgent materialisms."[20] However, that cultural insistence on the discrete human only serves to reveal, as Sheldon puts it, "a queer child figure whose humanity is always suspiciously intimate with other-than-human forms of life,"[21] a queerness now signified by Ig's perceived strangeness.

Perhaps, though, it is Luz who finally collapses the signifying structures of reproductive futures. Or rather, Watkins provides an allegory of collapse. In their escape with Ig, Ray and Luz's vehicle becomes stranded; Ray sets out across the desert in search of help but disappears, leaving Luz and Ig with a rapidly dwindling water supply in the face of extreme temperatures, a fierce sun, and the likelihood of dying of thirst. Luz and Ig are rescued by Levi Zabriskie and his cultish group who have chosen to establish a colony on the ever-moving dune sea. Levi is a fugitive research scientist who had stumbled across a government plan to detonate a nuclear device in order to stop the Amargosa in its tracks. Believing Ray to be dead, at least that is what she is told, Luz joins the colony and becomes one of Levi's lovers. He plans to reprise Luz's former role as the face of ecological preservation, this time incorporating Ig, to broadcast to America that the dune sea is not a dead space but inhabited and a habitat – and not just by and for humans.[22] This image would be resonant of Dorothea Lange's *Migrant Mother* (1936), a photograph iconic of Great Depression, Dust Bowl America, and, in particular, human survival amid the environmental disaster of crop failure – once again configuring the land as feminine. Luz refuses to play the role of Migrant Mother and she, along with a rediscovered Ray, escapes. They have little choice but to depart as the colony sets fire to their caravan (her precious biographies of explorers and engineers burnt in the process). They abandon Ig to the colony's collective care and flee in a stolen vehicle, which is subsequently caught in a flash flood following a rainstorm. In a suicidal act, Luz chooses to step outside into the gushing floodwaters:

> "I'm okay," Luz shouted back over the miraculous roar of water, all those prayers answered late. "I'd be okay," she revised, smiling before she slipped forever under, "if I could just get my feet under me."[23]

America's prayer for rainwater to mitigate the drought may have been answered, but the future is still in doubt, particularly if we think about what this scene might allegorize. It is a "resurgent materialism" that sweeps away the last vestiges of reproductive futurism, embodied by Luz, who once symbolized a hopeful (if reified) environmental future and who has abandoned rather than fostered her replacement, Ig, an equally unreliable signifier. The signification of the future, it seems, cannot gain a foothold in this environment.

This discussion of the novel's "resurgent materialism," "insurgent" future and estranged reproductive futurism firmly establishes Watkins's engagement with the agency of the nonhuman. Moreover, it is especially in this engagement that we see *Gold Fame Citrus*' self-reflexivity. This agency is writ large in the Amargosa itself. When Luz and Ray first see the Amargosa from a distance, it appears to them a "sandsnow mirage, hypnotized by fertilizer dust and saline particulate and the pulverized bones of ancient sea creatures, though they did not know it."[24] In this manifestation of the Anthropocene, deep time materializes (the bones of ancient sea creatures) and intermingles with the material remnants of humanity's imprint on the planet's chemistry (fertilizer), a cultivation that has historically strained the region's hydrological resources and ultimately contributed to the Amargosa and the exacerbation of climate change: "Still rose the dune sea, and like a sea now making its own weather. Sparkling white slopes superheated the skies above, setting the air achurn with funnels, drawing hurricanes of dust from as far away as Saskatchewan."[25] The intermixture of human and more-than-human worlds extends to human bodies, which are imagined in the Amargosa's hold over them: They "[d]id not know but felt this magnetic incandescence working the way the moon did, tugging at the iron in their blood."[26] Ray and Luz are not the only ones who "ascribed to it [the dune sea] a curious energy"; the feeling is widespread; its "pull" was "far beyond topographical charm. It was chemical ... elemental."[27] The unconscious attachment to the Amargosa experienced by Ray and Luz may be one way of imagining what Stacy Alaimo has described as "transcorporeality," in which "the human is always intermeshed with the more-than-human world, [which] underlines the extent to which the substance of the human is ultimately inseparable from the environment."[28] That, on the first page of the novel, the narrator remarks on the Santa Ana wind carrying Ray's and Luz's "particulate" as it courses through the southern Californian canyons, where they had been squatting, to mix with the dune sea, confirms this constant osmotic exchange between bodies and their environments.[29]

The conscious, collective feeling toward Amargosa, often expressed melancholically by those who have to leave its presence, tends to deny the human role in desertification in particular and climate change and the Anthropocene more generally.[30] In other words, this fetishization of the dune sea ascribes to it an agency more consequential than that of humanity. This geological fetishism finds its extreme in Levi's belief that "He felt, finally, a welling of harmony, a communion with the rock and the silt."[31]

Geologically attuned, or so he thinks, Levi's belief in the animism of the dune sea is belied by his sense of (his) human sovereignty over the so-called natural world (a disposition that brought about the Anthropocene in the first place). Upon addressing his cult, his proclamations "regrew the wild grasses, reran the rivers, cleansed them of their saline and fertilizer and choking algae, replenished aquifers ... swelled the snowpack, resurrected the glaciers, refroze the tundra, returned the seas to their perfect levels."[32] Levi's desire to terraform the natural world by naming it can be found in the pamphlet he writes (reproduced in the novel), "Neo-Fauna of the Amargosa Dune Sea: a primer," which contains drawings and descriptions of animals and carnivorous plants that Levi claims are living in the dune sea, some of which are, in reality, imaginary or regarded as mythical, some of which are exaggerations of real species, and some, variations of actual species.[33] For Luz, reading this animalarium while under Levi's spell invests the surrounding world with the immanent life and the "vibrancy ... of unseen wonders."[34]

While Watkins has foregrounded the idiosyncrasies of geological fetishism – as Luz says to Ray, "the uranium spoke to him [Levi]"[35] – the attribution of agency to the nonhuman still resonates with some slippages in ecocritical discourses. Jane Bennett's theory of "vibrant materialism" is widely drawn upon in ecocriticism and makes a useful case study for the purposes of this chapter. Bennett's theory can dissipate "binaries of life/matter, human/animal, will/determination, organic/inorganic," because of "the capacity of things ... not only to impede or block the will and designs of humans but also to act as *quasi* agents or forces with trajectories, propensities, or tendencies of their own."[36] Another way of putting this is that the human perturbation of the environment partially transfers agency to the nonhuman. Therefore, the "locus of agency is always a human-nonhuman working group," and so agency in this theory is *ad hoc*, an effect of an "assemblage" of "actants" that emerges temporarily and contingently depending on particular circumstances and contexts.[37] The idea is that agency is not an inherent or immanent property of a particular actant or thing or the matter from which they derive but is effected by the relation and configuration of things and matter. One might say that agency is a moment of critical mass in an "open-ended collective," or that an actant is neither subject nor object, but dependent on its particular position in an assemblage.[38]

If agency is so distributed, the problem faced by ecocriticism is how to distribute responsibility or culpability for environmental catastrophe. Watkins provokes the issue by staging a fetishization of the dune sea, in which human culpability for climate change is subsumed. Bennett, though, might beg to differ. She argues that the "notion of confederate agency does attenuate the blame game, but it does not thereby abandon the project of identifying ... the sources of harmful effects. To the contrary, such a notion broadens the range of places to look for sources."[39] While Bennett's new materialism does not deny the anthropogenesis of environmental catastrophe, arguably this theory's distribution of the agency by which catastrophic events unfold makes it increasingly difficult to discern the the the extent and distinctiveness of catastrophe's anthropogenesis. The problem lies in the idea that everything has the potential to make a difference – "everything is, in a sense, alive" because of its potential to be an actant in an assemblage[40] – and that means it becomes increasingly difficult to tell what makes the most difference and where differentiation originated. As David Farrier puts it, Bennett's theory delivers a "totally flat field of experience and potential,"[41] where what is really needed is a sense of "relationality." In rethinking the idea of assemblages, Thomas Lemke calls for an emphasis on "relationality" over agency, which would make it possible to see "how vital forces are mobilized and enacted, and to analyze what comes to matter (and what does not)."[42] More crucially, a sense of relationality yields "the specificities of power relations" that generate, drive, and frame environmental catastrophe.[43] Without the scrutiny afforded by a sense of relationality, some things (nonhuman actants) can seem unduly agential.[44]

Not only holding up nonhuman agency (and by implication causality) for scrutiny, Watkins's novel, through its narrator, laments the ways the human causation of the Amargosa, found in the terraforming of the Southwest by settler society from the nineteenth to the twentieth century, has been ideologically masked by "manifest destiny" and the legacies of belief in providence.[45] The narrator asks:

> Who had latticed the Southwest with a network of aqueducts? Who had drained first Owens Lake then Mono Lake, Mammoth Lake, Lake Havasu and so on, leaving behind wide white smears of dust? Who had diverted the coast's rainwater and sapped the Great Basin of its groundwater? ... Who had sucked up the Ogallala Aquifer, the Rio Grande aquifer, the snowpack of the Sierras and the Cascades? If this was God he went by new names: Los Angeles City Council, Los Angeles Department of Water and Power, City of San Diego, City of Phoenix, Arizona Water and Power, New Mexico Water Commission, Las Vegas Housing and Water Authority, Bureau of Land Management, United States Department of the Interior.[46]

The ironies of Manifest Destiny become more explicit as the narrator points to the reversal of the settlement of the West, marked by the evacuation of the town of Needles, where the residents' last stand against the dune sea has failed. These "Mojavs" – the name once described settlers of the Mojav desert region but now those who flee it as climate refugees – retreat to those parts of the US from which their ancestors began their journey westwards across the continent. In doing so, they concede that what has befallen them is of their own species' making. While westward expansion was deemed providential, now, if there is a force larger than humanity, it is climatic and geological but it has been set in motion by humans: "it had become increasingly difficult to distinguish the acts of God from the endeavors of men."[47]

If Watkins's novel stages nonhuman agency in order to reveal the actual human material and discursive origins and drivers of Amargosa, *Gold Fame Citrus* also reveals the ways that the discursive animation of things can distract attention from the human agency that effects state-orchestrated violence, no matter how environmentally mediated. After leaving Luz and Ig to seek help when their car becomes stranded in the desert, Ray is captured by rangers and imprisoned in a subterranean internment camp, officially known as the "Impermanent Retention Facility Nine," housed in what was known as "Limbo Mine" (a series of intersecting former talc mines). Detained there permanently, although under the state-sponsored fiction of temporary processing, are mainly those of Mexican origin, who were "siphoned off" as they evacuated California in the face of the Amargosa's progress. Their legal residential status and documentation was no defense against detainment "until their papers expired, or until nativist legislation could make them illegal," or against the perception they just "looked like . . . immigrant[s]."[48] Meanwhile, the undocumented were just deported straight away, back to climate-changed, socio-economically and ecologically collapsed Mexico.[49] Asked where those of Mexican and Central American descent had gone, if they were not in the evacuation centers, the Californian state government responded that most had gone home voluntarily due to lack of employment opportunities in a drought-ridden economy. In reality they had become "*Los detenidos fantasmas* – the ghost detainees,"[50] and before his escape from that place, Ray finds himself one of them.

As John Beck reminds us, the historical presence of detention centers in the Southwest, such as those in which Japanese Americans were interned, along with other forms of state violence – atomic and nuclear weapons testing and the subsequent irradiation of the land, uranium mining, the disposal of radioactive materials, contamination, and expropriation of Native American territory – has been facilitated by the ideological modulation of the West as some combination of wasteland, dead zone, empty, purely natural, or sublime space.[51] So, for example, while the so-called emptiness of the West compels its settlement, as wasteland and dead zone it can be contaminated and those deemed less than human can be interned there. Such ideological configurations have variously rendered Western space as other to the national identity and in need of discursive and material containment or securitization.[52] In *Gold Fame Citrus*, the animated dead zone that is the Amargosa is a hypervisible, inhuman threat that has reversed the historical trajectory of settler society but which serves to, as Beck would put, "hide in plain sight," internees (*Los detenidos fantasmas*) and which also buttresses the security state through its threatening otherness that renders it a military target.[53]

The securitization of the Amargosa is the culmination of a network of beliefs and discourses represented in Watkins's narrative (and resonant with the logic of certain ecocritical tendencies) that fail to account for the anthropogenesis of the dune sea (and therefore of climate change). The novel's self-reflexivity lies in dramatizing and giving geological form to these beliefs and discourses (and invoking correspondent academic theories) in order to reinscribe that anthropogenesis. More than that, self-reflexivity lies in the illumination of the human agency driving regimes of disposability otherwise obfuscated by the fetishization of the agency of a hypervisible geological other.

In the final section of this chapter, the argument turns to the matter of scale to consider the resonance in this novel of current debates about the ways that the criticism, theory, and practice of literature need to scale up to meet the representational challenges posed by the Anthropocene. Issues of scale in this novel focus on the Amargosa, which is composed of the fossilized remains, mineral deposits, and human remnants of previous epochs, now unearthed and amalgamated, along with the geological features of the present (mountains, hills, and deserts) scraped from the surface of the Earth. It also contains the pulverized structures of American modernity (roads, mines, towns, military bases, solar farms, and agriculturally cultivated landscapes) that once contoured the topography of the Southwest but which have been scoured and digested by the dune sea.[54] The Amargosa's amalgamation of materials compresses geological time: a process that "ought to have taken five hundred thousand years had happened in fifty," remarks the narrator.[55] In other words, changes to the Earth's surface that would normally take place over inhuman timescales have been compressed into very human temporalities. In fact, the fifty years of the Amargosa's activity is roughly correspondent with the recent identification of the Anthropocene's inception, in terms of the beginning of the

Great Acceleration (particularly of oil extraction and consumption) and consequent atmospheric concentrations of carbon dioxide and their climatic repercussions, along with sedimentations of radioactive isotopes in the Earth's strata from the fallout of atomic warfare and atomic and nuclear bomb tests.[56] Just as these stratigraphical signatures have been legible markers of our new geological epoch, Watkins's novel dramatizes the processes by which the material remains of human activity become geologically enfolded, to become inscriptions of humanity's imprint on the planet waiting to be unearthed and read – in the form of a futural, geological archive. In a speculative fiction of the near future, Watkins has presented a possibly more fully realized Anthropocene than that which the global North is currently experiencing and, from that future, demonstrates a sped-up geological history in the making. In other words, epochal change, from the Holocene to the Anthropocene, measurable in temporal terms that exceed human history, is here compressed so as to be imaginable within the humanist purview of the novel.

That said, this compression of time is at odds with the narrator's registration of a cultural anxiety induced by the scale of the Amargosa (and more generally the Anthropocene). When the Southwest is surveyed through the "pixel promises" of satellite imagery, the sublimity of the Grand Canyon seems to have been tamed. Its endless photographical reproduction – its excessiveness has been "dissolved in sodium chloride" – premediates this geological formation, which now readily lends itself to metaphor and figural containment: "See that red thread flagellum?" Not so the Amargosa: "Returning our gaze westward, the mind lurches vertiginous . . .. Another optical lurch as strata go shadows, as mountain goes mountains."[57] The "optical lurch" reveals the disjunctions between the scales on which the Anthropocene unfolds, or what Derek Woods might describe as "scale variance."[58] In other words, the Anthropocene materializes through matter, things and bodies, entities, processes and systems, species, the human and more-than-human, the co-emergent entanglements of all the above, and the multitude of temporal and spatial scales on which all of this happens. While the technology and optics of photography promises aerial visual mastery, even the ability to optically frame the planet, and the smooth transition from one scale to another as if viewed through a telescopic lens, the scale variance of the Anthropocene is not so frictionless. Despite focalizing the perspective provided by satellite imagery, for the narrator, the "mind lurches vertiginous," which suggests something akin to what Timothy Clark has described as "Anthropocene disorder." Such a disordered perspective is vertiginous because scales of perception, cognition, and representation corresponding with humanist horizons are no longer tenable, leading to "a loss of proportion *tout court* ... without a conceived alternative."[59] Here then Watkins's novel does not just recognize scale variance but confronts the failure of scale framing altogether. Or, as Watkins's narrator puts it, "When understood correctly, scale expresses itself mostly in the bowels."[60] Watkins's novel refuses an optical mastery that would imply the physical mastery of the planet proclaimed by human exceptionalism.[61]

Something akin to Anthropocene disorder has also been taken up by David Farrier, who argues that the "textures, processes and devices" by which modern experience is "articulated," including literature, can bear the imprint of a temporal thickening of the present.[62] Watkins's novel is no exception. For the Anthropocene has brought the prehistoric and the far future into contact with the present moment of fossil fuel extraction and consumption: natural resources millions of years in the making, themselves compressions of the evolutionary time of biodiversity, will have, when burnt, planet-changing atmospheric afterlives. That thickening has, as we have seen, been experienced in what Farrier would describe as various forms of geo-philia, from Levi's "harmony, a communion with the rock and the silt,"[63] to the gravitational pull of the Amargosa experienced by society at large, and it also registers in the novel's compulsive narration of geological processes. Generally speaking, this geo-philia could be understood as the attempt to find a geological bedrock as a response to the vertiginous experience of time – the conjunction of the deep past and the far future – and the realization that the ground is essentially fluid and mutable and that it is has always been reforming, albeit slowly.[64]

Watkins's novel constantly reminds us, though, that a preoccupation with scale, whether it be in this novel's diegesis, or in the practice, theorization, and reception of literature, risks overlooking environmentally mediated violence. And so, the narrator, ranging across the desertified Southwest of the novel, stumbles across the nuclear waste repository at Yucca Mountain and its Landscape of Thorns monument. In reality, Yucca Mountain has not yet been transformed into a repository;[65] the Landscape of Thorns has not actually been built and is still only one of the designs included in the Sandia National Laboratory report on nuclear semiotics.[66] In the novel, both repository and the monument have been realized; the latter a warning to those living thousands of years in the future of the still lethally radioactive material buried beneath their feet. That the International Commission on Stratigraphy's Anthropocene Working Group recently determined the epoch's inception as *circa* 1950, the beginning of the nuclear age (and the Great Acceleration in greenhouse-gas emissions), makes this landscape particularly relevant to the novel's concerns. The radioactive site is described from the collective point of view of the inhabitants of a small casino town, sitting on top of the repository and next to the monument. The narrator's repetition of the monument's inscriptions (also to be found in the Sandia report) implies that they, like the "pancultural" forms they adorn, are disingenuous signifiers: "This place is not a place of honor. No highly esteemed deed is commemorated here. . . . What is here is dangerous and repulsive to us . . . the center of danger is here . . . and below us."[67] These are warnings addressed to the far future but not to those victims of the radiological, "slow violence" of the present. As Rob Nixon puts it in his now familiar but extremely useful conceptualization: this is "a violence that occurs gradually and out of sight, a violence of delayed destruction that is dispersed across time and space, an attritional violence that is typically not viewed as violence at all [. . . in this case] somatized into cellular dramas of mutation that – particularly in bodies of the poor – remain largely unobserved, undiagnosed, and untreated."[68] The town's inhabitants have "long felt hard, lentil-sized nodes beneath our eyes, unshelled walnuts growing in our throats. Our water has tannins of uranium and we have sores that will not heal, dark motes floating in our fields of vision, yellowing sclera, blood in our stool. Our babies are born with webbed fingers and toes, or none."[69]

As if the representational capacities of realism were insufficient to record this slowly violent deformation, Watkins resorts to magic realism in her introduction of a mutated man found unconscious in the Landscape of Thorns, with "claws" for hands, "barbels," a "catfish maw," and translucent skin, and presumably an escapee from the repository where other similarly genetically evolved or engineered "someones, somethings" or "mole men" are imprisoned in order to tend the radioactive materials deposited there "thrice daily."[70] While the mole man figures the "cellular dramas" of the town's inhabitants that may not be seen – "we have long been unable to discern the poisoned from the yet-to-be poisoned"[71] – his description, along with that of the town's inhabitants, potentially overwrites the possible ethnicities of those living in close proximity to the real Yucca Mountain site. These would include the indigenous populations (e.g. the Western Shoshone and Southern Paiute) whose precarity came to light in resistance to the US Department of Energy's proposals for the Yucca Mountain repository.[72] The narratorial "we" does not explicitly refer to race or ethnicity, but it does describe the novel's fictionalized Department of Energy's advice to "kill" "contaminants" from the repository, underscoring the ways that the state renders some lives disposable in the face of environmental harms. The town's inhabitants do not follow these instructions and their care for the mole man demonstrates an understanding of a shared precarity. The narratorial de-ethnicization provokes the reader into excavating (historicizing) the lives deemed waste in what according to the novel's version of US Department of Energy is an "unpopulated" "wasteland" – one of the "desert repositories of this nation."[73]

In this excavation of environmental harms already done, rather than those abstractly consigned to the future, the novel once again exercises its self-reflexivity by invoking orthodox conceptions of the Anthropocene. Such conceptions do not account for the deep-rooted histories of the Anthropocene and its ongoing environmental harms – histories of colonialism, settlement, and expansion that the narrator has implicitly and explicitly articulated throughout the novel and which ground the scenes of disposability and environmental catastrophe that are narrated. (And it is such futural conceptions that have underwritten so much speculative fiction about climate change.) Reframing the Anthropocene, Watkins's novel moves toward what Kathryn Yusoff might describe as the socialization of geological thinking. Yusoff has written of the ways that the differentiation and nondifferentiation of human and nonhuman in early modern geological thinking was integral to processes of colonialism particularly practiced in the Americas since the Columbian exchange (of human, animal, plant, microbial life, and cultural and social organization) that, in contradistinction to the Anthropocene Working Group's findings, heralded the Anthropocene.[74] In other words, historically, geological thinking determined what and *who* was an extractable resource from colonialized territories, on the grounds of what (and *who*) could be deemed nonhuman. As Yusoff argues, such geo-logics have continued largely unexamined to the present day in the state's determination of who can act as a barrier to environmental harms, but also in the ways that geological science can, in its determination of stratigraphical signatures (the Golden Spikes marking epochal inception), subsume historical and ongoing environmentally mediated violence integral to the epoch. Even if *Gold Fame Citrus* is modest in its racialization of the epoch, the self-reflexivity of Watkins's novel works against the reinscription of such "disembodiment"[75] in the theory and practice of literature, by calling attention to the (geo)logical conclusions of representing scale and agency in abstract terms – logics that would dehistoricize the Anthropocene.

CHAPTER 9

Junk *Food for Thought: Decolonizing Diets in Tommy Pico's Poetry*

Nicole Seymour

> Humor [i]s an essential tool for survival.
>
> Tommy Pico[1]

The queer Indigenous poet, podcaster, and screenwriter Tommy Pico (Kumeyaay) is known for his biting wit. A sample declaration from his Twitter account, for example, reads, "my myers briggs is IDGAF" – as in, "I don't give a fuck."[2] The same seems to hold true for his speaker "Teebs," the "bratty diva [and] alter ego" who appears across the four book-length poems that Pico has published in as many years: 2016's *IRL*, 2017's *Nature Poem*, 2018's *Junk*, and 2019's *Feed*.[3] In the ironically titled *Nature Poem*, for example, Teebs reports, "I can't write a nature poem / bc it's fodder for the noble savage / narrative. I wd slap a tree across the face, / I say to my audience."[4] Aside from the humor sparked by the fact that trees don't really have faces, the poem hereby invokes tree-slapping as a kind of counterpoint to tree-hugging, that caricatured pastime of environmentalists.[5]

The LA-based Pico is certainly not the first poet to "resis[t] a Romantic focus on pastoral and wildness," as scholar Jean-Thomas Tremblay observes.[6] And Pico, who grew up on the Viejas reservation near what is currently San Diego, is not the first Indigenous artist to brazenly depart from the harmonious visions of nature circulated by the likes of Disney's *Pocahontas*. That is, he participates in an existing tradition of critiquing the well-worn cultural trope known as "the Ecological Indian." But as I will show in this chapter, Pico extends and refines this impulse to critique that we

I am grateful to Hiʻilei Julia Hobart for sharing her syllabus on Indigenous food sovereignty with me – thus both strengthening this chapter and helping me develop a food unit for my Native American Literature course – and to Tommy Pico for generously meeting with my undergraduate students. Thanks also to my colleagues Kyle Bladow, Amy Hamilton, Salma Monani, and Sarah Wald for inspiration and support.

find in *Nature Poem* in his subsequent book, *Junk*. He does so through a multivalent treatment of food – as a source of comfort, as a source of shame, as an indicator of settler-colonial trauma – and a related, explicit engagement with queer sexuality. In fact, the word "Junk," as Pico stylizes and deploys it, is itself multivalent; as critic Jacquelyn Ardam has noted, it indexes at least four things: "junk food, men's junk [as in slang for genitalia], junk shops" that poor folks shop at by necessity,[7] and a literary predecessor in A.R. Ammons's *Garbage*, an equally rambling, equally playful-yet-serious, National Book Award-winning poem from 1993.[8] In sum, Pico's poetry helps readers understand how issues of food, environment, colonialism, and queerness are deeply interrelated.

Critiquing the Ecological Indian

Before I proceed, a few words on the Ecological Indian trope are in order. Referring to romanticized portrayals of Native Americans as the original environmentalists, "one with nature," the Ecological Indian evokes a "nostalgic past and [constructs Indigenous] culture[s] as stagnant," to paraphrase gender studies and Indigenous studies scholar Mishuana Goeman (Tonawanda Band of Seneca).[9] Perhaps the best-known example is the infamous "Crying Indian" anti-littering commercial from Keep America Beautiful that aired frequently in the United States starting on Earth Day 1971. While a familiar cliché to many, it warrants a summary here for how it enacts those aforementioned categories of nostalgia and stagnation. The commercial begins with an Indigenous man in traditional-looking clothing paddling down a river in a canoe as dramatic drum music plays. Soon, we notice trash in the water. The camera pulls out to indicate evidence of modernity: first, power plants, later, a freeway. A car passenger throws a bag out of the window that appears to include the remnants of fast food (a particular concern of Pico's). The bag lands at the man's feet, and the commercial ends with a close-up as a single tear crosses his cheek – a stoic, nobly contained affect to which I will return later. Close to idyllic nature and horrified by modernity, paradoxically existing in that modern world but stuck in the past, this figure exemplifies the Ecological Indian.

Of course, Indigenous groups do possess valuable and unique ecological knowledge that should not be discounted. As environmental and Indigenous studies scholar Kyle Powys Whyte (Potawatomi) explains, "Anishinaabe and other Indigenous peoples have built knowledges of how to live adaptively with nonhumans and the environment, lessons that are shared and imparted most often through oral and performative

means."[10] These lessons combat a history of settler colonialism that has
sought to suppress or destroy that very knowledge, and which has damaged
environments and food sources more specifically; as ethnic studies scholars
Luz Calvo and Catriona Rueda Esquibel summarize, "[d]ecolonization
entails dismantling colonial systems of power and knowledge" that "structure and shape the economy, educational institutions, churches, and the
food system."[11] Examples include the damming and sport fishing practices
that have reduced access to native fish for tribes such as the Karuk and
Little River Band of Ottawa Indians,[12] and the forced relocation of Navajo
from Arizona to New Mexico in the 1860s, "onto land that couldn't easily
support their traditional staples of vegetables and beans," as writer Jen
Miller reports of the so-called "Long Walk."[13] As Miller expounds, "To
prevent the indigenous populations from starving, the government gave
them canned goods as well as white flour, processed sugar and lard"[14] – the
makings of what would become a uniquely Native, but particularly
unhealthy, dietary staple: frybread.[15] Here, one can think of what "Afro-
Vegan" chef Bryant Terry calls "the public health crises . . . brought upon"
non-White communities "by the industrialized, Western diet," and see
how food is a matter of both (de)colonization and of environmental (in)
justice.[16]

But the Ecological Indian *trope* is nonetheless harmful on multiple
fronts, as I have previously summarized.[17] For one thing, it potentially
undermines Indigenous sovereignty. As science studies scholar Kim
TallBear (Sisseton Wahpeton Oyate) points out, this trope "de-
legitimizes the efforts of tribes to govern ourselves if we are not perceived
as traditional according to a narrow, generic, and romanticized view of
what is traditional."[18] For another thing, it conceals environmental injustices experienced by Indigenous peoples. As environmental studies scholar
Sarah Jaquette Ray explains,

> Reserved tribal lands contain the majority of US natural resources and have
> been primary sites of nuclear weapons testing and nuclear waste
> dumping . . . Despite these realities, mainstream environmentalism has
> often relied on the symbol of the Indian as an emblem of healthy human-
> nature relations. Thus, the movement obscures Indigenous issues . . . even as
> it uses the Indian as a symbol for its own agendas.[19]

And perhaps the most striking explanation comes from Pico himself.
When he visited my two undergraduate classes in spring 2020, he rumin-
ated on the idea that the initial colonizers of what is currently the United
States saw Native Americans as mere extensions of the natural geography –

and, thus, their genocide as nothing more than, say, clear-cutting a grove of trees.

As I have noted, other Indigenous writers, artists, and activists have employed modes such as humor and irony to confront the Ecological Indian trope and its attendant expectations and complications. Examples include the 2009 poetry collection *Face*, by the well-known poet and novelist Sherman Alexie (Spokane/Coeur d'Alene), and sketches from the Indigenous comedy troupe 1491s such as 2015's "Pipeline Protest." As Pico has cited Alexie as a major influence,[20] and as Alexie blurbed Pico's first book *IRL*, it's worth comparing the two in some depth. In a poem from *Face* titled "Size Matters," Alexie makes fun not just of the Ecological Indian trope itself but also of his own craven interest in benefiting from it. As he eats lunch outside with a journalist, birds alight on his hand; "'These damn birds do this to me all the time,' / I said and sighed, the unspoken bullshit being, of course, / That animals love Indians more than they love white folks."[21] As we see here, Alexie and Pico share a penchant for humorous self-regard and a tendency to alternate between the melancholic and the irreverent, particularly when it comes to environmental issues. And both take sly pleasure in exploiting the preconceptions of predominantly White audiences, while *also* expressing angst over how those preconceptions make Indigenous artists more marketable. As Indigenous studies scholar Kyle Bladow has observed, the aforementioned line, "I say to my audience," reveals "that [Pico's] attesting to want to slap a tree is a public proclamation and a performance and implicat[es] the audience's influence on his professed refusal" to write a nature poem.[22] Such moments capture a particular bind, as I have noted elsewhere: "if one does not act like an Ecological Indian, one might not land a book deal or attract a mainstream audience. And if one does, that might mean betraying oneself and one's community."[23] At the same time, the *anti*-Ecological Indian could become a schtick all its own, a different kind of carnival attraction with shock value. Perhaps for these reasons, later in the poem we find Pico's speaker clarifying, "There is something smaller I say to myself: / I don't hate nature at all."[24] As Latin American and Indigenous studies scholar Hannah Burdette explains, "Pico takes issue with depoliticized images of the natural world and the settler-colonial logic embedded within them."[25] It's not nature that's the problem; it's nature poetry. It's not ecology; it's the Ecological Indian trope.

Comparing Pico to Alexie is at once reasonable and problematic, given the dynamics that have constructed the latter as *the* point of comparison for a contemporary Native American writer. These dynamics include White scholarly and curricular tokenization of Alexie and Alexie's own gatekeeping of Indigenous literature – which, apparently, included sexually harassing younger female Indigenous writers.[26] Returning briefly to Alexie's poem above, it could be said that there is more "unspoken bullshit" there, from the speaker's attempt at a flirtatious dynamic with the female journalist to the creepy penis joke that the poem's title seems to encode. (While Pico indulges in quite a few penis jokes of his own, these resonate quite differently given the dynamics of heteropatriarchy and of Alexie's particular behavior.) For all of the above reasons, I am wary of suggesting that Pico merely echoes Alexie's critique of the Ecological Indian and the cultural-creative binds it produces. Indeed, I hope to indicate below how Pico articulates even more complicated binds – diverging from the latter's critique with his focus on food and queerness, and with a different attention to gender/sexual dynamics.[27] I also want to resist the logics of literary and artistic historiography wherein White scholars and critics simply swap out one token non-White figure for a new one. On that note, it's worth mentioning that, while tokenization and gatekeeping have certainly not ended, Alexie's fall from grace has nonetheless coincided with the increasing prominence of a new wave of North American Indigenous writers, visual artists, and activists – many of whom are feminist, female, queer, and/or transgender.[28]

For all of the above reasons, I want to briefly put Tommy Pico's work in dialogue with that of feminist visual artist Wendy Red Star (Apsáalooke AKA Crow) – whom we might identify as a fellow member of the aforementioned wave – before moving into a discussion of Pico's *Junk*. Red Star's work is important in its own right, and carries its own specific tribal implications. But this dialogue will provide an overview of what I am characterizing as a recent divergence from established critiques of the Ecological Indian, and will thereby also contextualize Pico's specific interventions.[29] To begin with, the Montana-raised, Portland-based Red Star is playful, funny, and irreverent just like Pico, particularly when it comes to idealized visions of nature. For example, her breakthrough work *Four Seasons* (2006) features her posing in traditional regalia on Astroturf next to blow-up plastic animals, thus resisting that "rhetoric of a nostalgic past" to which Goeman refers and the specific trope of the Ecological Indian that articulates it. Further, like Pico, Red Star brings queer perspectives to bear on contemporary Indigenous issues – a crucial decolonial move, considering that homophobic and transphobic policing of Indigenous sexuality and gender expression is integral to the project of settler colonialism, as explained further below. For example, for a 2016 show at Oregon's Linfield College titled *Alterations*, Red Star presented fashions inspired by men's traditional outfits for the "hot dance," an Apsáalooke ritual so named because of its allusions to cooking food.[30] She brought in local drag queen Kaj-Anne Pepper – whose name provides another food allusion – to model the fashions, explaining to contemporary art publication *Daily Serving*, "I thought it would be fun to have Kaj-Anne activate my outfits. Too often Native dress is shown in pictures or on dress forms, but rarely in an animated state. This was an opportunity to see my work in action."[31] In addition to subtly invoking both food and queerness, Red Star thereby speaks back to that notion of Indigenous cultures as both stagnant and stoic; she "activates" or "animates" Indigenous cultures through the vehicle of contemporary drag performance.

In what follows, I will argue that Pico's *Junk* does much of that same work through its own unique ecopoetics. As I have hinted, what the poem offers is a deeply intersectional critique of the Ecological Indian, incorporating not just Indigenous/decolonial and environmentalist perspectives, but also perspectives informed by concerns of food/diet/fatness and queerness. Accordingly, my methodology for the rest of this chapter includes drawing on diverse scholarly sources that span Indigenous studies, food studies, fat studies, queer theory, and affect studies – because no one approach is sufficient unto itself to understand the project of *Junk*.

Junk's Food Tendencies

I'll proceed by outlining what I see as four interrelated thematic tendencies in *Junk*. To begin with, Pico satirizes trendy urban "foodie" culture. For example, his speaker Teebs disidentifies humorously, and defiantly, with the latter early on, playing off the notion of junk food: "I'm the opposite of a foodie I'm like a junkie."[32] Teebs elaborates on this disidentification a bit later, musing, "Why do people say they 'love food' / like it's a revelation A secret *I'm such a food-aholic* Oh, like / literally every other living organism in existence?"[33] Often this satirization of urban "foodie" culture intersects with the satirization, or even outright critique, of urban (White) gay male culture, as when Pico argues, "I'm not saying gay men are bad I'm just saying I don't like them They keep / saying they 'are paleo now, bitch.'"[34] This tendency of Pico's is affined with a third: his alternately humorous and serious references to his, or rather his speaker's, own eating habits and body-image issues – from, "I'm / not just going to turn down a donut unless sex in the derriere is / comin"[35] to "I will stop writing about the

conflict of my body when it goes away."[36] Finally, Pico references colonized diets and Indigenous health issues, again both humorously and
seriously. One non sequitur line reads, "'Comfort' food is a perky euphemism / oblivion food may be a touch too negs."[37] And an extended passage
recalls Teebs's and possibly Pico's childhood when

> there were three main industries on the rez (besides,
> of course, meth): fire dept, RV park, and the thrift shop Mom
>
> worked at each of them I spent whole ass afternoons among
> the busted watches and raggedly Barbies n rolling green candy
>
> bowls Sugar was first cultivated in India the trade became a
> major colonial industry I'd parade in faded dress and sweaty
>
> plastic pumps Candy is a simple way to make kids behave when
> you have three jobs Appetite is explained by simple biology
>
> "Sorry for the genes" is a phrase mom is often fond of saying
> You literally can't argue with Gobstoppers.[38]

This passage speaks, among many other things, to the fact that "Indigenous
communities often find themselves . . . with fragmented and precarious
food options that characterize systematically manufactured 'food deserts.'
Food deserts lack healthful food options and instead tout calorie-dense and
nutrient-poor processed fast foods as . . . alternatives to communities
economically impoverished by long histories of settler colonial
discrimination."[39] Food deserts and food insecurity are one, but certainly
not the only, factor contributing to a scenario in which, as the US
Department of Health and Human Services reports, "American Indian
or Alaska Native adults are 50 percent more likely to be obese than non-
Hispanic Whites," and adolescents, 30 percent.[40]

The Ecological Indian trope *absents* and *obscures* such realities by, as
suggested above, fantasizing about harmony between Indigenous humans
and their environments. Meanwhile, the interrelated movements of dietary
decolonization and food sovereignty aim to repair these realities. As
Indigenous studies scholars Elizabeth Hoover (Mohawk) and Devon
A. Mihesuah (Choctaw) explain,

> In response to high rates of diabetes and obesity, environmental destruction,
> pollution, resource depletion, poverty, and general lack of access to healthy
> food, tribes and grassroots organizations of determined tribal members have
> initiated numerous projects, including seed distributions, food summits,
> farmers' markets, cattle and bison ranches, landscape restoration projects,

community and school gardens, economic development initiatives, political activism, and legal actions. These enterprises are steps toward achieving what many food activists refer to as "food sovereignty."[41]

These movements focus not just on the right to *eat* healthy food, but also on the right to *produce* and *procure* it, through activities such as gardening, ranching, foraging, or hunting – which, as noted previously, have been variously suppressed, criminalized, or otherwise made difficult. Hoover and Mihesuah help us see again how the material environment is the literal grounds for both colonial violence and decolonial activism, with food a particular battle site for those forces.

Pico is theoretically aligned with movements such as dietary decolonization and food sovereignty. But he's doing something very complicated in *Junk*. He's not *just* decrying problems such as food deserts and food insecurity and their upshots such as obesity and diabetes. He's *also* pushing back against developments such as foodiesm and fatphobia – which might, at quick glance, seem to offer some corrective to those aforementioned problems, but which ultimately exacerbate them by imagining eating as a matter of individual choice. Indeed, *Junk* makes clear that food "choices" are historically and (sub)culturally constructed phenomena, as are feelings *around* those choices, such as self-consciousness, shame, and low self-esteem.

And here is where it becomes important to note that foodiesm and fatphobia just so happen to thrive in urban, often predominately White, gay male subcultures. I have already presented some of Pico's references to foodiesm, so I will take up fatphobia more explicitly now. Exhibit A might be the controversial pronouncement often seen on gay hookup apps: "No Fats, No Femmes." As media studies scholar Scott Beattie reports (drawing on Giles), "the openness with which some gay men feel entitled to belittle and demean fat gay men is similar to the open hatred expressed by homophobes."[42] But fellow gay men are not the only targets of gay male fatphobia. Exhibit B could be the well-publicized 2011 battle between self-identified fat female writer Lindy West and her gay male editor Dan Savage – which prompted queer writers such as Jeffry J. Iovannone to declare that "mainstream gay male culture is diet culture."[43] For Exhibit C I would propose the simultaneously funny and sad section of *Junk* in which Teebs ponders, "*Oh he def has an edible butt* says someone / out of the void which means some butts are edible and some / butts are inedible Incredible . . . I hate gay guys so much There's this / idea that only some bodies are worthy of desire."[44] A particular irony inheres here, of course:

while LGBTQ+ liberation movements have been premised on refusing the
burden of shame and rejection, some who fall under that umbrella may
shame or reject *others* for their bodies and/or their diets. (Or maybe it's not
ironic at all.) As dietician Phillip Joy and health scholar Matthew Numer
report, "dominant obesity and beauty discourses promote a lean, trim, and
muscled male body, and label gay men *outside* this ideal as less masculine,
undesirable, and unhealthy ... produc[ing] experiences of stigmatization,
feelings of isolation, low self-esteem, and disordered eating in men whose
bodies do not confirm to this aesthetics."[45] These scholars echo Pico's
comments on "edible butts," though less hilariously so.

Pico's poetry thus also functions to rectify – or to inspire scholars such as
myself to rectify – what transgender studies and fat studies scholar Lucas
Crawford calls "queer theory's scant interest in fat," even despite the fact
that, as Crawford argues, "fat has partly replaced queer as the figure of
decadent desire through which narratives of degeneracy and epidemic are
filtered."[46] But of course, the two elements, fat and queer, are inseparable.
Looking at a *Newsweek* cover on the "obesity epidemic" that features an
image of Earth superimposed on a large man's belly, Crawford claims that
the fact that "this imagery routes its fat panic through both the language of
epidemic and the symbolism of pregnancy means that it is routed equally
through sexual reproduction, gender, and the phantom of a recent and
ongoing history of HIV/AIDS as the 'epidemic' associated with deviant
forms of sex."[47] Another, perhaps more familiar, example of how gender
and sexual identities intersect with foodways might be the (misplaced)
panic over soy milk's potential to feminize male bodies.[48]

More broadly, scholars such as Elspeth Probyn have described how food
and sex are linked. Acknowledging that "[p]ractices of preparing and eating
food are ... highly sensual and sometimes sexual"[49] – stuffing a chicken,
for instance, or having a "mouthgasm" thanks to a particularly delicious
dessert – Probyn finds that popular discourse has heightened this connection to the extent that "food is now replacing sex as the ground of
identities, be they gendered, national, post-colonial, collective or
individual."[50] I would actually say that, as we see in Pico, food is *bound
up* in sexual identity; these things are all interrelated. Perhaps most relevant
to my discussion here, Probyn points out that fat pride movements employ
approaches drawn from queer political movements – decrying shame,
embracing pride, "coming out" as fat, and reclaiming "fat" and other
terms that have been used as insults, etc.[51] But we don't need a theorist
to tell us that food/dietary deviance and sex/sexual deviance *parallel* each
other when we have Tommy Pico to show us how they *intersect*, literarily if

not literally: he launches *Junk* with the image of his speaker "Frenching [French-kissing] with a mouthful of M&M's" in a movie theater.[52] With perfect ambivalence, Teebs continues, "dunno if I feel polluted / or into it."[53]

In considering these intersections of food and queerness, one must of course remember that Tommy Pico is an *Indigenous* queer person, and, further, that Indigenous studies scholars have shown that "heteronormativity [is] a colonial project."[54] That is to say, Indigenous expressions of gender and sexuality that don't fit the dominant Western models of binary gender and monogamous heterosexuality, such as "third gender" persons who serve important spiritual functions in a given tribe, have been punished and suppressed since colonization. We should therefore recognize Pico's explicit sexual references throughout *Junk*, to various bulges and "boners," handjobs and blowjobs,[55] as defiant and shame*less* attempts to bring contemporary queer Indigenous sexuality to the forefront. In light of these points, Indigenous studies and queer studies scholar Mark Rifkin's argument that "Native individuals' sense of their bodies is shaped by histories of settler invasion"[56] gives specific meaning to food studies scholar Tom Hertweck's claim that food, like sex, "brings the world inside and makes it part of us."[57] That is, it's not just homophobia that has been "colonially imposed and internalized,"[58] but also, quite literally, the industrialized Western diet. Pico's poetry highlights this connection – though, as I explain in further detail below, his sensibility regarding the latter issue is somewhat surprising.

Junk and Affect

The obnoxiousness of foodiesm and fatphobia helps explain why Pico does not condemn junk food or "bad" food more generally, as some might expect from someone clearly concerned with Indigenous health. But perhaps this ambivalent affect can be understood through some additional angles. For one thing, simply condemning "bad" food might further pathologize or dehumanize or frame as tragic those who eat it – as that grim US Department of Health statistic cited earlier potentially does. Indeed, scholars such as Hertweck and Sabrina Strings have described how "bad" eating has historically been associated with "bad" morals.[59] I would also note here the extensive research that shows that experiences of fatphobia or fatshaming lead to *worse*, not *better*, health outcomes.[60] Pico *also* seems to understand that it's not so simple to condemn certain foods or eating practices when they form part of one's contemporary culture. That is to say, "bad" food, such as Gobstoppers, or frybread, might feel more familiar and even more "traditional" to some folks than older, ancestral foodways – not to mention the fact that they offer pleasure in the face of pain. Here we might compare Pico's work to that of Indigenous poet Craig Santos Perez (Chamoru), whose "ode" to canned SPAM establishes the role of this US-military-introduced product in his ancestral homeland of Guåhån, or so-called Guam. Consider the first few lines:

> Guam is considered the SPAM® capital of the world. . . . Here SPAM® is considered a gourmet luxury and is often presented as a gift at birthdays, weddings, and funerals. Hormel even made a Hot and Spicy SPAM® especially formulated for Guam with Tabasco already added to it![61]

Perez's mock-wondrous tone here seems rhetorically affined with Pico's irony and ambivalence.[62]

I also suspect that Pico senses the ways in which decolonial dietary discourse can be exploited in the wrong hands. Consider, for a moment, ethnic studies scholars Luz Calvo and Catriona Rueda Esquibel's cookbook/manifesto *Decolonize Your Diet*, which cites epigenetic research finding that "the foods our grandparents ate and the toxins to which they were exposed can have a direct bearing on our own health."[63] As they assert, "We believe that what you eat now, what you put in your body, can have genetic consequences for future generations."[64] The point of that statement is very clearly to oppose the colonial frameworks that rendered one's ancestors' bodies disposable, and to break ongoing cycles of environmental injustices. But in a neoliberal, settler-colonial-capitalist context, and in a country that has sanctioned the separation of Indigenous children and their parents via residential schools and other means, to harp on the fact that "bad" food hurts not just oneself but also future generations could be a fraught move. And in fact, Lucas Crawford has pointed out that "questions of childhood fatness are tainted by accusations of child abuse."[65] Perhaps for those reasons, Pico's references to his parents are notably sympathetic, as with *Junk*'s aforementioned line, "Candy is a simple way to make kids behave when / you have three jobs"[66] and, from *Nature Poem*, "Let's say I was raised on television and sugar and exhausted parents / working every job that poked its head from the tall grasses of opportunity."[67]

The implications here are quite staggering if you pull back: settler colonialism has made traditional Indigenous foodways nearly impossible, so people have adopted the industrialized Western diet – only to find themselves then risking criminalization or at least stigmatization all over again. And even when Indigenous peoples *do* manage to engage in traditional foodways, they sometimes find themselves opposed by activists who seek to promote supposedly healthful behaviors such as vegetarianism and veganism, as with the case of the Inuit seal hunt.[68] And this is to say nothing of how "foodie" culture can turn traditional foodways into exclusive commodities, selling as "new" ways of eating ones that non-White people have long been practicing. In the words of Vincent Medina (Muwekma Ohlone), co-founder of the Bay Area Indigenous food pop-up Cafe Ohlone, "'Farm-to-table'" – that trendy term that began popping up in restaurant descriptions starting in the 2000s – "'is nothing new here ... To not acknowledge that is adding to [Indigenous people's] erasure.'"[69] It's enough to make one cry. Or, in Pico's case, both cry *and* laugh.

And here's where I should stress that there are *a lot* of laughs in *Junk*, a lot of enjoyably inappropriate affects and sensibilities, as readers of this chapter might have sensed earlier. For example, for however much shame Pico's speaker might have over eating "bad" foods, he clearly *also* takes gleeful pleasure in them – making grand pronouncements like, "Every bar frankly should have tostones [twice-fried plantains] smellin up the grill."[70] To riff on Crawford, Pico playfully displays "decadent desire" in terms of food as well as sex. Relatedly, we might also observe Pico's formal style. Returning to the long excerpt above, we see how Pico strictly invokes the couplet form, only to work against it. As Ardam points out, "Very few of his lines are end-stopped, so [*Junk*] is heavily enjambed. His syntactical units don't end where his lines end, so Pico's words are always running over the couplet structure."[71] In this way, the poem impishly embodies, rather than simply referencing, decadence and excess. Along with Pico's humor, this informal form works against the stoic and contained character of the Ecological Indian that I described at the beginning of this chapter.[72]

Further, Pico assiduously avoids the sincere utopianism found in theoretically aligned works such as Calvo and Rueda Esquibel's *Decolonize Your Diet*. While those authors imagine "a world in which everyone ... has access to organic, wholesome, ancestral foods that are grown in ways that respect the delicate ecosystems of our planet"[73] and declare that "It is vital to honor and respect the cultural and spiritual aspects of food,"[74] Pico is over here joking about dipping corn dog bites in nacho cheese. His speaker's "choice" of junk food thus speaks not *only* to tragic colonial legacies but also to a perverse, at least partly performative, desire to celebrate unhealthiness in the face of widespread dietary aspirationalism

marked by FitBits and the latest superfood. This is a highly risky, per-
versely contrarian stance. But I see Pico's "bad affect" as a unique solution
to a particular problem: how to decry dietary colonization without opening
oneself up to interpellation by smug, patronizing, privileged, and/or co-
opting takes on what "good" food is.[75] Put another way, Pico seems to
believe in the projects of dietary decolonization and food sovereignty, but
not in the affects or sensibilities they would seem to require.

Finally, then, I'm interested in how Pico's work invokes what Hertweck
calls "food affects" and "affective eating." As he argues, "Our choices,
rather than the foods themselves, have the potential to provide happiness
as much or even more so than sating the bodily need to eat;"[76] he concludes
that "we are all eating our feelings."[77] Pico's work chimes, though in really
ambivalent and unexpected ways, with these arguments, while also quali-
fying those sweeping "our"s and "we"s. Literary works such as *Nature Poem*
and *Junk* help readers to explore or even mediate the complicated emotions
invoked by colonial and environmental exploitation, and that arise from
the deep intersectionalities of eating – in this case, meaning the categories
of colonization, Indigeneity, queerness, and food/diet/fatness. Further,
such works allow readers to consider the question of how best to respond
to emotionally overwhelming problems such as colonized diets, food
deserts, and food insecurity – with prescriptions, literal or figurative?
with new recipes, literal or figurative? with seriousness and sincerity? Pico
suggests, with dark humor, satire, irony, and irreverence. And, of course,
poetry.

Conclusion

Perhaps it's no surprise that when Pico announced his newest book-length
poem (which, at the time of this initial writing, had not yet been released),
he disclosed, "[it's] about me creating a new food ritual and vocabulary,
after my access to indigenous ways of cooking and gathering food were
destroyed in my grandmother's generation."[78] Originally titled *Food* –
perhaps too on the nose? – the poem has since been renamed *Feed* in
Pico's typical punny style, evoking both the flows of food and of popular
culture and media, as in "newsfeed" or "Twitter feed." While *Feed* marks
the end of Pico's "Teebs" tetralogy,[79] we can expect that it will provocatively extend the conversation that he started with *Junk*, perhaps in
similarly *un*expected ways.

CHAPTER 10

Tender Woods: Looking for the Black Outdoors with Dawoud Bey

Susan Scott Parrish

In 2012, Black Public Media aired a documentary web series called "Black Folk Don't," offering an "irreverent" look at "certain assumed behaviour black folk are infamous for doing, or not doing."[1] One of the stereotypes the series addresses is "Black Folk Don't Camp." As in the other episodes, the title's declaration is gradually complicated and qualified. Some Black Americans in the show identify as "outdoor" people: as hikers, campers, and horseback-riders. But most who were interviewed spoke about there being no "comforts," or really, comfort, in the woods. Some explained the historically produced reasons for the danger they associate with, or actually feel, in rural outdoor spaces. One woman tells of how her husband – a civil rights attorney in Mississippi, a former Eagle Scout, and devoted camper – wears a Confederate symbol on his cap to signal to white southern campers that "we're friendly, we're here, we're with you, in order to make camping safer for us." Another woman confides: "Something about the sound of feet cracklin' on the twigs . . . I don't know, you just feel like, I don't know . . . mastah's comin' after you [nervous laughter]." A third person, a male urbanite, offers his analysis of why feelings about camping may differ with race: "there's something very . . . time-machiney about the nostalgia or love of camping, right, you want to 'go back to a simpler time.' Well, you know, for Black Americans, to go back in time anywhere in the previous four hundred years is gonna be hellish." He concludes: "You want to go forward, you don't want to go back at any point."[2] For these three, the space of the American woods – below and above the Mason-Dixon line – represents a threatening chronological transport. The woods seem so infiltrated by the violent, carceral plantation and Jim Crow regimes of the past that they either repel entry for Black Americans or require a sign of capitulation to those regimes to achieve (not even safe but) "safer" passage.

Generations of African Americans have commented on this historically produced relation, and often alienation, between people of African descent in the US and the nonhuman natural world. In the last thirty-five years, in particular, scholars, artists, activists, and founders of organizations have intensified their efforts to understand and respond to this abiding issue. Some scholarship has focused on how "the Great Outdoors," as a "cherished part of U.S. History," is coded white.[3] The environmental justice movement arose in the 1980s to reckon with the fact that the lasting logic of the plantation, and settler colonialism, continued to mark out people of color as racially appropriate targets for environmental harm in places of work, recreation, and habitation.[4] Looking into the roots of these problems, historians of the colonial and antebellum periods have demonstrated how European practices of land appropriation and resource extraction went hand in hand with their inventions of hierarchical human difference by continent of origin ("race"), all of which worked to European and Euro-American advantage. Historians have shown how "white" people, writing and acting in scientific, medical, legal, and literary modes, came to define these races as naturally different in kind and quality, and how "nature" was conjured up as a divine and diffusely material agent with social intentions favoring whites – favoring them with an earned title to productive and heroic American land while disfavoring "red" people through disease and vanishing mobility, and "black" people by casting them as a labor tool *on* the land who nonetheless were not *of* the land.[5] In other words, the labor and skill non-white people put into the land did not result in commensurate entitlements to that land or to national belonging but instead resulted in great proximity to environmental dislocation and risk.

More recently, scholars have placed these lingering settler-colonial and plantation legacies in a broader, planetary perspective. Some scholars suggest that the "Plantationocene" is a more apt descriptor of our geologic era than the "Anthropocene," given that not all of humanity in the modern era contributed to planetary degradation, or certainly did not contribute equally. These scholars point to the tremendous – previous and ongoing – socioenvironmental consequences of the plantation: the substitution of alien monocrops for previously biodiverse native ecosystems; massive deforestation and thus loss of a critical carbon sink; the ratification of a capitalist system and worldview based on practices destructive to non-European, typically tropical, places and peoples; and, in the case of cotton especially, the linkage with coal-powered manufacturing.[6]

While acknowledging the national and global legacies of the plantation and settler colonialism in ongoing environmental injustices, observers of Black environmental imaginaries and experiences in the US have, in the last twelve years, been trying to think *with* but also *beyond* the harm paradigm; they have done so in order to represent the complexity of the past and possibilities for the future. In 2009, the poet and scholar Camille Dungy published the anthology *Black Nature: Four Centuries of African American Nature Poetry*, making evident the variety of Black expressive responses to the natural world in North America. Chapters are devoted to poems on disasters, pests, urban and rural alienation, but also to poetry about environmental creativity, affinity, and belonging (in sections titled "Dirt on Our Hands," "Nature, Be with Us," and "Growing Out of This Land"). Just as Dungy herself moved – in her relation with American green environments – from "indifference to intrigued observation, to an engagement with the devastating realities of history, and finally into a space of renewed connection to the natural world," this anthology aims to provide readers an opportunity for reimagining both categories of the title "Black nature" and their interrelation.[7] In *Black on Earth: African American Ecoliterary Traditions*, Kimberly Ruffin observed in 2010 that while having to disproportionately live and work in the presence of environments made to "reflect racist exploitation" has produced "ecological alienation," there are also present longstanding Black cultural traditions that "enable – in fact, encourage – human and nonhuman affinity." This affinity with natural environments is partly born from African Americans' "deep knowledge about the human and nonhuman consequences of social systems," suggesting that a history of being treated as natural property conjoined with a history of agricultural labor created – for African American people – the capacity to think *with* nonhuman nature.[8] In *Black Faces, White Spaces: Reimagining the Relationship of African Americans to the Great Outdoors*, geographer Carolyn Finney argued in 2014 that "[w]hiteness, as a way of knowing, [became] *the* way of understanding our environment" and that Black Americans have been "limited in our role as victims in larger narratives." What continues to need articulation, Finney argued, is a "black environmental imaginary" that is not reductive – and is especially not reduced to victimization.[9] And most recently, in 2016, two scholars, J. Kameron Carter and Sarah Cervenak, coined the term "the Black Outdoors" when they convened a working group at Duke's Franklin Humanities Institute to explore the ways that blackness, having been "figure[d] as always outside the state, unsettled, unhomed, and unmoored from sovereignty," could also be a space – a Black Outdoors space –

through which to unmake and remake the modern western subject's formation, including its tenets of environmental ownership and domination.[10] Their work provides a theoretical dimension for earlier, and ongoing, efforts that have been more empirical and archival.

Scholars of the plantation have likewise worked to ascertain how people of African birth or descent were ideologically yoked *to* a commodified nature, but were nevertheless able to make refuge and expertise out of their nonhuman surroundings. Africans brought with them to the Americas a belief in – and practices of finding and using – the spiritually steeped material potencies of the natural world. Bound laborers went to the forests, canebrakes, and swamps not only to labor, but also to search for animal protein, plant-based medicines, and spiritual solace, as well as conduct unsupervised meetings. They sought to tap into nonhuman animacy and thereby assert a kind of ramified, creaturely, fortified personhood – or what Monique Allewaert calls "parahumanity."[11] In the Caribbean world, runaways used their environmental knowledge to establish maroon communities in the mountain forests of Jamaica and Suriname, from which they negotiated their freedom. Likewise, escaped men and women in the southern US turned swamps, woods, and caves into places of cover, and places from which to retaliate.[12]

Public outreach and organizing comprises another part of this movement to make Black Americans' environmental connections not only visible in the past but palpable in the present and increasingly robust in the future. Contemporary wildlife ecologist and self-styled "Black birder" J. Drew Lanham has, across many media platforms, communicated his love of, knowledge about, and identification with birds while drawing attention to the exceptional challenges Black naturalists encounter. Lanham explained: "It's critical that along with biodiversity we think about the human component as something just as important" – that we think about racial diversity in the natural sciences.[13] The Fledgling Birders Institute is one example of an organization getting that word out by providing support to young birders of color in the US.[14] As mentioned in the Introduction, a number of social media campaigns – #BlackInNature, #BlackBirdersWeek, and #BlackAFinSTEM, connecting naturalists of color to each other and making them more visible to the world – were launched in the wake of the racist intimidation of Black birder Christian Cooper in Central Park on May 25, 2020. Outdoor Afro is another organization that has created a nationwide network of sites "*where Black people and nature meet.*" Operating in thirty states, its leaders imagine that "outdoor" engagement, whether in urban, suburban, or rural spaces, can "inspire ... African American connections and leadership in nature. We help people take better care of themselves, our communities, and our planet!"[15] This last formulation – in which the health of self, community, and planet are all interconnected – typifies the way this movement has seen the strict biocentrism of past white efforts at wilderness protection as ill-suited to Black environmental habitation.

Across these realms of documentary, scholarship, and organization-building, then, is a multi-pronged effort to reckon with how the historical legacies of the plantation produce not only ongoing alienation and harm but also potential affinity and allegiance between Black Americans and nonhuman nature. Paramount to this effort is a prying apart of the malevolent or negligent *human* actions which brought and bring about environmental injustices from a *nonhuman* world which did not, and does not, innately operate on any race-based ideology. There is focus on the present and future: creating mutually supporting connections through birding, hiking, planting, and advocating for new legislation and standards. It is also crucial, though, that a wider public encounters the Black environmental past anew to establish the longevity and durability of these connections. Works of historiography and anthologies that gather a long history of Black nature writing, as I've said, have contributed to that process. A number of visual artists are also investigating, and using new media to imagine, ancestral Black environmental imaginaries. The public-facing orientation of their art makes it especially significant now.

For the remainder of this chapter, I will focus on how one contemporary visual artist is contributing to this effort to acknowledge, but move beyond, the harm paradigm – to separate out a human will-to-harm from a potential green tenderness.[16] Particularly intriguing to me is an artist whose work hasn't been, and still isn't necessarily, associated with "nature." Dawoud Bey has made a career photographing human subjects in cities. And yet, in 2017, he turned to the northern US countryside to consider anew the history of the Black Outdoors by trying to sensorially inhabit and mediate scenes from its past. Though he depicts northern woods, he explores the ways in which plantation jurisdictions and mentalities stretch far above the Mason-Dixon line, even as far as the Canadian border. Bey uses contemporary technologies of visual recording and reproduction in order to draw his audience into a more immersive, as-if-real experiment in re-entering historic woods.

The visual is a critical mode for this recovery of a Black Outdoors because it is especially through the visual that race has been invented and enforced. Frantz Fanon has been one of many commentators who have noted that for a Black person in contact with the historically produced and pervasive white gaze, one's "corporeal schema [can] crumble ... its place taken by a racial epidermal schema."[17] Not only was "nature" deployed by scientific racism to *visually* contend Black inferiority in the eighteenth and nineteenth centuries, but since then cartoons, stage acts, housewares, advertising, and packaging all made racist stereotypes of blackness a visual, tactile part of everyday public and private life.[18] Moreover, broadcast images during recent disasters (the Haitian earthquake, Hurricane Katrina, and the Flint water crisis) have made the connection between Black bodies and catastrophic environments seem essential rather than parallel symptoms of history. Just as the relation between American environments and Black people has been characterized as one of disfavor or harm, "the visual sphere has been understood in Black cultural studies as a punitive field – the scene of punishment."[19] Bey seems to recognize that to dismantle the naturalized racism that undergirds the US, he must disencumber nature of its white properties and Black bodies of their disastrous associations, as he investigates what it could mean for Black people to watch nature carefully, all the while feeling for its tenderness.[20] In a more abstract way, one could say that this artist is trying to get out from under European Enlightenment dispositions of subjecthood and objecthood, which associate whiteness with the mind, sight, and near divinity, and associate nonwhiteness with embodiment, visibility, and utility.

Enlisting nonhuman media technologies (that create and disseminate representations of life) to explore connections between African Americans and the nonhuman natural world suggests a compelling triangular relation here of the human and nonhuman. In other words, we don't see in Bey's recent work a simple backward-going dive away from the twenty-first century into pre-modern nature, but rather an exploration of how technologies might mediate Black biophilia, and how Black biophilia might in turn modulate technological modernity. Unlike the speaker at the beginning of this chapter who said, "there's something very ... time-machiney about the [white] nostalgia" for life in the woods, and something exclusively future-oriented about Black people, this artist *does* go back. And he uses contemporary visual technology as a kind of time machine to do so. His project is akin to the way theorist Susan Buck-Morss describes Walter Benjamin's goal for revolutionary democratic art in his classic 1936 essay, "The Work of Art in the Age of Mechanical Reproduction," namely: "to *undo* the alienation of the corporeal sensorium, to *restore the instinctual power of the human bodily senses for the sake of humanity's self-preservation,* and to do this, not by avoiding the new technologies, but by *passing through* them."[21]

Dawoud Bey, *Night Coming Tenderly, Black*

Practicing as a photographer of people in urban environments since his inaugural 1975 series, "Harlem, U.S.A.," Queens-born and Chicago-based Dawoud Bey explores decidedly new terrain, thematically and geographically, in this 2017 project. Bey explains that these photographs are "a visual reimagining of the movement of fugitive slaves" through Ohio toward the southern edge of Lake Erie on their route to Canada. "Using both real and imagined sites," Bey continues, "these photographs seek to recreate the spatial and sensory experiences of those moving furtively through the darkness."[22] *Night Coming Tenderly, Black* is comprised of twenty-five large-scale photographs, shot in daylight in 2017 but printed to intensify their darkness on 48- by 59-inch silver gelatin paper. The images were first exhibited in 2018 amid the pews of Cleveland's St. John's Episcopal Church, once known as Station Hope in the antebellum Underground Railroad. At the church, according to a press release, "the viewer must sit and lean forward to see the images, like praying. The works seem opaque and unyielding until the viewer commits to looking."[23]

In conversation with the photographs of Roy DeCarava, in which the dark tones of his prints made a home for his urban Black subjects, Bey explains that he too uses "material darkness [as] a metaphor for an enveloping physical darkness, a passage to liberation that was a protective cover for the escaping African American slaves."[24] The title of the project is drawn from a 1926 Langston Hughes poem, "Dream Variations," which ends with the lines "Rest at pale evening . . . / A tall, slim tree . . . / Night coming tenderly / Black like me."[25] These lines, through the rhyming of "tree," "tenderly," and "me," and through the work of the word "like," associate the speaker with everything around him or her – with the flora, time, affect, and shade of the woods. The skin descriptor "Black" does not isolate the human, but instead indicates a softly atmospheric, cyclically restful natural benediction. Bey, in the title of his exhibition, lobs off the last two words ("like me"), indicating a wider invitation in that wooded night, an invitation that precedes and exceeds the photographer. Along with this citation of Hughes, Bey – according to one reviewer – also drew on Frederick Douglass and other enslaved testifiers "to construct plausible slave vistas."[26] There are many vistas in Douglass's narratives of enslavement in Maryland, some of which include the imposing "stately beauty" of the Great House with its many outbuildings and "grand old trees," but likely the most telling is that vista within the woods that carried him from his grandparents' home of temporary freedom to the plantation house for which he had been all along destined. In those "somber woods," as Douglass relates, "several old logs and stumps imposed upon me, and got themselves taken for wild beasts" until a closer look revealed that these tree details which had seemed to be beastly eyes, limbs and ears only seemed that way "owing to the point from which they were seen." What Douglass learns, on his wooded route to the plantation, is that "the point from which a thing is viewed is of some importance."[27] This treescape teaches young Douglass to detect and resist imposition by learning a protracted, multi-angular visual epistemology.

As we turn to an example of Bey's images, the first thing to say is that, through them, the viewer is asked to *see as* a fugitive rather than *look for* one. Especially for Euro-American viewers, this represents a significant reversal of a formerly inculcated practice. In the eighteenth and nineteenth centuries, before the era of reproducible photography, runaway advertisements for enslaved people used generic woodblock prints and verbal descriptors to conscript a reading and viewing public in the slaveholders' efforts at capture. These ads, as Sharon Block and Hannah Walser argue, actually did a poor job of offering individuating details or heritage markers of fugitives; rather, they produced habits of white viewing that were both racially generic and forensic, in which detecting the racial sign of blackness and the criminal activity were one and the same – a practice still a feature of white-on-black viewing today.[28] During the Jim Crow era, photography was, at its worst, abused into being a medium of objectification and terror vis-à-vis Black Americans when used to memorialize and reproduce lynching ceremonies in the form of photo-postcards.[29] As a broader tool of social control, then, these visual technologies lent themselves to projection rather than detection, and to the misbegotten capture and exposure which followed.

In Bey's photographs, there is no body visually focused upon in the woods, and thus nobody who risks being seen as either errant criminal or inevitable victim or romantic primitive. Only is there an inferred presence moving and looking, moving amid the possibility of danger and looking for security. Bey uses the camera as a device of "reimagination" – a time machine that transports him to the 1850s, after the Fugitive Slave Act has been passed but before emancipation. In the woods with a contemporary camera, Bey tries to get closer to seeing and sensing as a person with urgent requirements of these woods and wooded houses. The rest of the photographic process (developing the silver-coated film, enlarging the negative, overexposing the paper and fixing the image onto the silver salts of the paper) then become *the viewer's* means of trying to sense the fugitive's experience of hazarding these dark woods into protection. With the Black body invisible in the woods, not only does Black embodiment recode as spatial perception and inferred motion, but the woods likewise become less an object and more a relation, or a process, into which the viewer is drawn. As Buck-Morss explains of the bodily foundation of aesthetics, or *aesthesis*: "It is a form of cognition, achieved through taste, touch, hearing, seeing, smell – the whole corporeal sensorium." Though *aesthesis* involves the whole body, it moves beyond "the body's limits. The circuit from sense-perception to motor response begins and ends in the world."[30] Likewise, in Bey's reimagining of an aesthetic relation between the fugitive and the woods, the Black human is "moving furtively" where and when they encounter a complementary subject, "Night coming tenderly / Black." This return to the bodily origin of aesthetics is not only required of the beings *in* the environment of the photograph, but also the viewers *of* the photograph, who must exercise patience and commitment with a landscape photograph that initially "seem[s] opaque and unyielding." Given this visual recalcitrance, people encountering these dark woods in the twenty-first century must summon from themselves a broader "corporeal sensorium," and participate in an intersubjective loop with the world before them. What the photograph is about is also what it asks of you.

Consider "Untitled #15 (Forest with Small Trees)" (Figure 10.1). Like many others in the series, it is almost four by five feet in size, big enough to allow the viewer to imagine the possibility of entry, and of having "spatial and sensory experiences" there. As in many of the images, trees are in the foreground. Or, to explain it from the fugitive's perspective, he or she draws close to trees while assessing where to move next. For viewers conditioned by western perspectival landscapes, we might look to the center, to a felt horizon line, for a meaningful event that the lines arrange. It is not forthcoming. Instead, the viewer needs to adapt to the utter "noniconicity" of what she sees.[31]

Compare Bey's Ohio treescape here with a 1958 image from the Euro-American landscape photographer Ansel Adams (Figure 10.2). In "Aspen, Northern New Mexico," the sunlight streams *at* the forest from behind the photographer, electrifying into skeletal alertness rows and rows of slender Aspen and setting in bright isolation one leafy tree in the foreground. The scene resembles a lit stage, with the star actor standing closest to the

Figure 10.1 Dawoud Bey, "Untitled #15 (Forest with Small Trees)." Gelatin-silver
print 44 x 55 in. 2017. Copyright Dawoud Bey, Courtesy of Stephen Daiter Gallery

footlights while the audience is struck into a state of sedentary wonder.
Unlike Adams's staged forest, where one beholds a stand of beauteous
bones, Bey's woods don't invite a looking at as much as a careful and
prolonged looking around – the seeking of a sheltering relation amid
possibilities of harm.

The various places of the photographs in this series – woods, lawns
around houses, streams, and lakes – all become, in Bey's words, "a tender
one, through which one moves."[32] To be tender is to be still growing and
vulnerable, even sore; it is to be loving and sympathetic; it is, as both noun
and verb, an offer or the act of offering. The tender proneness of the biotic
forms meets the motion of the fugitive in such a way that they become
temporarily "one." If runaway advertisements – set within the larger
structure of a slave society – helped, with the habits of viewing they
inculcated, to teach viewers that Black men and women were without
heritage, belonging, individuation, and depth outside the detector-
detected relation, Bey's photographs try to recreate fugitive seeing rather
than being seen. Because fugitive seeing looks for a way through, and for

Figure 10.2 Ansel Adams, "Aspens, Northern New Mexico." Print No. 6 from Portfolio VII, 1976. New Mexico. 1958. Gelatin-silver print, 17 7/8 x 22 5/8" © The Museum of Modern Art / Licensed by SCALA / Art Resource, NY and by permission of The Ansel Adams Publishing Rights Trust

temporary cover, more than for durable, drainable resource, it also happens to represent a more apt and tender way for humans to see nonhuman nature.

This artist asks viewers to reconsider *Black nature* – not as double jeopardy but as tendered allegiance – by coming to see antebellum Black experiences of the outdoors anew. As both historical, but also future-concerned, investigations of Black Americans' possible relations with the nonhuman world, Bey's photographs search for, and make visible, a "beautiful Blackness" that is an "affirmative value" reciprocated between fugitives and rural, crepuscular environments.[33]

***

To return to where we began. One of the people appearing in "Black Folk Don't Camp" remarked that even if she felt uncomfortable in the woods, she recognized that, because environmental "apocalypse might be coming, ... Black people should have [outdoor skills] if we're going to make it to the next level of earth."[34] This vision of a time when races are pitted against one another for survival on a suddenly less habitable earth, while apparently extreme, is not in fact an unreasonable appraisal of our national (and global) direction, nor, for that matter, its history. Absorbing environmental extremity differently (through invasive species and pathogens, or extractive practices, and in the form of flood, fire, or extreme urban heat) has in various ways since 1492 been a feature of the demarcation and stratification of human groups. As the environmental justice movement has made clear, the distribution of environmental advantages and disadvantages has been a technique of inequitable race-making. And yet, for Black Americans, environmental affinity, spirituality, and knowledge have also been a persistent part of their experiences since continuous African-descended habitation was established in the future United States in the early sixteenth century. Making the depth of that connection palpable, making it a resource for the future, and making it a bulwark against intensifying harm are all important goals of contemporary artists, naturalists, and organizers. One of the questions going forward is whether the particular conditions of past Black Outdoors affinity can help Black people not only "make it *to* the next level of earth," but also *make* the next epoch of earth.

PART III

Environmental Spaces, Environmental Methods

CHAPTER 11

Urban Narrative and the Futures of Biodiversity

Ursula Heise

The City in the Environmental Imagination

Cities pose a problem for the American environmental imagination. In Europe and North America, the city has conventionally been envisioned as the opposite of nature: either nature identified with an idealized countryside in the European context, as Raymond Williams has shown, or with a no less idealized wilderness in the North American context, which scholars from Henry Nash Smith and Roderick Nash to William Cronon have analyzed.[1] Yet the environments where most humans live now and will in the future are neither wild nor rural, but urban. Studies published by the United Nations, the World Health Organization, and other international organizations over the last decade and a half show that humankind crossed a threshold in 2008, the year in which, for the first time in history, more humans lived in cities than in nonurban areas.[2] Most humans now and in the future will either be born in cities or migrate there over the course of their lives. But even as cities grow materially, demographically, and in terms of their environmental footprint, they have only recently come to be envisioned as part of the environments that environmentalists seek to protect and preserve, and they remain in tension with what most average citizens experience and imagine as "natural."

This does not mean that cities have been ignored by environmentalists. The environmental justice movement has done much to integrate urban areas into environmental discourse and activism since the 1980s. It has highlighted the unequal access of affluent and poor urbanites to green areas, their unequal exposure to unsafe water, polluted air, and contaminated soils, and the disproportionate proximity of poor neighborhoods and neighborhoods of color to hazardous industries and waste dumps. Social and environmental disadvantages, in these contexts, have come to be seen as mapping onto each other in all too predictable ways, as texts from the report on "Toxic Wastes and Race in the United States" by the Church of

Christ Commission for Racial Justice (1987) and Robert Bullard's
Dumping in Dixie (1990) all the way to the work of Mike Davis, Laura
Pulido, and Kyle Powys Whyte have shown. Research that highlights the
interconnections between environmental damage and social injustice has
often focused on cities, where unequal access to environmental goods and
unequal exposure to environmental risks point in particularly stark form to
broader inequalities in the ways in which "nature" is used, distributed, and
perceived in the United States.

In tandem with the environmental justice movement, but often articulated in a more theoretical idiom, the field of urban political ecology has
since the 1990s explored the causes for these inequalities in the United
States and elsewhere. Theorists such as Nik Heynen, Maria Kaika, and
Erik Swyngedouw have proposed that urban structures as well as ecological configurations are coproduced by the same capitalist mechanisms
that "metabolize" natural resources. In this view, city and nature are not
opposed, but on the contrary generated by the same underlying economic
principles: "There is nothing a priori unnatural about produced environments like cities, genetically modified organisms, dammed rivers, or
irrigated fields. Produced environments are specific historical results of
socio-environmental processes. The urban world is a cyborg world, part
natural/part social, part technical/part cultural, but with no clear boundaries, centres, or margins."[3] As the idea of the "cyborg city" makes clear,
urban political ecology refuses to oppose urban systems to natural ones,
but approaches both of them as products of capitalist economic structures instead. In this perspective, the processes that produce social
inequality and make some groups more vulnerable to environmental
crises than others also produce certain kinds of nature, from urban
parks to mountaintop removal mines and wilderness areas. The city
turns into one combination of social and environmental patterns
among others that may appear quite different on the surface but are
generated by the same underlying processes. Like the environmental
justice movement, urban political ecology therefore seeks to integrate
the study of social inequalities with that of natural processes.

Urban natural processes themselves have increasingly become an object
of study in the natural sciences as well as in urban planning and design. The
German biologist Herbert Sukopp began his research on biodiversity in the
politically and geographically isolated area of West Berlin in 1970s, but it is
only in the last twenty years that urban ecology has turned into a rapidly
growing area of interest in biology and ecology. Cities tend to have
different soil characteristics and water systems than nonurban areas.

They are home to distinctive types of fauna and flora, and their own evolutionary processes. And they create their own microclimates (for example, the well-known urban "heat island effect"). In all of these dimensions, cities have become the focus of a vibrant discipline that explores them as environments with a distinctive ecological profile.

The increasingly visible impacts of climate change on cities ranging from Jakarta and Venice to Houston, Miami, New Orleans, and New York have also contributed to a change in the vision of cities' relation to nature. Cities and their growing populations contribute centrally to climate change. In return, rising sea levels, droughts, drinking water shortages, and the greater frequency of severe floods, hurricanes, and wildfires threaten urban areas and challenge the perception that cities occupy a realm outside of nature. However artificial and insulated from natural processes cities may appear, they are still part of global climate systems and vulnerable to natural forces at their most uncontrollable.

One might sum up these various developments across different forms of political activism, academic study, and cultural engagement over the last three decades by saying that if interest focused initially on nature *in* the city – the green areas, bodies of water, and vacant lots that could easily be seen as miniature ecosystems – it moved in the 1990s and early 2000s to nature *for* the city, and the question of how ecosystems services in urban areas could be improved and expanded. At present, the main focus has turned to cities *as* nature – the idea that cities are in fact "novel ecosystems," distinct from nonurban ecosystems but obeying ecological principles of their own.[4]

This shifting perception of cities and nature is also visible in urban writing. The historian Jennifer Price famously invited her readers to consider "Thirteen Ways of Seeing Nature in LA" in 2005. One of the most common perceptions she highlighted was nature as nonexistent: "LA ... has long been decried as the Anti-Nature – the American city with brown air, fouled beaches, pavement to the horizon, and a concrete river .... [T]his is the reigning nature story we tell in LA: there is no nature."[5] Excoriating a "stubborn aversion to cities" as the "central and most indicative failure" of American nature writing, she encourages residents of Los Angeles and other American metropolises instead to consider the many ways in which they encounter nature.[6] Earthquakes, wildfires, wildlife, even commodities such as "mango body whip" might jolt us into an awareness of how natural resources move in and out of the city, and what structures of dependence and exploitation govern our interactions with the nonhuman world.

Urban nature writing is no longer uncommon, and nonfiction prose more broadly has tackled the present and future ecologies of American cities in great detail, from studies of urban birds and parks to portrayals of urban futures in the age of climate change. Urban poetry and fiction have also begun to integrate the ecological with the social lives of the cities they revolve around. In what follows, I'll outline several different types of narrative that have dominated in American urban fiction and nonfiction of the last half-century. On one hand, stories that portray cities as risk environments have focused on toxicity – urban environments as sources of pollution and sites of hazardous industries that put residents' health or lives at risk – or on climate change, a context in which cities are typically portrayed as themselves exposed to lethal risk (section 2). Both of these story templates have been discussed in considerable detail in ecocriticism. On the other hand, some works over the last two decades have described cities as habitats for old and new types of multispecies communities. This more positive view of cities as sites of ecological opportunity rather than just ecological loss is still emergent and has to date attracted less critical attention. For this reason, I will outline the urban multispecies narrative in greater detail in section 3.

Cities as Risk Environments

When Lawrence Buell outlined the genre of environmental writing that he called "toxic discourse" in the late 1990s, he located its modern origins in Rachel Carson's *Silent Spring* (1962) and highlighted four of its narrative components: the protagonist's awakening to the reality of a polluted environment; totalizing images of a world in which there are no sanctuaries from contamination; the moral and political outrage of a socially and politically powerless group against the affluent and empowered class; and the gothic portrayal of bodies and landscapes disfigured by toxicity.[7] The basic elements of this "mythography of betrayed Edens" can be traced back,[8] according to his argument, to nineteenth- and early twentieth-century urban writing: the portrayal of industrial cities in England by Friedrich Engels and Charles Dickens, and of American urban poverty, squalor, and disease in the works of Charles Brockden Brown, Herman Melville, Rebecca Harding Davis, Jack London, and Upton Sinclair.[9] One could add to Buell's anatomy of toxic narrative the emphasis on parent–child relationships and the disruption of families, obvious in nonfiction accounts such as Lois Gibbs's *Love Canal: My Story* (1982) as well as fictionalizations such as Cherríe Moraga's *Heroes and Saints* (1990), a play about the consequences of exposure to agricultural pesticides for Latinx workers in the Central Valley of California. Religious imagery, which manifests itself prominently in Moraga's rural scenery, also surfaces more subtly in many accounts of urban "sacrifice zones."

Many of the narratives about toxic environments focus on rural areas, from the blighted farmland in the "Fable for Tomorrow" that starts out *Silent Spring* to Moraga's California and the toxic agricultural landscapes in the Midwest Sandra Steingraber portrays in her nonfiction book *Living Downstream* (1997). But urban environments have also figured prominently in pollution narratives, especially after the rise of the environmental justice movement. Lois Gibbs's nonfiction account of a community confronted with buried chemical waste at Love Canal, New York (*Love Canal: My Story*, 1982) served as the pattern for many similar stories of working-class residents' fight for health: for example, Susanne Antonetta's *Body Toxic* (2003), an autobiographical account of the effects of chemical exposure. Don DeLillo's novel *White Noise* (1985) with its account of an "airborne toxic event" in a Midwestern town, published right after the 1984 chemical accident at a Union Carbide plant in Bhopal, India, sets the tone for many other fictional accounts of toxic exposure. Ana Castillo's *So Far from God* (1993), for example, focuses on the lives of five Latina women in the small town of Tome, New Mexico, whose bodies and lives are affected by poverty, unemployment, and toxicity. In Todd Haynes's film *Safe* (1995), Los Angeles reveals itself as an environment saturated with toxins that increasingly impact the health of an affluent white homemaker. Richard Powers's *Gain* (1998), set in a Midwestern town similar to DeLillo's, portrays a woman who dies from cancer caused by an herbicide and the company that manufactures it. All of these texts foreground the victims' experience.

But in the narrative engagements with toxicity, the fight against the polluters is often as prominent as the suffering of the victims, as is already obvious in Gibbs's account of Love Canal. Jonathan Harr's nonfiction book *A Civil Action* (1988) and the 1998 film version describe the struggle to trace the causes of trichloroethylene water contamination in Woburn, Massachusetts, which led to a cancer cluster, and to bring the responsible companies to justice. *Erin Brockovich* (2000), a film directed by Steven Soderbergh and similarly based on real-life events, portrays the struggle of a single mother and legal clerk to bring Pacific Gas and Electric to justice for its contamination of groundwater with hexavalent chromium in the town of Hinckley, California. Neal Stephenson used events such as these for the plot of *Zodiac: An Eco-Thriller* (1988), an action-packed novel that follows the activist Tyler Sangamon as he seeks to expose a corporation for releasing polychlorinated biphenyls into Boston Harbor.

However innovative their themes and narrative strategies might be – DeLillo's postmodern satire and Antonetta's toxic memoir particularly stand out for their surprising twists on genre patterns and reader expectations – scenarios of urban toxicity tend to remain indebted to a pastoral literary and cultural tradition that has always cast cities as sites of corruption, contamination, and waste, in both literal and metaphorical senses. By describing cities as places where mothers miscarry, children fall sick, and adults die of cancer, or as conglomerates of multiple sources of pollution that threaten the human body, these works perpetuate a vision of urban spaces as incompatible with experiences of nature and healthy living. The city, in other words, remains the antinomy of the kind of nature environmentalists seek to protect.

Narratives of urban pollution have by no means disappeared, as the documentary *The Devil We Know* (2018), about the DuPont Corporation's contamination of Parkersburg, Virginia, shows. But since the early 2000s, climate change has claimed an ever-increasing share of narratives about urban environments and environmentalisms. This increase is not limited to the United States: writers from Australia to Finland and Germany to Brazil have focused on the fate of cities in the age of climate change. The risks that climate change imposes on cities vary widely: extended droughts and shortages of drinking water have turned out to be central challenges for Cape Town, Chennai, and São Paulo; subsidence and rising sea levels for Jakarta; wildfires for Brisbane and Los Angeles; hurricanes and floods for Miami, New Orleans, and New York. But in spite of this variety of changing regional climates and emergent riskscape, it is one image in particular that has dominated the urban literature on climate change: the drowned city.

As in portrayals of urban toxins and pollution, the narrative of the drowning or underwater city as a consequence of climate change reaches across the genres of film, fiction, and nonfiction. The giant tsunami that rolls through Manhattan in Roland Emmerich's *Day After Tomorrow* (2004), the first Hollywood feature film that addressed climate change, is one of the most memorable scenes associated with this climate change imaginary. But it was already a major theme in earlier cli-fi narratives and remained so in later novels, such as Bangkok under water in Paolo Bacigalupi's *The Windup Girl* (2009), and New York flooded in Nathaniel Rich's *Odds Against Tomorrow* (2012) and Kim Stanley Robinson's *New York 2140* (2017).[10] Nonfiction writers have equally seized on the city under water as the central synecdoche of climate change, as Jeff Goodell's *The Water Will Come: Rising Seas, Sinking Cities, and the Remaking of Civilization* (2017), Ashley Dawson's *Extreme Cities: The Peril and Promise of Urban Life in the Age of Climate Change* (2017), and David Wallace-Wells in *The Uninhabitable Earth* (2019) show. All of these books discuss major metropolises such as New York, Miami, Venice, or Jakarta to portray the risky futures of climate change.

In these epic accounts of drowning cities, a pre-Romantic conception of the relationship between the city and nature often reemerges. It is, once again, natural forces that endanger human settlements (a common vision before the turn of the nineteenth century) rather than cities degrading and polluting nature (a common trope of environmental writing since then). The epic sweep of large-scale destruction in many of these narratives tends to overwrite attention to climate justice – the question of who causes climate change and who suffers the consequences. But climate justice does sometimes inflect fictional as well as nonfictional scenarios of urban disaster. From the stark differences between the residents of corporate compounds and those of urban "pleeblands" in Margaret Atwood's *MaddAddam* trilogy (2003–2013) to Dawson's emphasis on "climate redlining" and the precarity of poor urban dwellers in the face of rising sea levels, many contemporary portrayals of drowning cities foreground that flooding does not mean the same thing for all urbanites. Some city dwellers are more exposed than others, some have better means to escape or counteract the consequences of climate change, and these differences follow well-established patterns of social inequality defined by class and race.

Narratives that emphasize climate justice resemble toxicity narratives in emphasizing the suffering of victims and their resistance to those who cause environmental disaster. At the same time, however, climate change narratives often turn cities themselves into the victims of humans' destruction of nature. As coral reefs bleach and polar bears' habitat thaws, cities drown in rising tides that authors and filmmakers often present as the finale to a particular way of life and sometimes even an apocalyptic end to human society itself. But in both toxicity and climate change narratives, cities are usually portrayed as associated – by way of causes or of consequences – with the destruction of nature at the hand of modern humans.

Multispecies Cities

A different type of urban environmental narrative has begun to emerge over the last quarter-century that seeks to understand cities as sites where nature is created and perpetuated rather than terminated. Cities are not just habitats by and for humans, in this approach, but also for a multitude of other species. In geography and urban planning, theorists such as Jennifer Wolch have therefore argued that cities should be reenvisioned from the perspective of "zoöpolis" that considers how urban structures affect nonhumans as well as humans.[11] Such a perspective invites a broadening of environmental justice and a radical urban democracy that include nonhuman species.[12] In anthropology, multispecies ethnographers have made a sustained effort to reenvision what we usually conceive of as human societies and cultures as multispecies assemblages that involve humans along with the fauna and flora that keep them alive, the animals and plants that form part of culture and religion, and the bacteria and viruses that variously ensure or harm humans' organic functions. Such multispecies ethnography has in some cases focused on urban spaces and species, as Deborah Bird Rose and Thom van Dooren's do in their study of penguins and flying foxes in Sydney.[13]

Such approaches to cities as multispecies communities have translated into several recurring narrative templates that emerge in fiction as well as nonfiction narratives. One of the most common of these is the awareness narrative, in which an individual or a group, gradually or suddenly, discovers the presence and sometimes agency of nonhumans in the city. Encouraging such discoveries is the goal of many "citizen science" or "community science" projects that involve urban dwellers without any formal scientific training in the search for and documentation of a wide variety of species, from insects and reptiles to birds and coyotes. The Natural History Museums of Los Angeles and San Diego, for example, co-organized "Reptiles and Amphibians of Southern California" (RASCals), a community science effort to document the adaptations of species in these two taxa to urbanization and habitat change.[14] Popular-scientific accounts of urban biodiversity often follow a similar impulse: John Marzluff's *Subirdia*, for example, seeks to create awareness of just how many species of trees and birds populate cities, and what principles govern which species thrive and which ones vanish from urban areas.

This awakening to the liveliness of urban environments resonates with the more general narrative of awareness that Scott Slovic has highlighted as characteristic of American nature writing.[15] It has also made its way into fiction: Buzzworm, an African American neighborhood councilor in Karen Tei Yamashita's novel *Tropic of Orange* (1997), for example, cares deeply about the omnipresent palm trees that dot the urban landscape of Los Angeles. Along with the material and existential support he lends to the city's poorer inhabitants, he teaches them to distinguish and take care of the seven different species of palms that sometimes thrive, but more often languish in the urban surroundings. T, the protagonist of Lydia Millet's novel *How the Dead Dream* (2008), begins to consider nonhumans after accidentally hitting a coyote on a desert road, and he gradually develops an awareness of the animal populations displaced by the real estate ventures he undertakes around Los Angeles. So intense becomes his interest in displacement and extinction that he ends up breaking into zoos to spend nights in the enclosures of "final animals," cut off from their conspecifics and sometimes the last of their kind.[16] Social isolation, grief, and alienation are no longer distinctively human experiences in this scenario, but shared across species in an urban space in which old social and ecological connections are replaced by new ones.

The multispecies awareness narrative sometimes combines with the narrative of urban return, which highlights how species that have vanished from cities return. This narrative forms one plot strand in Kim Stanley's Robinson's *New York 2140* (2017), which portrays a city that by the middle of the twenty-second century has experienced a fifty-foot sea level rise. In this scenario, lower Manhattan is completely flooded and has turned into an "aquatropolis" or "SuperVenice."[17] The drowned city that usually signals a civilizational ending in climate change narratives instead catalyzes New York's return to at least some of its original ecological profile. A character named only "the citizen" points out that New York is

> such a city that it used to take some looking to see it as an estuary. Since the floods that's become easier, because although it was a drowned coastline before, it is now more drowneder than ever. Fifty-feet-higher sea level means a much bigger bay, more tidally confused, Hell Gate more hellish, the Harlem River a wild tidal race and not a shipping canal, the Meadowlands a shallow sea, Brooklyn and Queens and the south Bronx all shallow seas.[18]

This unintended ecological restoration includes biodiversity: "And so the animals have come back, the fish, the fowl, the oysters, quite a few of them two-headed and fatal to ingest, but back," the citizen remarks drily.[19] At another point in the narrative, the same character outlines the biological resurgence in more detail and without such sarcasm:

> On the floors of the canals, the old sewer holes spew life from below. Up and down life floats, in and out with the tides. Salamanders and frogs and turtles proliferate among the fishes and eels, burrow in the mulm. Above them birds flock and nest in the concrete cliffs of the city ... Right whales swim

into the upper bay to birth their babies. Minke whales, finbacks, hump-backs. Wolves and foxes skulk in the forests of the outer boroughs. . . . At the center of the estuarine network swims the mayor of the municipality, the beaver, busily building wetlands. Beavers are the real real estate developers. River otters, mink, fishers, weasels, raccoons: all these citizens inhabit the world the beavers made from their version of lumber. Around them swim harbor seals, harbor porpoises. A sperm whale sails through the Narrows like an ocean liner. Squirrels and bats. The American black bear. They have all come back like the tide, like poetry.[20]

For all its continuing social and ecological problems, New York City has been transformed back into a vibrant multispecies ecosystem by way of climate change and rising seas.

In a different twist on the narrative of urban return, futuristic cities are not always repopulated by native species only. Often they include non-native plants and animals that combine with native ones into the "novel ecosystems" mentioned earlier. Terry Gilliam's science fiction noir 12 Monkeys (1995), a time-travel narrative, features moments that evoke such a new urban ecology. James Cole (played by Bruce Willis), a prisoner in the year 2035, is sent back in time to prevent the outbreak of a deadly pandemic that races around the globe in 1996 and extermin-ates most of humankind. An underground group called the Army of the Twelve Monkeys is suspected of having released the virus, but Cole discovers that these dissidents are far more interested in animal rights than genocide. In 1996, they release a large number of animals from the Philadelphia Zoo in an act of protest, placing the group leader's father, a renowned geneticist, in a cage instead. In "something like a fantasy of utopian possibilities in the present,"[21] in an otherwise largely bleak vision of the future, Cole sees these animals racing about and enjoying their freedom in the streets of Philadelphia. Indeed, some of these urban-adapted escapees still populate the film's ruined Philadelphia forty years later.

Gene technology inflects the biodiversity of the future in some narra-tives to such a degree that the city is no longer just a site of return but also of evolution. The Dutch ecologist Menno Schilthuizen has argued that cities are already places of natural evolution, as demonstrated by a mosquito species whose sole habitat is the London Underground: "What if [Culex molestus] is not an exception anymore? . . . What if our grip on the earth's ecosystems has become so firm that life on earth is in the process of evolving ways to adapt to a thoroughly urban planet?" Schilthuizen asks.[22] He argues that

[w]hile we all have been focusing on the vanishing quantity of unspoiled nature, urban ecosystems have been evolving behind our backs, right in the cities that we have been turning up our naturalist noses at. While we have been trying to save the world's crumbling pre-urban ecosystem, we have been ignoring the fact that nature has already been putting up the scaffolds to build novel, urban ecosystems for the future.[23]

Fictional texts do not typically focus on natural evolution in cities but instead tend to tell stories of technologically driven evolution. Genetic modification, including the mixing of genes from different organisms in a single species, is a common motif in contemporary science fiction, from Atwood's Crakers and pigoons in *Oryx and Crake* (2003) to the part-human, part-avian protagonist of Jeff VanderMeer's *Strange Bird* (2017). One of the best-known examples of this third type of urban multispecies narrative is Paolo Bacigalupi's *The Windup Girl* (2009). In this novel's storyworld, crops are regularly decimated by pests and plagues that trigger famine and disease in a global context of climate change and biodiversity loss. Agricultural and chemical corporations desperately reengineer the crops to make them plague-resilient, though these solutions only yield one or two viable crop cycles before the pests adapt. Bangkok, where the novel is set, swarms with gene-engineered plants and animals as well as new types of fungi, bacteria, and viruses. At the beginning of the novel, Anderson Lake, the representative of an American company, has to shoot a megodont – a genetically engineered descendant of mammoths – that is running amok in a factory. He also discovers a "ngaw" at a stand on a street market, a disease-free version of the rambutan fruit that he infers could only have been recreated from original genes that the Thai government keeps hidden away in a seed vault.[24] Through this genetic revival of a lost species, the narrative of biodiversity return here becomes historical rather than geographical, at the same time that the megodont stands in for the numerous newly created species in the metropolis of the future – including genetically engineered humans.

A fourth type of multispecies narrative that sometimes, but not always, involves technology focuses on innovative human–animal bonds. The social contract between humans, Crakers, and genetically engineered pigoons at the end of Atwood's *MaddAddam* (2013) is one example of a community that reaches across species. Sam J. Miller's *Blackfish City* (2018) gives this narrative template a more explicitly urban turn, as the story is set in an island city in the Arctic Ocean, Qaanaaq, which has become a magnet for climate refugees. One day, a mysterious woman named Masaaraaq arrives riding an orca, to whom, as it turns out, she is

bonded by nanotechnology; the polar bear who accompanies her is later
bonded with another character, Kaev, in a connection that is both physical
and psychological. These new individual and communal relations to
animals are not completely accounted for by the conventional figures of
the animal familiar, the pet, or the genetic relative. Rather, they signal the
emergence of innovative human–animal bonds in urban contexts where
social relationships between humans have been vitiated by ecological
disaster, corporate exploitation, poverty, and crime.

It is no accident, of course, that one of the animal characters in *Blackfish
City* is a polar bear, an animal species that is itself endangered by climate
change. Nonhuman species, especially endangered ones such as polar
bears, tigers, or bees affected by colony collapse disorder play
a subordinate but persistent role in the awareness and conversations of
the major characters in novels such as Jonathan Lethem's *Chronic City*
(2009) or Teju Cole's *Open City* (2011). They highlight how much a sense
of environmental crisis filters even into urban narratives that portray the
city as largely detached from nature, but its residents as haunted by the
knowledge that the natural world outside the city and quite possibly inside
it is both under threat and might put the very fabric of urban life at risk.

One of the recent American texts that most successfully combines this
sense of precarity with a celebration of multispecies communities does so
through the medium of lyrical poetry: Harryette Mullen's *Urban
Tumbleweed: Notes from a Tanka Diary* (2013). Mullen, who is neither an
environmentalist, a birdwatcher, nor a gardener, acknowledges that she
found herself without a ready-made language for the numerous encounters
with urban vegetation and wildlife she experienced in her daily life as
a pedestrian in Los Angeles: "Like ice plant, eucalyptus, and nearly all of
LA's iconic palm trees, I too am a transplant to this metropolis of motor
vehicles . . . Walking instead of driving allows a different kind of attention
to surroundings . . . Los Angeles, however urban, offers everyday encounters with nature."[25] Echoing Price's call for awareness of large cities as forms
of nature, Mullen explores such encounters as part of an urban landscape
also characterized by migration, homelessness, and incidents of racial
discrimination.

In *Urban Tumbleweed* (Mullen's metaphor for plastic bags blowing
down urban streets), encounters with plants, animals, and weather events
are as often marked by misrecognition or misunderstanding as by the deep
familiarity and expert knowledge that American nature writing tends to
celebrate.[26] "What of a poet who does not know the proper names of native
and non-native fauna and flora, who sees 'a yellow flower by a creek' – not

a *Mimulus?*" Mullen asks.[27] And yet, urban nature flourishes even in the absence of such knowledge and care, as thriving gardens and passing birds reveal:

> Why should I care about my neighbor's
> riotous dandelions? Does he concern himself
> with my slovenly jacaranda?[28]

> Caught a quick glimpse of bright eyes,
> yellow feathers, dark wings. Never learned your name –
> and to you, bird, I also remain anonymous.[29]

These brief encounters and loose connections between humans and non-humans, natives and non-natives lead to new urban ecologies and communities, even if they are ecologies of migration, displacement, and uprootedness. In one poem, native monarch butterflies are seen winter-roosting on introduced eucalyptus trees:

> Shady eucalyptus grove where sleeping
> butterflies cover each limb of every tree –
> A rest stop on their migratory flight.[30]

Human trash becomes a source of food for wildlife:

> Two seagulls face off in the parking lot
> between Costco and In-N-Out,
> quarreling over a half-eaten hamburger bun.[31]

Another poem (one among many) shows wildlife using urban infrastructures:

> Baby ducklings trailing mother duck
> can scarcely wet their feet in shallow puddles
> of this city's concrete rivers and creeks.[32]

And conversely, even non-native species provide human urbanites with an experience of nature:

> A scenic backdrop of young bamboo stalks
> growing in a corner of the yard, inspiring
> the children's tropical adventures.[33]

All these are glimpses of a socio-ecological cityscape where transplants, migrants, and homeless people are often as much "introduced" as urban plants or animals, and where all of them sometimes clash with attempts to create or recreate a social order or ecosystem that authorities perceive to have been disturbed. And yet, urban multispecies communities persist and often thrive – caught in lyrical fragments that sketch rather than spell out a full-fledged narrative of the futures of urban biodiversity.

Such narratives still remain rarer than the more familiar visions of toxic and drowned cities I discussed earlier, but as *Urban Tumbleweed* demonstrates, they are no longer uncommon even among writers whose primary orientation is not environmentalist. Nature in these narratives no longer resides outside the city, but is seen to inhabit urban spaces. Stories about pollution and climate change, as I outlined earlier, show how the entanglement of nature with urban areas produces risks for different groups of urbanites and for cities as a whole. Stories about biological evolution and the emergence of multispecies networks foreground a different kind of urban future in which the city itself is reimagined as a form of nature and reshaped into a habitat that makes room for different kinds of humans and of nonhumans. It is through such stories of multispecies communities that emerge – even from scenarios of inequality and risk – that American environmental literature demonstrates its relevance for an increasingly urban future.

CHAPTER 12

Japanese American Incarceration and the Turn to Earth: Looking for a Man Named Komako *in* Bad Day at Black Rock

Mika Kennedy

"I'm looking for a man named Komako," says aging veteran John J. Macreedy (Spencer Tracy) in John Sturges's 1955 film, *Bad Day at Black Rock*.[1] Black Rock is a flagging, would-be frontier town amorphously located in the American West, "crouching in isolation" in a desert flanked by mountains.[2] This town is the supposed home of Komako, the father of a fallen Japanese American soldier to whom Macreedy feels indebted. But when Macreedy discovers that Komako is nowhere to be found, the town kingpin, Reno Smith (Robert Ryan), shakes his head. He explains, "[Komako] got here in '41 – just before Pearl Harbor. Three months later he was shipped to one of those relocation centers." Smith's invocation of the United States' World War II Japanese American incarceration camps is fleeting, never to be mentioned again over the course of the film. Stranger still, this explanation turns out to be false, a cover-up for the true circumstances surrounding Komako's disappearance. Japanese American incarceration enters the film casually, even flippantly, as though it were an event innocent enough to serve as a cover story for a crime. But Komako's fate is not as disconnected from the incarceration as it first appears – nor, indeed is *Bad Day at Black Rock*.

Bad Day at Black Rock's narrative follows Macreedy as he endeavors to get to the bottom of Komako's disappearance. Komako was not incarcerated, but murdered. A racialized newcomer to a failing frontier town, Komako was sold a piece of useless land, only to dig a well and hit water – the motherlode, desert power, and salvation all rolled into one. To celebrate his success, Smith and the other denizens of Black Rock burned down his homestead with him inside it. They buried his body beside the well. Then Smith used the incarceration to explain away Komako's absence. Even after learning all this, Macreedy is ultimately ineffective in enacting justice on Komako's behalf – and indeed, could never have hoped to. *Black Rock* is a Western without a hero. Thus,

I propose a reading of the film that turns instead to earth, reading the landscape as a vital surround through which Komako and the incarceration physically and hauntingly manifest at Black Rock, even in the absence of human forms. This turn to earth links the Western and the West to narratives of Japanese American incarceration: both are bound to the settler-colonial impulse that seeks to consolidate US power and authority over land, water, and people in the West. Bringing awareness of the history of irrigation infrastructural development carried out by Japanese Americans at the camps situated on Indigenous land, I offer a reading, simultaneously indebted to ecocriticism and comparative race studies, that explores the ways *Black Rock*'s Hollywood Western becomes an incarceration tale – which in turn becomes a narrative of settler-colonial eco-imperialism.

A Western Without Heroes

In the opening scene of *Bad Day at Black Rock*, a train cuts through the desert. Its metal siding is almost brilliant enough to reflect the mountains that frame its passage. As though from the sky, suspended like a wind-hovering bird, we see it from afar. Then we're above the tracks, flying to meet the train head-on. We sweep up and over, hold our line over its black roof before we nestle into the brush and rock, now peering at the train from down low – low enough to catch a glimpse of shadowed undercarriage. As the opening credits roll, we return to the center of the tracks, facing the train head-on, but it's different this time. Rather than sweep up over the top of the train like a bird, we hold position. We maintain speed with the train, our backs toward the destination – an uncanny rendition of Walter Benjamin's *Angelus novus*, a figure that faces the carnage of history even as it is propelled blindly into the future.[3] It feels like a confrontation, with the straight shot suggesting that the train's coming is powerful and plot-driving.[4] The film's dramatic, brassy score rises to a sinister crescendo. When Macreedy disembarks, he inherits the train's defining presence, and captures the full attention of the townspeople. By all accounts, the coming of this train and its mysterious passenger seems a capital event.

But is it? A defining feature of travel by train is that it must always be, to some degree, expected. Trains run on schedules and stop at stations. To be sure, Black Rock's station is little used; the operator claims no one has visited Black Rock in four years. But the fact remains that Macreedy boarded a train on a regular schedule, which followed a designated route, and stopped at a predetermined station. His mystery is limited. Within minutes of his arrival in town, Macreedy offers his name and point of origin (Los Angeles), and shortly thereafter also divulges his reason for coming (he is looking for a man named Komako) – all markers of specificity that undo what little mystery he had. Neither is he the intrepid explorer, confronting the great unknown of a frontier. It's 1945, and the novelty of Black Rock is long gone. The town is quickly denuded of its remaining mystery, as well, because the circumstances surrounding Komako's murder are a secret so poorly kept that this revelation requires almost no sleuthing on Macreedy's part. Macreedy is meant to be the hero-protagonist – the man of action, the cowboy, the lawman, the Wyatt Earp.[5] Yet in the first third of the film, confessions come and mysteries unravel regardless of whether Macreedy undertakes any heroics; he doesn't actually need to solve anything. In the closing minutes of the film, Macreedy engages in a fiery canyon standoff against town kingpin Reno Smith, but the fight is quick, the denouement unsentimental. The resolution of Komako's murder mystery savors of anticlimax. And what is a Western without its thrilling heroics?

This question arises provocatively in *Black Rock* in part because of the film's unique placement in the filmography of the Western. Produced well after the silent, half-reel Bronco Billy Westerns, and before *Black Rock* director John Sturges's better-remembered *Gunfight at the O.K. Corral* (1957) and *The Magnificent Seven* (1960),[6] *Black Rock* entered a scene where the Western had never stopped being produced, persisting well past the *fin de siècle* – but had also largely continued staging the nineteenth century. *Black Rock*, by contrast, is set in 1945, and the lingering specter of World War II looms large – Indian Wars and ranchers and stagecoaches accosted by outlaws give way to thoughts of gas rations and lingering OPAs (Offices of Price Administration), scarcity rather than resource-rich lands and boundless opportunity.[7] In *Black Rock*, the threats are more contemporary, less freely fantastical; the atmosphere is muted.[8] In keeping with this tone, film historian Dana Polan additionally notes that the generic influence of film noir in *Black Rock*'s West also lends a brooding, cynical tone to its Western outpost sick with secrets.[9] Not only is the climactic drama of the Western missing, but so is the grandeur that explorers of the Sierras such as John Muir once touted. Rather than abundance, Black Rock's tall peaks and wide open emptiness connote absence and subterfuge. Although most of Black Rock's residents seem to make their livelihood from ranching, no ranches or livestock appear in the film. Shoot-outs must happen under the cover of darkness, and never at high noon. Ambitions for empire or even pioneering self-sufficiency have come and gone – even Reno Smith admits to journeying to Los Angeles "now and again." Laden with these twentieth-century concerns, *Bad Day at Black Rock* stages a very different West than might be expected of the genre.

The cynical, fading, morally ambiguous West of *Black Rock* is captured by the "post-Western," a subgenre that would rise to prominence in the 1960s and 1970s, which American Studies scholar Neil Campbell suggests are cinematic attempts to contend with "a West living in the presence of its mythic afterlife."[10] But *Black Rock*'s is not a generic post-frontier malaise, and its mythic afterlife is laden not only with the closing of the frontier, but also the close of World War II. Though Komako never appears in the film, he is not faceless: his face is Japanese. Mushroom clouds split the skies over Hiroshima and Nagasaki; camps were filled in the US interior West; fire raged in Pearl Harbor. Komako's Japanese face matters, even if we never see it. And while Smith's invocation of the incarceration camps may have been a game of smoke and mirrors, it wouldn't be the first time a mythic afterlife has been conjured, only to far exceed the conjurer's original intentions. If the post-Western holds within it elements of the "classic Hollywood" Western, hybridized with a touch of contemporary darkness, I argue that we, as viewers, have been invited to name *Black Rock*'s darkness more specifically. *Black Rock* becomes a Japanese American incarceration film the moment Smith uses the camps to excuse Komako's absence.

Of course, *Bad Day at Black Rock* is also an atypical incarceration film, though not primarily for the reasons you might expect. Even mainstream Hollywood films more overtly about incarceration have tended to relegate the actual realities of the incarceration to the background, and have instead tended to privilege narratives focalized through non-Japanese characters. In this respect, Macreedy would not be out of place. In fact, this pattern held true well into the 1990s, after the passage of the Civil Liberties Act of 1988, which acknowledged the injustices of Japanese American incarceration and established a process for redress. Legal scholar Taunya Lovell Banks argues that even these later films, such as *Come See the Paradise* (1990) and *Snow Falling on Cedars* (1999), focus on the interracial romance between a white man and a Japanese American woman, displacing any social commentaries about the incarceration in favor of tales of white infatuation and the power of white heroism.[11] Banks also dismisses *Bad Day at Black Rock* as one of these narratives, citing Macreedy's character as yet another effort to "reestablish white innocence after internment."[12] Similarly, media critic Marita Sturken views *Black Rock* as a film about "a morally bankrupt America [that] is redeemed only by Macreedy, the wounded veteran with a sense of justice."[13] Again, as far as the premise of the film goes, *Black Rock* does not appear to be a black sheep. Macreedy is the "good white man," the man repulsed by the racist acts of others, who has returned from the war with accounts of the valor of the 442nd Battalion. Speaking derisively of Komako, Smith scoffs, "Loyal Japanese Americans – that's a laugh. They're mad dogs. Look at Corregidor – the Death March," to which Macreedy replies, "What did Komako have to do with Corregidor?"[14] He means: Komako had nothing to do with Corregidor, thereby positioning himself as the good white man who is able to distinguish "loyal Japanese Americans" from enemy Japanese. He has come to Black Rock to deliver Joe Komako's medal; he is here to denounce the troubled histories of anti-Asian racism and incarceration while also redeeming the role of the white man.

Yet I argue that the point at which *Black Rock* diverges from the conventional Western is also the point at which it diverges from the Hollywood incarceration narrative: Macreedy may be *Black Rock*'s post-Western leading man, but he is no hero-savior. In fact, he is demonstrably *bad* at the role. When Macreedy confronts Smith in the film's final scene, Komako's presence in the film has receded so far into the background Macreedy can no longer pretend to be a white savior avenging the injustice of Komako's death. By that point, he's trying to save his own skin; he's trying to avenge a more recently murdered white damsel; he's just one of two white men trying to set each other on fire. As Macreedy boards the train and departs the town, the triumphal bombast of the film score resounding over Black Rock's desertscape rings as hollow as the opening score's promise of mystery and portents.

I'm inclined, then, to follow Komako to the edges of the narrative. When Smith invokes the wartime incarceration of Japanese Americans as an alibi, he unwittingly lends a weightiness to Komako's death. Smith calls the incarceration camp a "relocation center," echoing the United States' euphemistic take on the forced relocation of more than 110,000 persons of Japanese descent, and their subsequent disenfranchisement and imprisonment. To his mind, the incarceration can serve as alibi because it was a lesser evil. It was impersonal and, most importantly, state-sanctioned. Yet the incarceration is an ignominious piece of history that the United States has typically been unwilling to narrate accurately, and more inclined to euphemize or cover up – particularly in the decades immediately after World War II. To pair Komako's death with the incarceration is not a cover-up; it is a compounding. Once interpellated into the history of the incarceration, Komako's death is no longer at liberty to be the product of one bad day at Black Rock. What Macreedy stumbles upon at Black Rock is larger than one town, one body. Only by connecting the drama of

Macreedy and Komako to this larger history can the audience begin to make sense of the film's spectacle. A film is more than its plotline, and what is valuable about the nature of Macreedy's failure is the emptiness it leaves in its wake, the anxious thrumming with which it leaves the audience. *Black Rock* is about what arises in the wake of Macreedy's failure. It is about the alternative narratives that become part of the Western that is not a Western, the war story after the war, and the incarceration narrative without incarcerees. To admit this is to recognize a much longer, insidious history of racism in the United States – and the ways that the mythic freedoms of the West are built less on manifest destiny than dispossession and exclusion. And so Komako's death wells up.

The Turn to Earth

Let us return to the train. We know who is riding the train, and we know where it is headed. We know how that story ends. Ignore the anxious film score, the motion blur, and turn instead to the place the train is passing through. Turn to the desert scrub and the dry valley, to the hazy mountains in the distance conveying muted majesty, for their tallest peaks are clipped, victim to a murky fog. Like Macreedy and *Black Rock*, the mountains savor of anticlimax, too. So look lower, to the base. Turn to the earth, an attention that *Black Rock*'s own cinematography seems to invite, with shots from the vantage point of low-lying boulders. The train arrests the viewer's attention as it traverses the desert, yet the train also becomes background. Thirty seconds into this train sequence, just after the film's title card displays, a series of three shots brings a different element to the fore.[15] In the medium shots that comprise the bulk of the opening scenes, the black rocks that give the town its name are framed in the foreground. These shots follow the traditional rule of thirds, establishing depth by using objects in the foreground to frame the larger scene. But who is framing whom? In these shots, the train becomes more leading line than subject, cutting the frame diagonally to draw attention to the foreground. It's the black rocks, not the train, that we see in focused, front-and-center detail.

"Without the land, American mythmaking would not exist," writes Deborah A. Carmichael, on the role of landscape in Hollywood Westerns.[16] *Black Rock* is no exception. But perhaps what is most interesting about *Black Rock*'s landscape is not the bold and obvious ways it signifies the West, but the ways in which this landscape conjures what cannot be seen – at least, not entirely. *Black Rock*, post-Western, is past the point of mythmaking. It's tasked with imagining a mythic afterlife.

In order to probe the intersection between *Black Rock* as Western and *Black Rock* as Japanese American incarceration film, I propose we turn away from the train and its passenger, Macreedy, and turn instead to earth. That is, to approach the landscape as an active presence in the text, one that is as critical to the narrative as the shooting script or stage business. The landscape, after all, is the site of mythmaking and the resting place of mythic afterlives. In the turn to earth, *Bad Day at Black Rock* doesn't begin with a train, nor does it end with a gunfight. Komako is dead and buried long before Macreedy arrives, and his body will remain long after. So let the train recede toward the vanishing point and focus on the black rock that frames its passage. These rocks are pock-marked and igneous; they are evidence of volcanic activity – of an environment that is always in motion as the Earth's crust drifts and tectonic plates shift. These rocks mark the landscape as dynamic space, actively unfolding the mystery plot at Black Rock, albeit on a longer and more capacious timescale than one bad day.

On his way to Komako's former homestead, Macreedy wheels a borrowed utility vehicle through the Alabama Hills, among the rocks. He and the car are small in the scene, dwarfed by great quartz monzonite protrusions and erratic boulders, brought by glaciers long ago. Observe the scene as Macreedy does: first, the charred remains of Komako's former home. Then the patch of wildflowers, growing against all odds in the hard, dry ground. Bend down and pick them, and roll the stems between your fingers. Turn to earth, and find that Komako is present after all, because Macreedy informs Smith that he'd seen flowers bloom like that before. During the war, he'd seen wildflowers mark the earth where the dead were buried. It's no great leap to imagine whose body sustains them here. We turn toward Komako, and find him turned into earth. He does not appear in human form, but he is damningly, physically manifest. The anticlimax of the film seems to whisper, *The frontier? A Japanese man? Well, of course he was killed.*

Drop a stone down a shaft dug deep into earth. Listen for a wet *plonk* as the stone hits water. Reno Smith decided that a story about the incarceration of 110,000 Japanese Americans made for easier listening than the sound of that stone.

Komako, turned to earth, was not incarcerated. Nevertheless, his body holds space for the carceral. Contemplating the work of sculpture artist Ruth Asawa, Iyko Day describes the way Asawa's pieces act as "a visual metaphor for the negative space within and surrounding Japanese

internment in North America."[17] Komako's body functions similarly in
Bad Day at Black Rock. At first, Komako himself is negative space, a missing
person. But when Macreedy discovers him dead, manifested as soil and
wildflowers, the film's sense of things unsettled only magnifies, as we then
need to make room for Smith's lie. His lie can no longer pretend to explain
away Komako's absence, but the incarceration it has conjured still remains.
The camps become *Black Rock*'s incongruous missing piece, haunting the
negative space in every scene.

In his commentary on *Bad Day at Black Rock*, Polan notes the film's
unusual preponderance of interior scenes – unlike the traditional Western,
wed to wide open spaces and the freedoms they signify.[18] For Polan, the
effect is claustrophobic. He imagines this as a visual invocation of the
frontier's closing, of freedoms ending. As both closed Western and incarceration film, however, *Black Rock*'s claustrophobia signifies doubly. If
we're meant to understand Black Rock's declension as tragic, we also
know that the town killed a man; they are not innocent. We know they
are aware of the Japanese American incarceration camps nearby. They are
willing to use them, in more ways than one. Even when *Black Rock* sets
scenes outside, creating space with long shots and capturing the valley's
sharp blue sky, the mountains themselves become carceral to Black Rock,
a sharp fence that is less majestic than imperious. Standing in the shadow of
these mountains after 1945, viewers must reckon with what came before.
They find themselves imprisoned in the mythic afterlives of the event.
Through Smith's invocation of the camps, *Black Rock* becomes such
a space, as well. In my reading of *Black Rock*, I turn to earth because
the film's environment, its landscape, speaks what the script will not.
Smith's lie falls from his lips and settles in the dust. Komako was "shipped
to one of those relocation centers," he says, exactly once, and no more.
But the earth's memory is long. Once planted, the idea of the camps grows
like wildflowers, as though it were *Black Rock*'s unspeakable thing
unspoken.

Texts like *Black Rock* also invite us to contemplate the ways that our
understandings of the World War II incarceration of Japanese Americans
change when they are mediated by the environment and mythic landscapes of the West. The call to think more regionally about the sites of
Japanese American incarceration has begun to be answered by scholars
across disciplines – for example, in Western studies by John Beck, in
Asian American studies by Stephen Hong Sohn, and in environmental
history by Connie Chiang. Beck discusses the camps' entanglements with
the Southwest and its role in the development of a US national security

state; Sohn explores the deserts of Julie Otsuka's *When the Emperor was Divine* through (and beyond) the lens of regional modernism; Chiang draws attention to the ways Japanese American incarcerees historically understood the environment of the camps, and the multitude of ways they interacted with it, from outdoor recreation to irrigation labor.[19] Each of these projects understands the camps as part of a landscape that exceeds their fencelines, linking their creation, maintenance, and legacy to the particularity of the region that surrounds them. Similarly, in *Black Rock*, Smith's attempt to divert attention from Komako's disappearance onto the state-sanctioned disappearance effected by Executive Order 9066 only serves to draw the two into closer relation with one another. We see the progression of Komako's murder and the building of the camps as tributaries from the same source: that is, the United States' colonial impulse to exclusively own and dominate the land it calls the frontier West. After all, the camps are not only what happens within them, or what happened between the bombing of Pearl Harbor and the destruction of Nagasaki. They are part of a larger and longer European, and then United States, history of colonization and dispossession.

What I find uniquely captivating about *Black Rock* is that although the camps are mentioned only once, Smith's lie is geographically capacious. He manages to summon the environmental particularity of *both* the Manzanar and Poston camps to *Black Rock*'s landscape simultaneously. This doubled environment places *Black Rock* not only in its immediate surround but between/within multiple places, which invites us to examine the fascia that connect them – that is, the struggles for land and water that make *Black Rock* a frontier story, but also a Phoenix story; a Los Angeles story; a Washington, DC story. Various critics, such as Marita Sturken in her seminal reading of *Bad Day at Black Rock*, appear to assume that Black Rock is a fictionalization of the town of Lone Pine, the town nearest the Manzanar incarceration camp. This assumption makes sense, given that the movie was filmed at Lone Pine.[20] Yet Black Rock was named for a small town in Arizona, not California. Additionally, in the original film script, a stage direction describes a road sign that proclaims Black Rock's nearest landmarks: Phoenix, 156 miles. Sand City, 32 miles.[21] While this sign does not appear in the final cut of the film, Rea Tajiri's experimental documentary *History and Memory* (1991) also uses clips of *Black Rock* as an intertext, to visualize and locate her mother's experience at the Poston incarceration camp. Poston is roughly 150 miles west of Phoenix – almost exactly the distance from Phoenix to the fictitious Black Rock, if the road sign is to be believed.²² Where is Black Rock? Amid both Manzanar and Poston at once?

The ambiguity seems as though it must be in direct contrast to the tenets of place-based examination. If environment is so critical to our reckoning with carceral history – and so paramount in unearthing *Black Rock*'s second storyline, its anxious and claustrophobic surround, the camps it hides, and the bodies it fails to – what does it mean when that landscape cannot be singularly identified? After Smith justifies Komako's absence by claiming that Komako had been shipped off to an incarceration camp during the war, Macreedy asks him which camp. Smith tellingly replies, "Who knows?"

While it is easy to imagine that *Black Rock*'s refusal to name the town's nearest landmark of incarceration would function instead as a refusal to engage that history, perhaps what is most important about the turn to earth is that it is not only the turn to Manzanar, or the turn to Poston. It is a turn to *earth*. *Black Rock* exists at the interstices of so many things that are considered separate from one another, at the moment at which, against all odds, they overlap: it is a Western and an incarceration film, action playing out adjacent to either Manzanar or Poston, or both at once. The effect is unsettling, both in the sense that something is not quite right, and in the sense that the landscape again becomes dynamic space. *Black Rock*'s location adjacent to both Manzanar *and* Poston emphasizes the doubling not only of Japanese American bodies displaced/disappeared, but also of the pivotal role that land and water play in motivating each disappearance. Imagining *Black Rock* at both Manzanar and Poston simultaneously is like layering two topographic maps, one atop the other, and finding the points at which their topographies match, twinning high peaks and deep canyon troughs. For example, while water is part of the narrative in both places, its role becomes most salient when we examine these places together, drawing connections between and across places in order to foreground their mutual condition as sites of US nation-building and environmental transformation.

"We don't even have enough water," Smith says of Black Rock, staving off a confrontation with Macreedy. He suggests that to be Western is to discover the lengths a town will go in order to keep that water in their "rightful" hands. The West will be won whatever it takes, from murder to mass incarceration. And the West is a war for water.

This isn't a new story, nor is it unique to Black Rock, or even to the camps. Take Manzanar: while the camp is often characterized by its arid climate and punishing dust storms, its name derives from the Spanish for "apple orchard." Before an incarceration camp was built there, Owens Valley Paiute hunted, fished, and gathered in the Valley. They also developed irrigation systems that would support farming.[23] Then, in the 1860s, white settlers chased mining opportunities and other natural resources into the valley, colonizing the area by use of military force, driving the Paiute from their lands.[24] By 1913, however, another settler power established itself in the valley – the Los Angeles Department of Water and Power (LADWP). In order to meet the escalating energy needs of the city of Los Angeles, the LADWP diverted enormous amounts of water from the Owens River, piping it 230 miles westward; by 1929, the LADWP owned all the land and water in the valley. This crippled the region's agricultural capacity, resulting in decades of tension that would again come to a head when the War Relocation Authority began building the Manzanar incarceration center there – another incursion from the coast, this time in the form of a prison for potential "enemy aliens" whom the city found undesirable. The United States repeatedly cannibalizes its own settler projects. This is the history that rises to the fore when we see the incarceration as a story in and of the West. And, as has been visualized by filmmakers such as Ann Kaneko and her documentary *Manzanar, Diverted* (2021), this matters not least because the story is ongoing.[25] World War II is over and the camps are closed, but the Owens River Valley remains a site of contestation between the region's Indigenous peoples, white settlers, and the city and people of Los Angeles.

Similar patterns echo at what would later become Poston. In 1865, the Colorado River Indian Reservation was established in western Arizona, along the Colorado River. It was home first to Mohave peoples and later joined by Chemehuevi. While the United States' goal was to populate the reservation with "10,000 American Indians," this plan did not account for the fact that all Indigenous peoples are not, in fact, the same; the Mohave fought to assert their exclusive right to the land, not to be given to others. Furthermore, most of their neighboring peoples had no desire to leave their lands and move to the reservation.[26] Additionally, a series of poorly engineered irrigation projects also kept the reservation from achieving its stated development goals, until in 1940 the Headgate Rock dam was finally built to keep the waters from destroying the banks every time the floodgates opened.

Interstate conflict over the right and management of water were also brewing. Upriver from Headgate Rock, another dam, the Parker Dam, had been built between 1934 and 1938. From California's perspective, the dam was a New Deal gift of water that allowed for the expansion of Los Angeles and its surrounding urbanizing area. From Arizona's perspective, the dam was unauthorized and the water was stolen. When the building first began, then-Governor of Arizona Benjamin B. Moeur dispatched Arizona's National Guard to halt the project and guard the river. While the US Supreme Court ultimately ruled against Arizona's objections, control of the waters remained – and continues to remain – embattled.[27]

In 1940, with California and the rest of the Southwest thirsty for the river, the Colorado River Indian Reservation was in jeopardy of losing its water rights. It had not built the irrigation systems that could justify their claim, nor did the area have a large enough population to demonstrate their need.[28] In 1941, Japan bombed Pearl Harbor. Then came the camps. In the eyes of John Collier, Commissioner of Indian Affairs, this presented an opportunity: with the added population and the sudden availability of Japanese American labor, building the camp at Poston functioned as an active bid to retain water rights in the area (albeit one made by the Office of Indian Affairs (OIA) without the full approval of the Colorado River Indian Reservation's (CRIR) tribal council).[29] At its peak, the Poston camp held over 17,000 Japanese Americans – nearly double the "10,000 American Indians" the OIA had aimed to move to the CRIR, and what at the time made Poston Arizona's third most populous "city." Over the course of World War II, imprisoned Japanese American labor built more than thirty miles of irrigation canals, in addition to over fifty miles of accompanying irrigation and drainage ditches, though these projects still fell short of what had initially been promised to the tribal council.[30]

Today, the Parker Dam is still in active use, as are the roots of the irrigation infrastructure Poston's prisoners developed during World War II. As in the Owens Valley, the Parker Dam and its associated pipelines divert a portion of the Colorado across state lines, over the Sierras, and into Los Angeles County. Whatever their geographic distance and seemingly separate cultural spheres, follow the water and Manzanar and Poston end up tributaries to the same colonial machine. To invoke them both at Black Rock, where water is worth killing for, implicates Komako's death in far more than the doings of one small-time tyrant and a town left for dead. These are the vital histories that manifest at the interstices between the Western and the incarceration, and which must be centered if we are to tell the story of either in full.

To begin at Black Rock and turn to earth brings Komako's burial – the reason for it and the excuses layered atop it – to the fore. It also invites a critical reframing of the incarceration narrative that emerges in the negative space of the film. The incarceration haunts the West, but the

West is part of the incarceration, too. For example, while the locations of the camps in the interior West are typically framed as wastelands, far from the populated coast, they were also sites with potential for development – wastelands to be tamed and "improved," rather than abandoned. The War Relocation Authority sought to place the camps on public land, so all such improvements would accrue to the federal government, but letters from private citizens also flooded in, volunteering their own lands to house the camps – and to be developed by Japanese American incarcerees.[31] This detail becomes essential to narrating the incarceration because it renders the camp not merely punitive and not merely about Japanese American "enemy aliens." They become not only negative non-space, but places critical to the project of exerting ownership over land – particularly at the expense of the Indigenous peoples that already lived there.

Such exertions, as I've demonstrated in my brief glimpses of Manzanar and Poston, highlight the way the camps exist in relation to the long war for land, water, and sovereignty in the West, and repeat settler-colonial patterns that preexisted and persist after the camps. In *Black Rock*, the myth of the frontier shows its hand and the wartime incarceration of Japanese Americans haunts the margins of the town and the mountains that frame it. But the warp of the Western and the weft of the incarceration film should not feel like an unlikely intersection, given how tightly both are bound up in the mythic afterlives of the frontier – not only in Hollywood's interpretations of the incarceration, with their focus on white heroes, but also in the ways Japanese Americans define our own histories and heroism. War Relocation Authority pamphlets welcomed Japanese Americans to camp as "pioneers," a euphemism most Japanese Americans found as convincing as "evacuation" or "relocation center."[32] At the same time, however, the Japanese American Citizens League still hoped its members might confront their camp experience as an opportunity to demonstrate "better Americans in a greater America."[33] The success of agriculture in the camps is often hailed uncritically as Japanese American exceptionalism, but rarely speaks to the ways this history is also entangled with the destruction of Indigenous lifeways. (Prior to Poston's agricultural triumphs, prior to the dams, and prior to the reservation, the Mohave farmed pumpkins, beans, and maize in accordance with the Colorado River's natural flood patterns.[34]) There is no right way to live in a colonizing incarceration camp, and this is by design. There can be no heroes there, just as there can be none in *Black Rock*. The notion of the hero belongs to a mythic frontier that never existed.

Ultimately, the turn to earth is not an act of unearthing, as in an excavation of a secret. The relations are tangible and manifest. They are part of the very landscape, our surround. Following the ecocritical notion that a text need not explicitly take on environmental themes to be an environmental text, I argue that reading environmentally can also highlight additional critical fascia that might otherwise have gone overlooked, such as those that join the Western and the incarceration film, the West and the history of Japanese American incarceration. Black rocks draw attention from a train; wildflowers mark an unmarked grave. The sound of a stone meeting water provides evidence of motive for a crime. Linking the incarceration with the West is an invitation to reexamine the role land and water play across them – both to question the seeming disappearance of non-white (immigrant *and* Indigenous) bodies from what is Western, and to imagine the ways that placing the incarceration squarely in the West requires further examinations of what it means to be in relation to land, water, citizenship, and sovereignty.

So listen for the wet *plonk* of a stone hitting water at the bottom of a well dug deep into earth. Listen to the silence of the Parker Dam, holding the waters of the Colorado in abeyance and diverting them westward, over the mountains and toward Los Angeles. Speak the name "Manzanar," and wonder who could possibly grow apples here, in a place so dry as this.

Turn your ear to the ground and listen for the water below.

CHAPTER 13

Leisure over Labor: Latino Outdoors and the Production of a Latinx Outdoor Recreation Identity

Sarah D. Wald

When asked about his relationship to nature, Gabe Vasquez told a story from his childhood. He explained,

> When my family and I first got to Caballo Lake in New Mexico we threw our lines in the water and it wasn't long before a Game & Fish officer came to check on our licenses. Because it was our first time fishing and we were from Mexico, we didn't realize we needed a license. The officer claimed he couldn't understand what my Dad was saying, so he called Border Patrol. Border Patrol detained my Dad that afternoon at a county jail in Truth or Consequences. They released him several hours later because he had not done anything wrong. Despite that harassment, my dad told me to stay strong and that the outdoors were a place for everyone. We got our fishing licenses that afternoon and went back to the river. Since then, I've tried to spread the same message . . . *the outdoors are for everyone*.[1]

One of the many ways Vasquez has spread his outdoor equity message is as the New Mexico coordinator for the organization Latino Outdoors. A grassroots nonprofit organization founded in 2013, Latino Outdoors seeks to increase Latinx access to the outdoors and nature, to build a network of Latinx conservation professionals, and to mobilize Latinx advocacy for expanded public lands protections. In 2019, Latino Outdoors organized 190 outings for 3,300 participants with more than 90 volunteer leaders in over 20 locations across the US, and collaborated with over 250 distinct organizations.[2] Latino Outdoors responds to the historical and ongoing exclusion of people of color from outdoor recreation and the conservation movement, challenging the racial construction of nature, the environment, wilderness, and public lands as white space.

Vasquez's story echoes many contemporary narratives of people of color in outdoor spaces. In a viral incident in 2020, Christian Cooper, a Black birdwatcher, asked Amy Cooper (no relation), a white woman walking through the Ramble in New York City's Central Park, to leash her dog (see

Introduction). Amy responded to his request to obey clearly posted rules by threatening to call the police and tell them she was in danger from an "African American man," a threat upon which she then acted. When Amy finally leashed her dog, Christian stated "thank you," and walked away. The interaction, which Christian filmed, gained notoriety for the cavalier way in which Amy weaponized her white womanhood to endanger Christian's life. In specifying to police that it was an "African American man" who supposedly jeopardized her safety, Amy revealed her expectation that the police would punish Christian for his Blackness even though she was the one breaking the leashing law.[3]

The video captured the danger that people of color, especially Black people, experience in white spaces of outdoor recreation. As geographer Carolyn Finney wrote, "I wish I could feign surprise at what happened to Christian Cooper when he encountered Amy Cooper in Central Park. I wish I could imagine it to be a blip in the United States's history; an accident, an outlier, not at all reflective of the truth of how [B]lack people are all too often treated. But I can't."[4]

The exclusion and danger that people of color experience in outdoor recreation and on public land is one that is both shared and racially and ethnically specific. The white womanhood that placed [black birder] Christian Cooper at risk of bodily harm relies on the context of US anti-Blackness shaped by slavery and Jim Crow (see Introduction). When Vasquez found himself facing the Border Patrol while trying to fish, it was partly the result of a long history of reading Latinx peoples as what Sarah Jaquette Ray terms "ecological others," perceived simultaneously as foreign and as environmental threats.[5] Native American recreationists face still yet other forms of invisibility and danger in outdoor recreation and public lands, lands historically occupied by their own people and on which treaty rights guarantee certain traditional practices.[6] Both these differences and the shared context of racial exclusion matter.

Latino Outdoors is just one star in a constellation of organizations and initiatives that emerged in the first part of the twenty-first century to address issues of equity, diversity, and inclusion on public lands and in outdoor recreation. Grassroots organizations such as Latino Outdoors and Green Latinos aim to increase the visibility of Latinx leadership in conservation, develop new Latinx outdoor recreationists, and claim a seat at the conservation table for Latinx communities.[7] Groups such as Outdoor Afro and Black Girls Trekkin' seek to create comfortable environments for Black recreationists by hosting events for hikers, swimmers, and climbers.[8] These organizations represent access to nature as environmental right. They counter popular visions of people of color as unlikely environmentalists, recognizing their longstanding relationships to nature, outdoor recreation, and public lands (see Chapter 10 by Susan Scott Parrish).

Yet, these efforts to diversify outdoor recreation on public lands also raise vexing questions, given the ways outdoor recreation in the US emerged in relation to settler colonialism. Narratives about national parks, national forests, and wilderness adventures in the US have justified a settler-colonial logic by erasing Indigenous claims to those very lands. As scholars such as William Cronon, Carolyn Finney, Jake Kosek, Paul Outka, and others have argued, visions of a sublime and romantic wilderness have further served narratives of white supremacy that promote a right and wrong way of engaging with nature.[9] Moreover, backpacking and adventure culture have fed a frontier mythology built on white heteronormative masculinity and a eugenicist investment in able white bodies, as scholars including Gail Bederman, Sarah Jaquette Ray, Dorceeta Taylor, and Alexandra Stern have shown.[10]

How then do we approach a movement that seeks to include Black, Indigenous, Asian, and Latinx recreationists in these spaces deemed white after settler-colonization? What cultural work occurs when an organization such as Latino Outdoors depicts the traditional proving ground for white heteronormative masculinity and US national identity as Latinx leisure space? Do such organizations reshape the definitions of wilderness and nature? Or do they simply expand access to them in ways that leave the fundamental troubles with wilderness, outdoor recreation, and public lands intact?

In this chapter, I consider efforts to increase racial and ethnic diversity on US public lands and in US outdoor recreation through a case study of the organization Latino Outdoors. I argue that Latino Outdoors works to upend the exclusion of Latinx peoples from outdoor recreation and public lands through constructing and disseminating a *Latinx Outdoor Recreation Identity*.[11] In doing so, Latino Outdoors disrupts a US cultural logical which incorporates the labor of Latinx peoples while denying their substantive citizenship as well as their political and ecological belonging. In contrast to legacies of Latinx outdoor labor, Latino Outdoors embraces Latinx leisure, and specifically Latinx outdoor leisure. Furthermore, the organization emphasizes historical forms of Latinx environmental knowledge, and thus environmental belonging. Latino Outdoors creates new forms of Latinx environmental belonging founded on leisure rather than labor. These forms of environmental belonging operate within Latino

Outdoors as a proxy for political belonging and the grounds for political action.

Public Land and Outdoor Recreation

Latino Outdoors has an explicit focus on public lands in both the outdoor recreation and the advocacy it encourages. This is unsurprising given that the majority of outdoor recreation in the US occurs on public lands, and that public lands have played a foundational role in the conservation movement to which Latino Outdoors strives to contribute a Latinx voice.[12] Understanding Latino Outdoors' interventions in outdoor recreation and public lands advocacy requires some knowledge of both the historical and contemporary debates over public lands in the US.

One-third of every acre of land in the US is local, state, or federal public land. The federal government holds 635 million acres or 27.9 percent of US land.[13] Public lands have long played a key role in how scholars have narrated both US environmental history and the history of environmentalism in the US. As political scientist Stephen Davis recounts, "Over the course of the nineteenth century, the federal government would acquire an astonishing 1.6 billion acres, or nearly 70 percent, of the land in the United States."[14] This land was acquired through layered strategies of genocide including massacres, forced removal, and forced assimilation. The federal government privatized over one billion acres of the land it claimed, distributing it to homesteaders, military veterans, and railroads as well as other industries. Throughout the nineteenth and early twentieth centuries, conservation and preservation movements worked to shift federal public lands policy, by retaining lands, particularly West of the Mississippi River for conservation (scientific and rational management) and preservation (untouched nature) purposes.[15]

The debates into which Latino Outdoors most powerfully intervenes are those shaped by environmental humanities scholars, who have shown enduring interest in US public lands. From the 1960s through the 1980s, a celebratory account of public lands, especially national parks and wilderness, dominated environmental humanities scholarship. Works such as Roderick Nash's *Wilderness and the American Mind* (1967) provide a grand narrative through which the American public comes to recognize the inherent worth of wilderness over time. Environmental historian Ramachandra Guha forcefully criticized this approach in his frequently cited essay, "Radical American Environmentalism and Wilderness: A Third World Critique." William Cronon's edited volume *Uncommon*

Ground (1995) further disrupted this celebratory teleology with his influential essay, "The Trouble with Wilderness," which positioned wilderness as socially and materially constructed rather than an objective material reality, nature in its Edenic original state. Cronon contended that the concept of wilderness was often more harmful than helpful in the ways it drew the public's attention away from the presence of nature in the everyday to focus disproportionately on the nature "out there."[16]

Some of the most forceful critiques of US public lands have targeted public lands and outdoor recreation as forms of settler colonialism. Settler colonialism describes the processes, ideologies, and power dynamics that occur when colonizers settle with the intent to stay on land inhabited by others. As sociologist Kari Norgaard summarizes, "This particular social formation of colonialism is characterized by the elimination of the original inhabitants; elimination of Indigenous knowledge, and political, social, and ecological systems; and their replacement by those of settler society."[17] Settler colonialism involves not only land theft and displacement, but also the disruption of Indigenous ecologies and cosmologies.[18] US ideas of wilderness, or a priori nature originally uninhabited and created without human intervention, rely on a settler-colonial logic that ignores Indigenous relationships to the more-than-human world and erases Indigenous cosmologies. US conceptions of wilderness in the late nineteenth century through the twentieth century understood nature as fully separate from human. The 1964 Wilderness Act codified this vision of wilderness as land "untrammeled by man, where man himself is a visitor who does not remain."[19] Such a vision is incommensurable with many native worldviews based on ideas of relationality, or what scholars call kincentricity (distinct from both anthropocentricity and its opposite, biocentricity).[20]

As historians Karl Jacoby and Mark Spence argue, the US conservation movement has gone hand in hand with native dispossession. The federal government established national parks and national forests around the same time as they established Indian reservations. Treaties often guaranteed tribes' rights to traditional uses of unsettled federally held lands, including rights to hunt, fish, and access sacred sites. When the federal government sought to prevent such traditional uses on newly named national parks and national forests, they met with strong resistance. Settlers believed native peoples to be incapable of managing land intelligently and perceived traditional uses as destructive to nature. Preventing traditional uses of these lands operated not only as conservation policy (creation of uninhabited wilderness by removing inhabitants and their traditional management activities) but also worked as military strategy to reduce Indigenous mobility (restricting Indigenous peoples to reservations) and forced assimilation (cultural genocide) by removing traditional sources of sustenance and livelihood.[21]

Federal public land management fundamentally disrupted Indigenous ecological relations. The federal lands that became national parks and national forests were recently dispossessed landscapes. Indigenous inhabitants shaped these landscapes for millennia. As Norgaard explains, "Indigenous knowledge and management generated the abundance in the land that formed the basis of capitalist wealth across North America."[22] The dispossession of native populations from traditional lands and the restriction of Indigenous land management practices altered ecosystems. Federal management represented a dramatic change from Indigenous communities' traditional management practices. In the case of Yosemite, these restricted Indigenous practices included activities such as hand removal of young trees and controlled burns that prevented a thick understory from developing. As journalist Dina Gilio-Whitaker (Coville Confederated Tribes) reports, "Within a few short decades of bureaucratic management Yosemite Valley would become almost unrecognizable to its Indigenous inhabitants."[23]

Federal management continues to enact what sociologist J. Bacon terms "colonial ecological violence."[24] Norgaard, through a case study of the Karuk, argues that this colonial ecological violence "takes place through the alteration of land, the alternation of species composition and ecological structures, and the alternation of relationships between people and the more-than-human entities known as nature."[25] These ecosystem changes alter the Karuk's ability to engage in significant cultural practices. Moreover, federal management policies, such as regulations around fishing, hunting, and fire, continue to deem many culturally significant Karuk practices illegal.[26]

Such linkages between colonialism and conservation are not unique to the US, despite narratives of American exceptionalism often used to explain the US conservation movement, especially the creation of national parks. Guha, for example, shows a similar colonial dynamic at work in India, contextualizing the popular Chipko movement (known for women hugging trees to prevent logging) as part of a longer history of peasant resistance to colonial forestry. Furthermore, scholars have exposed the ways that both European models of conservation and US national parks and national forests (whose creation was influenced by European models) have been exported internationally in ways that reinforce colonial dynamics in countries ranging from Kenya to India. This critique appears in Amitav

Ghosh's novel *The Hungry Tide* (2006) as well as Mark Dowie's journalistic *Conservation Refugees* (2011); both texts highlight the displacement Indigenous people have faced as the result of conservation projects.[27]

More recently, however, promising alliances have been forged between Indigenous communities and conservationists collaborating on US public lands. The Bears Ears National Monument is a frequently cited example of such an alliance. In mobilizing to protect areas of cultural and ecological significance in their ancestral lands, the Bears Ears Inter-Tribal Coalition, which brought together five sovereign tribal nations (Navajo Nation, Hopi Tribe, Pueblo of Zuni, Ute Mountain Ute tribe, and Ute Indian Tribe), worked in alliance with mainstream conservationists. They met with temporary success when President Barack Obama established the Bears Ears National Monument in December 2016.[28]

The tenuousness of the ideological solidarity between public lands advocates and the Bears Ears Inter-Tribal Coalition became apparent in response to the Trump Administration's substantive (85 percent) reduction of the monument, a move now under lawsuit. The outdoor clothing company, Patagonia, Inc. blasted the Trump Administration's move with an advertisement published in the *New York Times* and centered on their website that read "The President Stole Your Land." As environmental humanities scholar April Anson points out, Patagonia's settler environmentalism was on full display in its response. The possessive move to "your" land prioritizes a settler subject with threatened property while erasing the Indigenous relationships to the lands at the heart of the Bears Ears movement. Additionally, in focusing on "The President," Patagonia erases the complicity of and benefit to white settler environmentalists in the initial act of "stealing" the land by placing it into federal control (an insight Anson credits to an Inupiaq woman attending an early talk on her topic).[29] As Anson's analysis, as well as work by Nick Estes (Lower Brule Sioux Tribe), Julie Sze, Elizabeth Hoover (Mohawk/Mi'kmaq), and Gilio-Whitaker suggests, solidarity work by settler environmentalists with Indigenous nations is necessary to address public lands not only as a legacy of settler colonialism, but also as an ongoing settler-colonial project.[30]

Ecological Legitimacy and Expanded Public Lands Access

In the first part of the twenty-first century, environmental writers and environmental humanities scholars published a series of works that sought to redeem public lands without dismissing their troubling history and moral complexity. Such works include Stephen Davis's *In Defense of Public Lands*, Margaret Grebowicz's *The National Park to Come*, Jennifer Ladino's *Memorial Matters*, Terry Tempest Williams's *The Story of an Hour*, and Stephanie LeMenager and Marsha Weiseger's call for collaborative public lands management.[31] These projects share a desire to protect public lands and invest in their future without ignoring their histories of material and ideological violence, often by centering the voices of those whose claims to the land have been marginalized, contested, or erased.

Latino Outdoors is a part of this redemptive effort. Latino Outdoors seeks to mobilize a Latinx constituency to protect public lands. In doing so, it seeks to transform those public lands in ways that recognize Latinx pasts and produce Latinx futures. Latino Outdoors broadens the definitions of nature and outdoor recreation at the heart of public lands management debates. They upturn racially exclusive histories of conservation and recreation on public lands in foregrounding Latinx environmental knowledge and Latinx environmental histories. In doing so, they mobilize the tension between Latinx outdoor recreation and Latinx outdoor labor to argue for Latinx political and environmental belonging.

Latino Outdoors successfully challenges the wilderness model at work in the traditional conservation movement. The organization's website features dozens of "Yo Cuento" blog posts in which staff and volunteers explain their relationship to nature and the outdoors. As Latino Outdoors explains, "Yo cuento" is a versatile phrase, signaling, "I count," "I matter," and "I tell my story."[32] In 2019, more than a hundred individuals contributed to the "Yo Cuento" project.[33] The posts themselves are at least partially crowd-sourced.[34] Their narratives provide a rich tapestry of environmental experiences, includes the urban, agricultural, domestic, and pastoral. For example, Laura Torres writes, "My earliest memory of the outdoors is connected to living in Georgia and having fruit trees, growing some veggies, and a pond within walking distance of our home." She later explains, "My story is one of learning to connect with Nature wherever I am. Whether I am in a rural space or a sprawling city."[35] Jasmin Antonia Estrada further extends this definition of nature, describing a moment in her childhood, sitting in a "red plastic chair with the words Coca-Cola written on the top, in the heat of Guatemala City." The corporate capitalism of the Coke label, the artificiality associated with plastic, and the urbanism of the city elicit much that mainstream environmentalists depict as nature's opposite, the ills to which wilderness supposedly offers humans respite. Yet in this moment, Estrada insists, "I was part of nature deeply, the mix of concrete and potted plants was the beginning of my understanding that there is no right way to be the part of nature that you are."[36] Estrada rejects a binary in which nature and humans are distinct, perceiving herself as no less "part of nature" seated in a plastic red chair than she would be on a hiking trip through a federally designated wilderness area.

Luis Villa, Latino Outdoors' executive director, moves beyond redefining nature to challenge common definitions of "outdoor recreation." He contends that his afternoon at a low-rider event is just as much outdoor recreation as his morning spent hiking at Bear Creek Redwoods Open Space Preserve. For Villa, what is essential is "leisure" and "fun." Furthering his case, Villa points out that low-rider events frequently take place at local parks, beaches, and other public spaces, the same locations as picnics, walks, and other activities more conventionally accepted as outdoor recreation activities.[37] His choice of an activity centering the automobile explicitly challenges perceptions of motorized recreation as fundamentally anti-environmental. Instead, he showcases how even low-riders afford Latinx communities opportunities to gather and enjoy outdoor public space.

Certainly, some Latino Outdoors blog posts do embrace a more typically colonialist narrative of discovery and expedition in a sublime landscape defined through its opposition to the human. However, this is not the dominant mode of storytelling in Latino Outdoors' online presence. Posts like those by Villa, Estrada, and Torres are far more common.[38] Indeed, the narratives of nature that are most frequently highlighted in Latino Outdoors' online and social media accounts often serve as forms of what Priscilla Solis Ybarra terms goodlife writing.[39] Goodlife writing depicts relationships with nature that transcends possession and instead focuses on, as Ybarra writes, "simplicity, sustenance, dignity, and respect."[40]

Latino Outdoors' definitions of nature and outdoor recreation emerge from the organization's presentation of Latinx identity and Latinx culture. The use of the singular here (identity rather than identities, culture rather than cultures) reflects the way that Latino Outdoors presents Latinx identity and Latinx culture (or cultura). Terms such as Latino, Latina/o, Latin@ and Latinx often obscure important differences in class, race, nationality, and citizenship status. In using such broad terms as "Latino culture," Latino Outdoors does not reflect some singular, authentic, and essential Latindad. Rather, Latino Outdoors engages in the production of a new form of political identity, a Latindad that emerges from shared outdoor engagement and advocacy: a *Latinx Outdoor Recreation Identity*. The singular is used across Latino Outdoors materials not as a way to obscure the diverse and varied experiences of Latinx individuals and communities, differences the organization often celebrates, but rather to emphasize this shared new political identity.

As part of the Latinx Outdoor Recreation Identity it produces, Latino Outdoors emphasizes the inherent environmentalism of what it presents as Latinx culture. For example, Latino Outdoors founder José González has stated: "In their heart of hearts, Latinos are conservationists and environmentalists."[41] In other documents, Latino Outdoors talks about "Unearthing our Conservation Cultura" and "showcase[ing] how conservation roots have been ingrained in Latino cultura for generations."[42] This echoes Ybarra's claim in *Writing the Goodlife* that Mexican Americans disidentify as environmentalists because colonialism and modernity (specifically the Cartesian split) form the conditions under which environmentalism became necessary.[43]

Latino Outdoors' strategy echoes the Chicana/o environmentalism that Randy Ontiveros describes emerging along a more mainstream environmentalism in the 1960s and 1970s. As he writes in *Spirit of a New People*:

> Like their peers, Mexican Americans in the 1960s and 1970s were growing increasingly concerned about the impact of industrialization on the nonhuman natural world ... Chicano/a progressives felt alienated, though, by mainstream environmentalism's sharp philosophical distinction between human and nonhuman need. ... But if they ignored environmental issues, they did a disservice to themselves and to their communities. Their response was to formulate a distinctive Chicano/a environmentalism, one that drew on Mexican American traditions and that joined ecological concerns with social concerns.[44]

Likewise, Latino Outdoors emerges out of the desire to create a conservation movement based in what organizers present as Latinx values and culture, distinct from the mainstream environmental movement and its "hidden attachments" to whiteness (to borrow Denis Cosgrove's term).[45] To echo Ontiveros: to ignore conservation issues does a disservice to Latinx communities, but to engage with mainstream conservation groups proves alienating (not least because of what Park and Pellow term "environmental nativism").[46] Thus, Latino Outdoors, in their words, "unearths a conservation cultura" in order to develop a Latinx community who will "stand up and roar" when "the bulldozers come next."[47]

Latino Outdoors' claim to "conservation cultura" aligns with their catchphrase "Estamos Aqui" (we are here). As José González explains: "And by that we mean that the Latinx community has been here in the Western United States for hundreds of years, and the landscape belongs to us as a culture as much as it belongs to anyone."[48] The Latinx claim to the land through indigenous heritage and generational lineage also appears in Vasqeuz's "Yo Cuento" blog post, quoted at the essay's start: "We celebrate our history here [in New Mexico], not just as Latinos but as Mestizos, as people with mixed indigenous blood, roots and beliefs. We count here because we've been on this land for thousands of years, we're not outsiders here."[49] Latino Outdoors' claims to environmental belonging are capacious, incorporating the recognition of Indigenous peoples among Latinx migrants to the US, claims to indigeneity as part of mestizo identity/ mestizaje, and critiques of US imperialism, such as the loss of Mexican territory to the US.

"Estamos Aqui" aligns with "Yo Cuento" as narrative strategy. We are here, we count, and our stories matter. Telling diverse Latinx stories that showcase the ways that Latinx voices matter to conservation is a central strategy of the organization. Latino Outdoors specifically names storytelling as an important part of Latinx culture and thus an important strategy for their own work, as David Flores and Karmon Kuhn have elucidated.[50] Scholars such as Carolyn Finney argue that it is important to see people of color as environmental stakeholders. When only white people or wealthy people are recognized as concerned with the environment, then only their environmental concerns are seen to matter.[51] This is part of Latino Outdoors' work. By telling stories that position Latinx individuals as politically present and environmentally engaged, Latino Outdoors establishes Latinx communities as essential environmental stakeholders, therefore increasing the power afforded Latinx conservation leaders.

In this way, drawing on the work of Laura Pulido, we might read Latino Outdoors as establishing a strategic environmental essentialism aimed toward ecological legitimacy.[52] "Ecological legitimacy" is a phrase Pulido coined to explain how some are granted the power to make environmental decisions while others are denied this power, in part because they are perceived as lacking concern for the environment. Pulido argues that the Hispano community in Los Ojos, New Mexico about which she writes claim a closeness to land and nature as a "cultural essentialism" to gain an ecological legitimacy long denied. Latino Outdoors' emphasis on Latinx "conservation cultura" deploys the strategic environmental essentialism geared toward the ecological legitimacy Pulido describes. This works in concert with the organization's expanded definitions of nature and outdoor recreation to increase the range of activities and beliefs which would indicate Latinx environmental belonging and thus legitimate Latinx communities as environmental stakeholders in the context of exclusionary mainstream environmentalism.

Labor over Leisure

The stories that Latino Outdoors tells explicitly counter environmentalism's exclusionary understandings of environmental identities and an ecocultural logic that naturalizes Latinx outdoor labor while criminalizing Latinx outdoor leisure. Consider Vasquez's experience fishing with his father, quoted at the start of the chapter. In this narrative, Vasquez acknowledges the multiple strategies of exclusion that work to keep Latinx peoples out of outdoor recreation spaces. This includes policing and legitimate fear of policing along with subtler ways of communicating that Latinx people are not welcome to recreate in outdoor spaces. It speaks to the ways in which mainstream environmental discourse figures Latinx people as pollutants or containments to the purity of both nation and nature. It is significant that the lack of fishing license evokes a call to Border Patrol. Policing the proper use of outdoor spaces by the proper normative bodies operates as a form of policing the nation. This is the cultural logic of what Ray terms "the ecological other."[53]

Vasquez's return to fishing, his refusal to be deterred, enacts a claim to national and environmental belonging. It also expands the grounds upon which such belonging operates. Latinx studies scholars have long argued that the US seeks to incorporate the labor of Latinx peoples without granting them full substantive citizenship. This is the essence of much US immigration policy, which realizes the tension between capital's desire for cheap labor and national racial rhetoric about the cultural purity of the body politic.

The act of fishing Vasquez describes is particularly radical because it is not productive. It is an act of leisure. It is not about profit. It is about pleasure. In *The Nature of California*, I argue that part of the butterfly's power as a migrant rights symbol is that it is welcomed for its beauty, rather than its use value.[54] It counters the type of economic arguments made by films such as *A Day without a Mexican* or the United Farm Workers' Take Our Jobs campaign. These works suggest that the primary problem with exclusionary immigration efforts is that the US needs Latinx labor. Latinx migrants belong because they take jobs white people will not take. In contrast, Latino Outdoors insists on the possibilities of Latinx leisure. The organization implicitly refutes a narrative that argues inclusion based on labor and economic contributions.

Let us return to Vasquez's phrase, "the outdoors are for everyone." Recreation is the unstated assumption that makes this statement work. Latinx peoples are overrepresented in spaces of outdoor labor, such as farms and construction sites.[55] Latino Outdoors' Program Director Ruby Rodríguez, in a conversation with Luis Villa, describes "the appeal of more relaxing forms of recreation" for communities who often "perform physically demanding jobs in their everyday lives." According to Villa, "Ruby further posits leisurely outdoor recreation as a sort of activism against a hyper-productive society, a peaceful protest actually."[56]

Environmental humanities and Latinx studies scholars have long sought to reconfigure the relationship between labor and environment. Historian Richard White exposed the ways labor itself is a category that has been constructed in opposition to conservation and environmentalism, as made clear in the very title of his well-known article, "Are You an Environmentalist or Do You Work for a Living?"[57] White argues against the position that all work is environmentally destructive by challenging the distinction between wilderness out there and the nature closer to home, including the electricity that powers the computer on which he types. He also argues that work offers a valid and valuable form of knowledge about nature.

Since White's essay reshaped the scholarly terrain of labor and nature, historians have further examined forms of working-class environmentalism on public lands. Most relevant is historian Mario Sifuentez's work which positions Mexican and Mexican American forestry workers as essential actors in Oregon's environmental history. Sifuentez's scholarship stands alongside anthropologist Anna Tsing's discussion of mushroom harvesting to insist on a complex engagement with race, citizenship, and privilege as part of environmental labor on federal public lands.[58] The move to outdoor Latinx leisure made by Latino Outdoors implicitly builds on Sifuentez's scholarship by developing the relationship between these naturalized and invisible forms of Latinx environmental labor and the right to Latinx environmental leisure. Jasmin Antonia Estrada, for example, writes of her undocumented uncle in her "Yo Cuento" blog post:

> He and many people who don't have access to interacting with nature as a leisure activity deserve to have moments in nature that are not in passing nor fear. Moments that are not plummeted in the history of the wild and dark being used as a place for violence against themselves and their ancestors, for trauma, or seen as dirty for being in it – but as a place of positive connection, for growth, for home and exploration, a place that can be a refuge.[59]

Here Estrada rejects the logic of the ecological other that positions Latinx laborers as "dirty," an environmental contaminant. She criticizes the logic that would limit the access to nature that undocumented workers like her uncle have to scenes of exploitation and oppression, trauma and violence. In positioning the environment instead as a site of "positive connection," Estrada claims leisure, pleasure, and belonging (home and refuge) as Latinx environmental right.

This, too, is part of the work of the Latinx Outdoor Recreation Identity that Latino Outdoors produces. The strategic environmental essentialism of a Latinx Outdoor Recreation Identity grants Latinx communities a seat at the conservation table. It justifies the expansion of nature and outdoor recreation at the heart of much Latino Outdoors programming, including the type of outings Latino Outdoors offers, the representational work of their web and social media presence, and the advocacy work they do to ensure greater access to resources and representation from non-governmental organizations as well as state and federal agencies. The claim to nature and environmental belonging enacts a form of political belonging. The focus on leisure further develops this political belonging by implicitly rejecting models of Latinx inclusion based primarily on economic contributions. It leverages broader understandings of pleasure, leisure, and joy to build non-fungible forms of inclusion and belonging for Latinx individuals. These forms of political belonging offer the grounds not only for national inclusion, but also for a reworking of the notions of nature, land ownership, and economic relations on which the nation was founded.

CHAPTER 14

Sanctuary: Literature and the Colonial Politics of Protection

Matt Hooley

Literature at the End

"If there were a theme song for the year 2019," writes Nanjala Nyabola, "it would be a dirge for the end of asylum."[1] The year during which nearly 100 million people were displaced by political and environmental crises was also the year the US principally traded its refugee system for an archipelago of privately run migrant detention centers.[2] As Nyabola notes, the end of asylum is a disavowal of the liberal political vision of a "post-World War II International order"; an order defined by a commitment to afford relief to those threatened by persecution and by the right of displaced people to return home again.[3] It could also be argued that in the years leading up to and including 2019, changes in environmental policy sounded an end to environmental refuge. While the US rolls back targeted policy protections (of Bears Ears National Monument and the Arctic National Wildlife Refuge, and of clean water and endangered species), even more troubling is the sense that protections targeting any discrete form of land, water, or life are futile while the very nature of land, water, and life is irreversibly changing. In this sense, one way to understand the currency of "the Anthropocene" – a geological periodization that has come to symbolize global ecological crisis – is that it names a world we can no longer protect from ourselves or protect ourselves in.

"The end of" is a structure of political affect, a framework for thinking about how we are connected and disconnected amid changing conditions of harm and relief. As such, it has organized recent political responses in the US to social and environmental crises. The end of state-based and international structures of protection has inspired new democratizations of protection: sanctuary movements based in cities and on campuses that refuse cooperation with federal immigration police and that provide temporary housing and healthcare, and a new environmental populism that seeks to redress global climate crises via local aid and infrastructure reform.

"The end of" is also a cultural logic that marks a shift in literary responses to global climate crisis. Perhaps most notably, the new speculative genre cli-fi imagines adaptation and loss in the context of catastrophes to come. Like sanctuary, cli-fi is an adaptation of genre, a change in the kind of political and cultural forms necessary "when," as Stephanie LeMenager writes, "the affective expectations we hold for how things unfold . . . do not make sense anymore."[4] Cli-fi is a genre that thinks about new trajectories of expectation and, specifically, about expecting not to know what to expect in a catastrophically changing world.

"The end of" is also a falsely universalizing framework that obscures inequitable distributions of loss and relief – as scholars of Black, Indigenous, and diasporic studies have long observed. Concepts such as the Anthropocene depend on theories of humanity and environmental change that, far from being universally descriptive, have themselves been engines of recurrent maldistributions of harm.[5] Similarly, attending to the end of political orders of protection can forget the violence those orders enacted in the first place, as well as the practices of human and more-than-human care they displaced.

Amid intensifying crises of displacement, this chapter asks if or how forms of refuge fortify the colonial politics of protection and what those forms might reveal about the future of human and environmental care. It also asks if literature is a form of refuge – a way of providing kinship, comfort, or memory – when state structures of relief are withdrawn. As in the other chapters in this volume, these questions are situated in the context of US political and cultural history. For that reason, I proceed with two premises about how forms of refuge occur. First, although both sanctioned and insurgent forms of refuge typically name the kind of (social or environmental) relief they provide, I assume that all displacement and all refuge are always both social and environmental; and further, that apprehending that entanglement should be an imperative of ecocriticism. In the context of colonial capitalism, human displacements are always connected to the transformation of land into resource. Similarly, environmental harm always has a differential social impact. Second, I treat "the end" as a recursive temporality within US colonialism. I clarify this premise further in the next section of this chapter, but broadly, I am interested in attending both to the fact that the history of colonial expansion has always been world-ending for the people and ecosystems it has targeted and to the way that the proposition of a universalized end has been deployed as a justification to reinvest in violent political systems.

Although sanctuary and displacement are ancient and recurrent, both feel immediate, and urgently so. It is precisely that urgency that is so resonant about the framing, "the end of." This chapter does not want to diminish that reality as it asks what, following Lisa Lowe's formulation, is affirmed and what forgotten when environmental literature uses "the end of" to resurrect attachments (e.g. the colonial family or property) that precipitated crisis in the first place.[6] Further, thinking about sanctuary as a form that bears a relation to colonial power is not to dismiss every way it is used amid political upheaval. Rather, it is to ask how literature participates in systems of displacement and relief and how we might imagine alternatives to them.

In the context of the interwoven histories of US environmentalism and colonialism, the politics of protection has a specifically spatial aspect: colonial protection occurs through forms that make and remake national space. Formations such as national parks, for instance, protect particular spaces and spatialize an ideology of national protection. And it is for this reason that the colonial politics of protection has been a primary interest of American environmental literature, from the nineteenth century to the present. The environment is an avatar for a set of spatial contradictions at the heart of the American project – between wilderness and settlement, access and ownership, location and dislocation – that formations of protection purport to resolve. Therefore, for writers such as Wallace Stegner ("national parks are the best idea we ever had") or Henry David Thoreau ("in wildness is the preservation of the world"), understanding how the US protects land is essential to understanding how that land is American.[7]

At the same time, formations of American environmental protection are always spatial enactments of Indigenous displacement and dispossession.[8] In both the grand, inaugurating rhetoric of the national park system and in Thoreau's more parochial practice of retreat, wilderness as displacement is itself displaced through history and ideology. At any scale, Indigenous relations with spaces coded as wilderness are recast as sites original to American history or to Americanness.[9] In today's climate crisis discourse, this displacement occurs in well-meaning arguments for expanded US environmental regulations or for a new American green economy in the name of saving "all humanity" – a category whose coherence depends on displacing the ongoing history of Black and Indigenous exclusions from the human from understanding the cause of or the urgency to stop climate change.

Canonical ecocriticism has often addressed the contradictions intrinsic to the politics of protection through the logic of reform. For instance, in

Writing for an Endangered World, Lawrence Buell identifies wilderness as the common ground between the otherwise "irreconcilable" late nineteenth-century projects of Jane Addams's Hull House (a "mission to bring civility to the urban wilderness") and John Muir's national parks (a "mission to preserve wilderness").[10] Buell argues that both projects "valued open space as therapeutic" and defined open space as militarily protected forms of refuge in which "sympathetic immersion and discipline in place was key to personal wellbeing" and to the wellbeing of American democracy broadly.[11] For Buell, these projects suggest a political capacity of environmental literature to imagine more democratic social and environmental protections to improve how Americans live on and with land. However, what notions of reformable systems of protection elide are questions about the US's claim to land in the first place and whether the reform of a democracy predicated on the ongoing displacement of Black and Indigenous people from land could yield anything other than the rearticulation of those displacements.

As such displacements protract, how can we imagine and practice care beyond the colonial politics of protection? What can literature provide at the end of international orders of protection, other than their reenactment? What follows is a reading of sanctuary as a form through which displacement and refuge are both enacted and interpreted in the context of US colonialism. The first section, "The Sanctuary Interval," shows how forms of refuge mark the space and time between cycles of expanding colonial power. Here, using Terry Tempest Williams's *Refuge*, I describe how sanctuary operates as a "genre of liberalism" in which colonial narratives of kinship and healing reconcile a crisis of social and environmental protection.[12] In the last section, "Waiting for Decolonization," I resituate the question of sanctuary in the context of decolonization. Here, I read Joan Naviyuk Kane's collections of poems, *The Straits* and *Milk Black Carbon*, in the aftermath of the King Island diaspora and as a poetic and social experiment in thinking beyond state-sanctioned modalities of safety, return, and kinship.

The Sanctuary Interval

In social and environmental contexts, a defining feature of sanctuary is that it is singular. In the Christian sanctuary tradition, the word suggests a particular act performed in a particular space to produce a legal exception. Sanctuary takes on the status of law through the transformation of political gesture (made sacred by sacred space) and religious space (made

political by political gesture).[13] In an environmental context, this transformation occurs via uniqueness, rather than sacredness. Founders of the
US national park system argued for the preservation of Mariposa Grove
and Yellowstone by describing them as sanctuaries for singular ecosystems.
As Theodore Roosevelt put it in 1903, at the opening of Yellowstone
National Park, the park is "absolutely unique in the world ... [whose]
preservation ... is a credit to the nation ... [and] noteworthy in its
essential democracy."[14] Preservation is exceptional because of the special
quality of the space and the space is democratic because of the political
quality of its preservation.

Sanctuary is a legal exception because of the quality of space where it
occurs. However, as recent scholarship on sanctuary cities and conservation sites demonstrates, that status is not subversive or separate but supple-
mentary to colonial power; the reason sanctuaries do not aggregate into
new, or subtract from existing, jurisdictions. What I call "the sanctuary
interval" refers to two ways the exceptional status of sanctuary (including
spaces of environmental refuge) organize colonial power. First, it indicates
a recurrence of colonial power after an existing system of state protection
ends – an effect I call the localization of care. Second, it describes a space of
therapeutic passage for subjects marked for salvation, what I term the
pastoralization of the interval. In this section, I use these frameworks to
track the politics of protection in Terry Tempest Williams's *Refuge: An
Unnatural History of Family and Place* (1991).

In the spatial grammar of US power, the exceptional status of sanctuary
can be understood as a recourse to the local. In the case of sanctuary cities,
for instance, Peter Mancina shows how noncooperation with federal
immigration policies does not stop those policies but protects local government efficiency.[15] Similarly, establishing national monuments to conserve land under the Antiquities Federal Land Policy and Management
Acts does not assert unilateral federal jurisdiction over such spaces but
coordinates their conservation with local economic and extraction
interests.[16] In this sense, sanctuary is a localization of care in that it locates,
or spatializes, relief and that it excepts without opposing colonial jurisdiction. In *Refuge*, the Bear River Migratory Bird Refuge is the location
through which environmental protection and settler kinship cooperate.
The refuge, an early addition to the National Wildlife Refuge System, was
created in 1928 to protect freshwater marshland from development,
encroaching salinity, and an outbreak of avian botulism. The refuge is
also, for Williams, a space of homemaking, where caring for and about land
serves the reproductive ideology of the colonial family – "a matter of

rootedness, of living inside a place for so long that the mind and imagination fuse."[17] The book's narrative is organized by uncertainty about whether the refuge will survive both as a space of environmental protection and colonial domesticity.

What threatens the refuge as a space of environmental protection is the flooding Great Salt Lake, an action marked by measurements at the beginning of each chapter that increase from 4204.70' to 4211.85' before retreating back to 4204.70'. This flooding is a function of the industrial development that surrounds the lake, which both restricts its hydrology and creates the framework through which rising saltwater is interpreted as dangerous. And eventually it is concern for that development (rather than for birds) that saves the refuge, in the form of a $60 million system that pumps the floodwater into a holding pond to be used by magnesium producer and the nation's largest air polluter, AMAX.[18] What threatens the refuge as a space of stable settler homemaking is cancer:

> Most of the women in my family are dead. Cancer. At thirty-four, I became the matriarch of my family. The losses I encountered at Bear River Migratory Bird Refuge ... helped me to face the losses within my family. When most people had given up on the Refuge, saying the birds were gone, I was drawn further into its essence. In the same way that when someone is dying many retreat, I chose to stay.[19]

Here, the trajectories of history and harm are layered and complex. What causes the brutal recurrences of cancer in Williams' family is probably US nuclear testing. Williams points out that her family's and the birds' presence was ignored "when the Atomic Energy Commission described the country north of the Nevada Testing Site as 'virtually uninhabited desert terrain.'" "[M]y family," she continues, "and the birds at Great Salt Lake were some of the 'virtual uninhabitants.'"[20] Immediately following this, Williams reports a dream in which "women from all over the world" "[dance] wildly" around a fire in the desert, singing "a song given to them by Shoshone grandmothers."[21] And then, to end the book, Williams describes an act of protest: crossing the Nevada Test Site border as "a gesture [made] on behalf of the Clan of the One-Breasted Women." The memoir ends with the protest participants being removed by police and dropped off short of Salt Lake City: "the officials thought it was a cruel joke to leave us stranded in the desert ... what they didn't realize was that we were home."[22]

Williams does not see her claim to protected belonging or her cultural appropriation as the denial of Shoshone claims to territorial or cultural protection. Instead, these gestures of what Alyosha Goldstein calls "settler expectation" are localized by the refuge.[23] For Goldstein, forms of public land like the refuge mediate competing colonial constructions of public and private property. Using the example of the Bundy family occupation of the Malheur National Wildlife Refuge (a space that appears late in *Refuge*), Goldstein shows that conflicts between federal and individual land claims express the same theory of property, defined as a structure of permanent future expectation. Here, "expectation" describes the accumulation of territorial capital and the promise of settlement guaranteed even after the end of one or the other form of land claiming. Public land, whether it is set aside (e.g. from Indigenous people) for "democratic" use or claimed for violent (e.g. Bundy family) or non-violent (e.g. Williams family) private use, is thus a "jurisdictional imaginary" that secures colonial futures indefinitely.[24]

Williams' investment in the refuge is also an example of what Eve Tuck and K. Wayne Yang call "settler nativism." Settler nativism is an "attempt to deflect settler identity while continuing to enjoy settler privileges on stolen land."[25] For Williams, settler nativism occurs through the troubling comparisons between her family with migratory birds and with Shoshone people (for whom the social and political consequences of nuclear colonialism have been incomparably more vast) and through her claim to "home" on the basis of religion. Williams's family were among the "original 'pushcart companies'" of Mormon settlers, for whom sanctuary in the desert was both a US nationalist and Zionist project.[26] During the same decades of growing US support for Israeli colonialism in Palestine, Mormon leaders imagined a religious sanctuary ("a New Jerusalem" in the desert, on a river they named the Jordan) as a prophetic fulfillment, even as the Indigenous genocide and land seizure it required was explicitly funded by and served the interests of a growing US colonialism.[27] The land Williams calls "home" in *Refuge* is, on one hand, marked as separate from the American project – where "Brigham Young raised his hands above the Salt Lake Valley and said 'This . . . is the place that the Lord has appointed, and we shall stay here until He tells us to go somewhere else.'"[28] On the other hand, it is a place where Mormons rehearsed the most brutal tactics of US colonialism to seize that land from Indigenous people.[29]

Refuge is the space between harm and relief, and between the brutalities of colonial displacement and placemaking. And one reason *Refuge* has become a classic of contemporary US environmental literature is because it records life in that space, in between. For Williams, that space is personal even as it is organized by systems (jurisdiction, capital, ideology, biology, ecology) that are always more-than-personal. However, *Refuge* is not just a narrative of living within in-between spaces but also about passing through them. In social and environmental contexts, forms of protection are also forms of passage. For environmental writers like Williams, that passage can be described, using Buell's term, as "therapeutic": as a movement toward a healing relationship between humans and wilderness. In the context of migration, sanctuary is presented as a passage toward a benevolent relationship between noncitizens and citizenship. In both cases, sanctuary is a narrative structure as well as a space: a way to narrate the passage of unprotected places, species, and people into colonial protection. What I call the pastoralization of the interval refers to two ways that sanctuary formalizes passage into colonial protection. First, sanctuary involves a theater of care that reproduces "pastoral power."[30] Second, passage through sanctuary affirms narratives of salvation rather than narratives of the recurrent, world-ending colonial violence that causes displacement.

For Williams, the Bear River Refuge is a social and an environmental sanctuary; a place where family and wildlife are protected. The central drama of the memoir is whether the refuge will be lost to development and with it, the successful migration of birds and the continuity of colonial kinship. And as a permanent formation, it *is* eventually lost – flooded by saltwater in the same chapter Williams's mother dies of cancer, an unmooring coincidence: "The birds have abandoned the lake. Borders are fluid, not fixed. There is no point even driving out to the Refuge. For now it is ocean. I hardly know where I am. Since Mother's death ... I have nothing to hope for because what I hoped for is gone."[31] This is an experience of personal loss compounded by the sense that Williams also loses the spatial form through which she learned to interpret experiences of loss.

Randy Lippert uses the term "pastoral power" to describe how sanctuary spaces conduct the politics of protection through the roles of the shepherd and flock – expressive and receptive postures of care that organize the management of need.[32] Throughout *Refuge*, ideological development occurs as Williams, her family, and the environment around them move between such postures. Early in her life, the refuge is where, beyond the Mormon patriarchal social order, Williams is cared for by women as they care for the wild. Later, during the flood, Williams is dislocated not just from those trajectories of care but from the possibility of recovery as a function of care. Mourning, in the passage quoted above, is a suspension of change, an inundation, an "ocean."

As the flood and her grief peak, and Williams confronts the legacy of militarization in the Great Basin, care is democratized as conservation. Opposing the ecological and biological effects of weapons testing, Williams argues for expanded protection of wildlife habitats – a gesture made personal both by her own loss and by the idea that wilderness is therapeutic. "A blank spot on the map," she writes, "is an invitation to encounter the natural world, where one's character will be shaped by the landscape. To enter wilderness is to court risk, and risk favors the senses, enabling one to live well."[33] Even in the face of loss, wilderness furnishes a quality of "grief [that] dares us to love once more."[34] Land conservation is one way liberalism reproduces through care, ideologically and narratively. Through the refuge, national histories of protection and harm become personal narratives and personal histories of care and loss become democratic – a dialectic the book itself reproduces for readers who enter themselves into its theater of care. What both refuge and *Refuge* forget is that US protection and violence are convergent, not contradictory; and that distributions of care are always directed by the colonial state.

At the end of *Refuge*, as the flood waters are pumped away, the state builds a "bomb catcher" to keep undetonated explosives dislodged by the water from being drawn back into the Great Salt Lake – a body of water newly incorporated into the Western Hemisphere Shorebird Reserve Network. Williams admits that "none of these [refuge] sites is secure. Conservation laws are only as strong as the people who support them," framing them as forms of last resort against development.[35] But this concept of refuge obscures what the receding water reveals: that, in the history of US colonialism, cycles of conservation and militarism are overlapping, not opposed; and that colonial expansion proceeds both through violence and relief. Indigenous people were violently displaced from the land around the Great Salt Lake to make it a refuge for settlers and wildlife; many of the testing sites that now leak bombs and cancer-causing radioactivity are recommissioned nature preserves; and spaces such as the Desert National Wildlife Refuge and Bears Ears National Monument are being opened further to military and industrial development. As a form, refuge does not mark the end, but rather the interval between cycles, of colonial expansion.

To think of sanctuary as an interval, as a form describing the recurrence of colonial power, does not mean we dismiss the care that occurs there. But it does mean attending to the histories of movement sanctuary organizes beyond individuals passing into protection. For instance, Jodi Byrd and Nicole Waligora-Davis read forms of state protection to track histories of displacement that narratives of pastoralization forget. They ask how, beyond narratives of individual salvation, we describe histories of what Byrd calls "imperial transit" – the forced moveability of Indigenous and racialized peoples in the Americas "through which U.S. empire orients and replicates itself . . . through the continual reiterations of pioneer logics."[36] For Waligora-Davis, this means remembering racial histories of suspension and deferral that always coincide with state expansions of belonging (e.g. emancipation, refuge, and citizenship). Sanctuaries for Waligora-Davis are "throughways, interregnums, thresholds . . . [and] corridors ineluctably demarcating boundaries" that coincide with vast shifts in state power but that also drag, bend, or "[suspend] state time."[37]

Social and environmental sanctuary formations obscure the vast transmutations of land and life they enact and redress. They also affirm narratives of care or catastrophe in which investing in state protection may seem the only recourse. In the final section of this chapter, I turn to Joan Naviyuk Kane's *The Straits* and *Milk Black Carbon* to consider writing that opens out after the end of sanctuary toward practices of care that do not reactivate cycles of colonial expansion.

Waiting for Decolonization

In 1929, the year after the Bear River Migratory Bird Refuge was established in Utah, the US built a Bureau of Indian Affairs (BIA) School and a Catholic mission on a small island forty miles west of Alaska. The rocky shores of Ugiuvak (renamed King Island by James Cook in 1778), rise steeply a thousand feet out of the Bering Sea. It is a place that perhaps seemed to Cook overexposed to sea, ice, and weather, but was, for 2,000 years, a place Ugiuvangmiut people safely and reliably sustained relation with each other and with an abundant marine ecosystem. A century and a half later, it was precisely those relations US officials targeted through the school and mission – institutional forms of protection that disguised a colonial politics of space. The school and mission were designed to compel the passage of Indigenous people into Christianity, English, and capitalism, and thus enacted territorial dislocation via ideological improvement.

As with the expansion of national parks between the late nineteenth and mid-twentieth centuries, missions and boarding schools administrated a colonial resource rush. As thousands of settlers chased Alaskan gold and oil, laws such as the Organic Acts (1884, 1912) and the Nelson Act (1905) sought a balance between settler extraction and state governance. The colonial protection of Indigenous people was instrumentalized to this end; most famously in the 1971 Alaska Native Claims and Settlement Act (ANCSA), which declared millions of acres state land and afforded "land benefits" to tribal Village Corporations; and the 1980 Alaska National Interest Land Conservation Act (ANILCA), which conserved 157 million acres under a provision of the ANCSA. The ANILCA is the authorizing policy for parks such as the Arctic National Wildlife Refuge, targeted for oil extraction by the Trump Administration. Between the initial onrush of settlers and late twentieth-century policy reforms, the mission and the school marked a sanctuary interval. That interval ended in 1959, months after Alaska became the forty-ninth state, when the BIA closed the school on Ugiuvak and forced Ugiuvangmiut families to relocate to Nome or risk family separation. By 1966, all residents were evicted to a mainland settlement without utilities, where Ugiuvangmiut language and lifeways were actively endangered by settler schooling, policing, and economics.

Prior to relocation, generations of Joan Naviyuk Kane's family lived on Ugiuvak, including her mother. Kane herself could not visit the island until 2014, when she organized a return trip for herself and three elders. Kane examines the experience of returning to Ugiuvak in two volumes, *The Straits* and *Milk Black Carbon*. However, "return" in these texts does not mean recovery either through the trip or its poetic record. Kane writes, "I come from a recently displaced people. I can never restore King Island through language. I cannot even adequately catalog all that is lost, or has been lost, or what we are losing still. Certainly, I cannot pretend that repatriation is easy, or possible."[38]

Where sanctuary forms stabilize recovery via passage into ideological and spatial protection, Kane's traversal of the Bering Sea does not resolve the contradictions of security and location intrinsic to colonialism. Where *Refuge* finds ideological definition in passage through loss, Kane attends to the "exponentiation" of care and loss when passage through is impossible; when under colonialism, dislocation is indefinite.[39] Kane's poems are short and syntactically spare, paced in unrhymed stanzas usually four or fewer lines each. The poems open space for imagination and sound to refract and gather again; poems that reverberate rather than resolve. In Kane's poetry about Ugiuvak, land and sea are rigorously unmetaphoric. The island, its steepness, its plants and weather, are a method; as is the turbulent sea, "not winedark," Kane writes, "Its bright break a page of script repeating."[40] Land and sea are relations for making meaning, even after colonial protection ended everyday Inupiaq life there.

A poem titled "Incident Light," about arriving at the shore of Ugiuvak, begins by dispensing with the separateness of forms through which that arrival would align with ideological restoration.

> I went for relief
> of the mind, to move
> into currents of worry
> I did not know
> what the body held.
>
> I thought I would turn
> through broken ice
> and disappear
>   the features
> of apprehension and influence.
>
> If only I could betray
> the brute matter.
>
> If only the seas had
> not erased the facture,
> ladder, the easy reach.

One way to read these opening lines is as pointing to the immateriality of expectation. Recovery does not accrue via forms – the ideological coherence of the body, the spatial completion of arrival – familiar to narratives of colonial passage. The terms of the landing in the poem are nontranscendent; untranslatable from "brute matter." Thus, the poem's subjects proceed not through but out into a world never so still that it could be confused for a system (the national park, the settler family) for measuring ideological realization.

> Instead we sank
> into snow,
> four women ascending
> together the deep furrow
> worn by water
> returning to water:
>
> Ayagaduk, Uyuguluk,
> Yaayuk, Naviyuk.
>
> I was startled, at once
> aware that the far road
> had fracted, done
> under by the fault
> we fought to bury.

As the poem ends, these vectors of tectonic and oceanic motion outswell even the idea of individual restoration or disappointment:

> Land arises
> beyond a treble
> of strong currents.
>
> The boat that bears
> us rises in them.
> With invisible stars
> we share blood.
>
> Those seas, increased,
> might scour and reflect –
> those seas, increased,
>
> rephrase us.[41]

Where social or environmental sanctuary recycles recovery and loss, recurrence here conveys a radical "increase[ing]." Kane's return does not restore but "rephrase," a word that signals a performative and ephemeral quality of transformation. Liberal forms of sanctuary are present in this poem as the conditions of displacement – Alaska's promise of settler homemaking, conservation, and institutionalized care for Indigenous people. The poem denies that these forms determine what happens during conditions of (legally) permanent colonial displacement. Specifically, care occurs not via passage through spaces of difficulty and relief but by staying in them; and there, proliferating relation beyond the terms of colonial governance.

Within sanctuary systems, the protraction of passage itself is coded as therapeutic. In her work on the temporal politics of sanctuary cities, Jen Bagelman calls this practice of suspension a "state of waiting" – the way the time and space of the deferral of relief is recoded as productive, as a period during which refugees "become good, aspirational citizens."[42] Kane's lingering, exponentiating attention to the materiality of relation, land, and language enacts an altogether different practice of waiting. In part this is due to a clarity about the falseness of narratives of fulfillment offered by US structures of protection. Ugiuvak, as Kane describes in a poem by the same name, is a place from which such structures have displaced human and environmental relation; a displacement that is material, never fillable or instructive:

> Elsewhere ice is forming on rocks along the shore
> [...]
> Another daughter I will not have will not get there.

> She will never gather wood for whittling
> nor noose rabbits. Along with the brother
> I live without [. . .]
>
> Roots remain ungathered, points of navigation
> resolve to nothing, arbitrary.[43]

But waiting in these texts is also distinguished by the space Kane makes for it to mean something other than passivity or progress. Waiting is a practice of remaining that is intentional but not predictive, an attendance with place and relation. In the context of US colonialism that proceeds through both displacement and protection, waiting is also a refusal to dematerialize care via recuperative logics of the local or pastoral. In "Iridin," a poem named for the chemical element in irises that is both a poison and a balm, Kane opens the space between the island itself and the narratives that would reduce it to home lost or recovered:

> A coastline, a transitional place
> bears evidence of others dwelling:
> a house pit in the shape of a nest,
> another like a knife, a noose
> not lost not in time. Ours

That space between land and narrative is not a gap. Kane is not interested in an interval, a space in between, but rather a space for holding together as a practice of immeasurable and impermanent intimacy:

> a useful relationship though not a tight one
> for between us we knew there was something to lose.

The poem ends quietly, in the open possibilities of sense that the subjects stay with each other and land, unguarded by the language of comparison and salvation:

> Fragrant in June heat & a field of confusion
> nothing like a metaphor: moss campion
> minute orchids, sweet
>
> sweet vetch.[44]

Ending with such a small moment may seem inapt given the broad stakes of the politics of sanctuary this chapter has tried to suggest – stakes that include the history of US environmental literature and the future of climate disaster. However, as a moment of rigorous attention to the materiality of relation that thwarts the aesthetics of colonial expectation, its smallness opens significant analytic and imaginative possibilities for readers of environmental writing. The structures of social and environmental protection I have bookmarked with the terms sanctuary and refuge depend both on affirming colonialism as care and forgetting the materiality of Indigenous social and environmental relations. Texts such as *The Straits* and *Milk Black Carbon* hold open space for practices of attendance and imagination that distinguish the work of decolonization from the terms of colonial protection. In such texts, waiting for or with decolonization is anything but emancipatory; it is dangerous, unheroic, and mutual, "tenuous and uncountable," in Kane's words.[45] It is the lived and literary work of remaining with possibility and loss after the end of sanctuary and without the political promises of protection.

CHAPTER 15

The Queer Restoration Poetics of Audre Lorde

Angela Hume

Two years after Hurricane Hugo, which in 1989 devastated the unincorporated US territory St. Croix, and one year prior to her death from cancer, African Caribbean American poet Audre Lorde wrote a poem called "Restoration: A Memorial – 9/18/91." The poem grew partly out of a series of journal entries that Lorde made in the wake of Hugo on St. Croix, her home at the time, and bears witness to the storm's catastrophic aftermath, which, in Lorde's view, was "man-made."[1] In her journal Lorde suggests that the Caribbean island had been made sick by the capitalist US government, which exploited it for its resources and then neglected it after the disaster – just as her own body had been made sick by pollution from US industry on the mainland and then sicker by the profit-driven "Cancer Establishment." In this chapter, I will explore Lorde's concept of restoration in both her poem and her journals. The concept empowered her to confront and resist the environmental injustice she saw affecting the environment around her along with her individual body.

Throughout her writings, Lorde addresses environmental injustice. She writes about how her childhood home of Harlem, for example, with its sparse city parks and "sooty-pebbled" riverbank, was often dirtied by industry.[2] Lorde also describes how the pollution of her adult home on Staten Island – water contaminated by refinery runoff and air thick with industrial fumes – threatened people who were already vulnerable: poor women, women of color, and queer women. In what Lorde named a "woman-devaluating culture,"[3] where women of color bear the brunt of environmental hazard, the erotic, creative "lifeforce" of women is perpetually under assault.[4] For Lorde, the stark message for her as a Black lesbian with cancer was that she was never meant to survive.[5]

When Lorde left the city and went to live on St. Croix, she made connections between her long battle with breast cancer and the disaster that was Hugo, concluding that both were the result of environmental racism. In light of her critique, I hope to show how Lorde's concept of restoration, central to her understanding of environmental justice, enables her to express and navigate the unpredictable process of home (re)making in the aftermath of bodily and environmental trauma, along with the material limits to this remaking.

By definition, restoration is the act of returning someone or something to a former state, or to a condition of health.[6] To restore is to give back, set right or repair from decay or damage, or return.[7] Unlike the ecological concepts of resilience and resurgence, restoration does not necessarily entail a lively rebounding, robustness, or increase.[8] It suggests reparation, but does not require a spring forward in chronological time or an arc of progress. Restoration can be muted and gradual. What I am calling Lorde's restoration poetics builds on these definitions. It seems to me that, for her, poetry's task is to return, or restore, the reader to a historical moment that has been lost, in the service of a future. For Lorde, restoration is not a progressive, ends-oriented activity, but rather a nonlinear, highly contingent one that, however empowering or healing, can offer no promise of repair or cure.[9] Thus, Lorde's conception of restoration, a kind of homemaking, can help illuminate and complicate queer theories of (un)happiness and home. Before turning to Lorde's writings, it is helpful to consider the broader environmental justice context in which she wrote.

Environmental Justice: Toward a Historical Approach

In recent decades, environmental justice literatures have proliferated. The environmental justice movement itself emerged at the end of the twentieth century, confronting how suffering as a result of environmental violence disproportionately burdens poor, racialized, feminized, and LGBTQ+ communities. As the narrative often goes, a defining early moment for the movement occurred in 1987.[10] In this year, a report by the United Church of Christ Commission for Racial Justice found that more than half of African American, Latinx, Asian/Pacific Islander, and Native American communities lived near toxic waste sites. To describe these findings, executive director Benjamin Chavis inaugurated the phrase environmental racism.[11]

In October 1991, delegates of the First National People of Color Environmental Leadership Summit in Washington, DC adopted seventeen "principles of environmental justice," further catalyzing the movement. In their "preamble," the delegates wrote of their intention to build a national and international movement of all peoples of color to fight the destruction and taking of our lands and communities . . . [and] to secure our political, economic and cultural liberation that has been denied for over 500 years of colonization and oppression, resulting in the poisoning of our communities and land and the genocide of our peoples.[12]

Here the delegates align environmental justice with decolonial, anti-capitalist, and liberation politics. That is to say, they commit environmental justice to exposing structures of colonial power,[13] critiquing the extractivist logics of the economic system, and demanding freedom for historically enslaved and oppressed peoples. In this chapter I will show how Lorde's Hugo journals in particular convey the anti-colonial sentiment that would inform environmental justice statements such as this one.

Within American ecocriticism, literary critics began writing about environmental justice literatures in the late 1990s. In 1998 Lawrence Buell named environmental justice literatures, along with writings about them, "toxic discourse."[14] In the last two decades, a number of articles and books have been published on the topic. In 2002 Joni Adamson, Mei Mei Evans, and Rachel Stein's *Environmental Justice Reader* helped establish environmental justice as a field. In her (2010) *Bodily Natures*, Stacy Alaimo introduced the influential term "trans-corporeality" to characterize toxic embodiment.[15] And in 2011, Rob Nixon's *Slow Violence and the Environmentalism of the Poor* provided a framework for articulating violence that is "incremental and accretive, its calamitous repercussions playing out across a range of temporal scales," from climate change, toxic drift, and deforestation, to radioactive fallout, acidifying oceans, and more.[16]

Today descriptive and theoretical accounts of environmental justice literatures appear with even greater frequency. But within American eco-criticism, there is much room for historical work that charts the emergence and evolution of environmental justice in literature. I hope to show what such a historical approach might look like. To do so, I will account not only for Lorde's published nonfiction and poetry, but also for unpublished journals, historical documents, and ephemera that, taken together, provide another story about environmental justice's emergence. My approach wagers that literature becomes meaningful when read in relationship to other historical events and artifacts. We can read literature to recover – or restore – neglected or lost histories, such as the struggle of descendants of colonized and enslaved peoples living on St. Croix, or of Black women disproportionately affected by the American breast cancer epidemic of the late twentieth century.

The Black Women's Health Movement and the American "Economics of Disease"

One political and literary movement that has been understudied for its critical contributions to what would later come to be called environmental justice is Black feminism. Black feminism in the 1970s and 1980s, and in particular Black women's health activism, articulated the "troubling inter-relationships [that] exist between racism, poverty, health care, and health status" for African Americans, especially Black women.[17] In her keynote address at the First National Conference on Black Women's Health Issues at Spelman College in summer 1983, Dr. June Jackson Christmas linked high infant mortality rates, chronic disease, and high levels of stress among Black women to a discriminatory and exploitative health care system along with environmental factors including "occupational hazards [and] damaging environmental conditions (such as exposure to toxic wastes)."[18] The goal of the Conference on Black Women's Health Issues was to improve the lives of Black women of all ages by demanding their right to care and "heal[ing] a sick system."[19] The event grew out of health activist Byllye Avery's work on the National Black Women's Health Project. Before first conceptualizing the Health Project around 1980, Avery cofounded the Women's Health Center in Gainesville, Florida, in 1974.[20] Through her work at the health center, Avery saw how Black women's silence around health issues inhibited their process of self-empowerment. She started the Health Project to facilitate "talking [as] an ongoing process" through self-help groups: "[W]e sat down, and kicked our shoes off, and started to break the conspiracy of silence that kept us apart."[21] (See Figure 15.1.)

Black feminists' turn to the social and environmental injustice of chronic disease was inspired in part by Audre Lorde. Three years prior to the Conference on Black Women's Health Issues, Lorde published *The Cancer Journals*, chronicling her recovery after a modified radical mastectomy. Lorde would spend the next decade of her life advocating awareness of the relationship between racism, the "profit economy," and the attrition of Black women's bodies and the environment.[22] In her *Cancer Journals*, Lorde confronts how the medical industry isolates and exploits breast cancer survivors by pushing prostheses and reconstructive surgeries. She writes, "I believe that socially sanctioned prosthesis is merely another way of keeping women with breast cancer silent and separate from each other … what would happen if an army of one-breasted women descended upon Congress and demanded that the use of carcinogenic, fat-stored hormones in beef-feed be outlawed?"[23] Lorde

Figure 15.1 Poster for the First National Conference on Black Women's Health
Issues, Boston Women's Health Book Collective Subject Files, Black Women's
Health Project folder, Harvard Medical Library in the Francis A. Countway Library
of Medicine.

suggests that the profit economy, including the "Cancer Establishment,"
requires that breast cancer be invisibilized so that it (the economy) may
continue to generate capital through toxic industrial meat processing. As

Avery would echo, Lorde argues that Black women must break the silence and come together to fight their atomization and disempowerment. Later, she writes, "I may be a casualty in the cosmic war against radiation, animal fat, air pollution, McDonald's hamburgers and Red Dye No. 2, but the fight is still going on, and I am still a part of it. I refuse to have my scars hidden or trivialized behind lambswool or silicone gel."[24] Crucially, Lorde asserts that the fight for the recognition of breast cancer as a form of injustice is inseparable from the fight for environmental justice more broadly.

Throughout the 1980s, Lorde continued to write about her experience with cancer, which by the end of 1985 had returned in her liver.[25] She often reflected on the possible links between illnesses like hers and the industrial pollution around her home on Staten Island from metal and oil refineries in New Jersey. In a poem she first drafted in the early 1980s titled "On My Way Out I Passed Over You and the Verrazano Bridge," Lorde writes, "now sulfur fuels burn in New Jersey / and when I wash my hands at the garden hose / the earth runs off bright yellow."[26] Lorde knew in her body that the subjugation of Black women and the "poisoning of the earth" were interconnected.[27]

In the 1980s Lorde began visiting St. Croix. She also traveled around the Caribbean, Germany, and elsewhere in Europe to meet and organize with Black women of the anti-imperialism and anti-apartheid movements and to explore alternative cancer therapies.[28] Lorde believed that cancer was a "political weapon" wielded against women of color and integral to the American "economics of disease."[29] Moreover, she developed a theory that battles against cancer and racism around the world, waged by Black women of the African diaspora, were intimately related. Lorde writes, "Racism. Cancer. In both cases, to win the aggressor must conquer, but the resisters need only survive. How do I define that survival and on whose terms?"[30] Cancer *was* a kind of apartheid, in that it was utilized by the dominant structure (in this case, the capitalist state) as a mechanism for separating off, alienating, and attenuating women and women's power. Consequently, surviving cancer was a political act.

In 1988, as she battled metastatic breast cancer, Lorde went to live on St. Croix with her partner, Gloria Joseph. After leaving her longtime home of New York City behind, she embraced the natural world of the island, gardening and raising bees.[31] In the next section, I will show how Lorde's queer restoration poetics in her journals and poetry constitute early environmental justice literatures.

Colonial Power and Environmental Racism: Lorde's Hugo Journals

Living through Hurricane Hugo on St. Croix and seeing the storm's devastation firsthand had a profound effect on Lorde's environmental thinking. In the aftermath, Lorde's ideas about the relationship between racism and environmental health came to fruition. In a series of journals that she contributed to Gloria Joseph and Hortense Rowe's anthology about Hurricane Hugo, *Hell Under God's Orders* (1990), Lorde critiques the US government's role in both creating the conditions for and failing to respond to the Hugo disaster. She also begins to elaborate connections between the sick island post-disaster and her own sick body.

On September 17 and 18, 1989, Hurricane Hugo struck the Virgin Islands. The storm wreaked havoc, with winds higher than 140 miles per hour, and passed directly over St. Croix.[32] On St. Croix, the hurricane damaged or destroyed 90 percent of homes.[33] Because the local territorial government was not adequately prepared to perform first-responder activities, people began looting in order to obtain emergency supplies.[34] The local government's response was further hampered by the storm's depletion of its resources and manpower; the island's infrastructure was completely ravaged.[35] For weeks, most residents went without basic utilities.[36]

In her published journals, Lorde provides her own testimony and reflections. She opens her series of journals with a letter to an anonymous friend: "Dear Friend: Those who do not learn from history are doomed to repeat their mistakes. It is necessary to remember the nightmare experience and extraordinary heroisms of the hurricane."[37] It seems to me that Lorde conceives of her journals as historical artifacts that would tell the story of what had happened. By providing a written account, Lorde seizes the facts away from culture's unreliable short-term memory and insists on their place in a more permanent register.

In the published version of a journal entry dated September 18 that reconstructs her experience of the immediate aftermath of the storm, Lorde describes her and Gloria's ruined home. Like many people's, their roof was partially blown off in the high winds. "[T]he porch is totally gone except for only a concrete slab," Lorde writes; "The living room is completely open on two sides."[38] She recalls how, stepping outside, the landscape was unfamiliar to her: "We can now look straight out to sea ... Nothing green is visible ... There are no leaves left on trees, no flowers, no bushes. Everywhere, burned, blasted landscapes of sparse and tortured broken trees."[39] In a subsequent entry, she observes "the absolute lack of color – no flowers, no leaves, no color on our beautiful island."[40] Here Lorde repeatedly uses a negative construction to emphasize the extent to which the storm had emptied the island of its abundance. In her September 18 entry she writes, "It looks like some mean-spirited and powerful monster has gone on a jealous rampage through our home."[41] In Lorde's account, the storm is hateful and unrelenting, part of but ultimately antagonistic toward nature. All the green that indicated health and vitality had been stripped away, leaving behind a diseased landscape. Like the cancer that had invaded Lorde's body, Hugo ravaged the island's fragile ecology, leaving it vulnerable and exposed. "I am dying and that is the closest I have come to death in my life," Lorde handwrote on September 19 in her original Hugo journal, acknowledging not only the irony of her situation but also, quite simply, that she and other human inhabitants were not separate from the island's ecosystem.[42] At the end of the published September 18 entry, Lorde writes: "There is little time to think about anything other than physical safety and survival. We have stepped out into a world forever altered."[43] Lorde, who had spent much of her life theorizing Black women's survival as a political act, suddenly found herself fighting to survive post-disaster in the most basic, literal way.

In March 1991, the United States General Accounting Office issued a report to Congress assessing the federal, state, and local responses to Hurricane Hugo and also the Loma Prieta earthquake, which struck only a month after Hugo. The report found that government preparedness and response were lacking at all levels (local, state, and federal). But notably, with regard to the response on the Virgin Islands, the report primarily faulted the local government.[44] Ultimately, the report concluded, the Federal Emergency Management Agency (FEMA) was overwhelmed by the demands of the two simultaneous disasters, and because it was tasked with being the first responder on St. Croix when the territory's emergency plans proved ineffective, it faced a "particularly challenging situation."[45]

Shortly after the storm, the local and federal governments decided that a strong federal presence was needed, so President George Bush Sr.'s administration sent 1,200 Army personnel, FBI agents, US Marshals, and other law enforcement personnel to intervene. The report to Congress suggested that the federal government's military response was necessary to "help restore order" in the wake of looting on St. Croix, which it characterized as quickly devolving into the looting of "nonessential items."[46]

Lorde's own firsthand account is starkly different from that of the 1991 government report to Congress. It was not until the third day following the storm that the US military arrived on St. Croix, and when they did, they quickly began policing the island, shoving M-16s in people's faces if they dared to talk back.[47] According to Lorde, the federal government came to St. Croix to police, not aid, people, and did not offer emergency supplies, food, or water.

According to some critics, the highly militarized response only exacerbated racial tensions on St. Croix that had existed for many years. One anthropologist, Ann Brittain, argued that Virgin Islanders had been relegated to a permanent underclass of people who were forced to work for wealthy, white mainland vacationers. Brittain suggested that the looting was the reaction of a population that harbored resentment toward a tourism industry that had imposed a high cost of living while simultaneously denying islanders its jobs.[48] Lorde's own comments register this sentiment: "We pass from the stun of crisis to the interminable frustrations of long-range coping with a profit-based economy." She also writes bitterly of the anger people felt about how the government treated them, like a problem in need of fixing, or a "hostile population," not survivors of a disaster. As she puts it, "Obviously, the first and primary mission of the U.S. military upon arrival is to protect property ... No matter what."[49] Lorde cites the example of how the military focused its efforts on protecting Hess Oil company, which had government contracts. She compares the government response on St. Croix to its response in Northern California in the wake of Loma Prieta in order to drive home her point that the colonized people of St. Croix were subject to environmental racism: "The level of concern and outpouring of aid to that community is in such marked contrast to the treatment deemed acceptable for St. Croix, that few could miss the costly lesson of what it really means to be in a colonial relationship to a super power."[50]

Throughout the journals, Lorde articulates what she saw as a key nature–culture dynamic, in which nature is made ugly by human activities. With regard to the island's destruction, Lorde writes that it was a "man-made ugliness."[51] She elaborates: "Hurricane Hugo was a terrible natural disaster, but nature heals herself. It is what we inject into her like tumors that fester and grow loathsome."[52] Human intervention in nature makes nature sick, throwing its ecosystems out of balance: "The bees and the jack-spaniels, yellow-jackets, are everywhere, stinging and furious."[53] Lorde's references to a nature–culture dynamic are self-conscious ones that resonate with the insights of ecofeminism.[54] Her descriptions immanently critique Western culture's justification of the subjugation of women, perceived racial others, queer people, and animals and plants by placing them on the nature side of the binary, thus making them culture's other.[55]

Moreover, Lorde's descriptions imply that liberating oppressed and sick-ened people and liberating oppressed and sickened environments are part of the same project. This perspective is one that Greta Gaard would later name a queer ecofeminist one.[56]

In her final published journal entry, Lorde employs an environmental justice perspective in order to make her call to action: "We must also learn to live in such a way that the effects of these natural events are minimized, and the after-effects of such occurrences are absorbed by realistic pre-planning that include[s] all members of our society." She warns that human activities were eradicating rainforests, polluting the atmosphere, and heating up the oceans, referencing the phenomenon of global climate change, the same year Bill McKibben would bring the issue into main-stream consciousness with the publication of *The End of Nature*. But the earth, Lorde suggests, is capable of restoring itself: "Our earth is healing herself. Again. And we pay a price for the violence we have done to her in the name of scientific progress."[57] Ultimately, Lorde argues, the earth can be preserved if humans commit to doing so: "Each one of us has some power that can be used, somewhere, somehow, to help save our earth."[58] What begins as a series of journals about the specific disaster of Hurricane Hugo ends up being an environmental justice manifesto, in which Lorde links Hugo to the broader violence of the Western capitalist state's racia-lization, marginalization, and degradation of vulnerable human popula-tions and environments.

Queer Restoration: Environmental Justice as Homemaking

Just as surviving cancer was, for Lorde, a political act, so was surviving Hugo. In both cases, survival constituted a repudiation of capitalist state-sponsored environmental injustice. In her poem "Restoration: A Memorial," collected in her posthumously published *Marvelous Arithmetics of Distance* (1993), Lorde links survival to restoration; both are figured as multitemporal, ongoing processes that take place in the ravaged landscapes of the sick island and the sick body. For Lorde, restor-ation entails looking backward in order to heal and go forward, despite uncertainty. Restoration may occur simultaneously in the past, present, and future, or in their interstices. In this final section, I will show how Lorde mobilizes an environmental justice perspective to elaborate a queer restoration poetics. I use the word poetics here to refer to Lorde's poetry. I also use the term in its classical sense – from the Greek *poiesis*, meaning to make – to refer to her poetry's philosophy of making (or remaking). In this way, I am suggesting that a queer restoration poetics can also be an activity of *queer remaking* through writing.

For Lorde, restoration is not a cumulative activity. Rather, it is a highly uncertain one that can lack continuity. By writing through the unpredictable time of restoration, Lorde anticipates what disability theorists describe as "crip time." As Ellen Samuels writes, with reference to her experience living with a disabling illness, "Crip time is time travel. Disability and illness have the power to extract us from linear, progressive time ... and cast us into a wormhole of backward and forward acceleration, jerky stops and starts, tedious intervals and abrupt endings."[59] In Lorde's poem, however, she is not cast, passively, into a wormhole; rather, she is an agent who embraces the inconstant time of her post-Hugo life.

The poem begins:

> Berlin again   after chemotherapy
> I reach behind me once more
> for days to come
> sweeping around the edges of authenticity
> two years after Hugo blew one life away
> Death like a burnt star
> perched on the rim of my teacup
> flaming the honey drips from my spoon
> sunlight flouncing off the gargoyles opposite.[60]

Lorde writes from Berlin, a city she spent time in between 1984 and 1992. There she taught at Freie University, organized with Afro-Germans, and received cancer treatments from a naturopath.[61] In her poem, Lorde opens with a caesura in the first line, emphasizing that she writes in the time and space following her treatment. She also suggests that it is only by looking "behind" oneself at what is past that one becomes capable of "sweeping" around in time toward "authenticity." It is not obvious what Lorde means by "authenticity," despite her assertion that it has shape and "edges." Perhaps she wishes to achieve correspondence between her feelings and her expression of them, in spite of poststructuralism's condemnation of notions of authorship, self-presence, and authenticity itself. Or perhaps she desires to feel real and actual, despite the illness that had overtaken her body.[62] Maybe Lorde feels that, even two years later, she has not yet found the words to write authentically about the reality of Hugo's devastation – one life blown away, whether literally or figuratively, "like a burnt star." In her handwritten journal, Lorde simply calls the storm "indescribable."[63] It is also unclear to whom the "death" in the sixth line belongs: it could be a storm victim's, or it could be Lorde's own, "perched" right before her, seemingly closer than ever before. Lorde ends the stanza by describing her proximity to the teacup whose lip twinkles in the sunlight. Here the language's heightened materiality – its sibilance and repetition of the lippy "p" consonant sound – underscores Lorde's place in the physical world, conveying again, perhaps, her desire for authenticity. Throughout the stanza, Lorde holds open the gap between past and present, tarrying in the space between.[64]

In the next stanza, Lorde writes,

> Somewhere it is Tuesday
> in the ordinary world
> ravishment fades
> into compelling tasks
> our bodies learn to perform
> quite a bit of the house is left
> our bedroom spared
> except for the ankle-deep water
> and terrible stench.[65]

The time and place of the second stanza are ambiguous. At first it seems that Lorde is referring to the present time of Berlin, with the "ravishment" of chemotherapy beginning to fade. Not until line six of this stanza is it clear that the present of the poem is actually two years prior on St. Croix. Lorde writes of her and Gloria's ruined home following Hugo, and in this new present, "ravishment" is no longer due to chemo, but rather the storm. In fact, Lorde adapted some of these lines from a handwritten journal entry from September 19 ("It is Tuesday afternoon in the ordinary world," she wrote), just two days after the storm, a moment when she felt "devastation after the relief at being alive and the shock of what we have lost."[66]

One might interpret Lorde's sudden temporal leap into the past as reflecting the tendency of a sick body-mind. For those who are ill, time can become slippery and lose its linear structure; time can become a "wormhole," to recall Samuels. One might also read Lorde as intentionally reinhabiting the authenticity of feeling that came with facing death more head-on than she ever had before, in order to feel more alive, despite her illness.

She continues:

> Would I exchange this safety of exile
> for the muddy hand-drawn water
> wash buckets stashed
> where our front porch had been
> half-rotten vegetables
> the antique grey settling over your face
> that October?[67]

Lorde poses a rhetorical question in order to emphasize her longing to return home to St. Croix and Gloria, despite the island's unhealth. Like Lorde, the island is sick, littered with rotting objects. Everything is muddied and pallid, including Gloria's face. Lorde characterizes her experience of being in Berlin as "safe," but one that felt like being banished from her home; ironically, what keeps her from her sick home is her own sick body. Once again, Lorde points to how the institution of cancer, as a disease to be "properly" treated in the medical clinics of the Western world, keeps women from each other and their homes and strips them of their power.

Next, Lorde writes:

> I want you laughing again
> After the stinking rugs are dragged away
> the crystal chandelier dug
> from the dining-room floor
> refrigerator righted
> broken cupboards stacked outside
> to dry for our dinner fire.
>
> A few trees still stand
> in a brand-new landscape
> but the sea road is impassable.
> Your red shirt
> hung out on a bush to dry
> is the only flower for weeks.
> No escape. No return.
> No other life
> half so sane.[68]

Here Lorde imagines the restoration of her and Gloria's home along with their spirits, believing that domestic repair work might help return their lives to some kind of normalcy. At the end of the fifth stanza, Lorde describes the difficulty of her relationship to St. Croix. From Berlin, St. Croix feels inaccessible. But from the other present of the poem, the St. Croix present, she is trapped on the wrecked island, unable to leave. She emphasizes her feeling of containment through her use of the present tense: "the sea road *is* impassable." Moreover, she knows that, at her disease stage, she will never be able to "escape" or "return" to her previous state of greater physical health. It is a double bind. And yet, she cannot imagine any other way of being. Thus, the final lines – "No escape. No return. / No other life / half so sane" – might be read as a declaration of self-acceptance and self-love. The contradiction of Lorde's position – where the place that feels most like home is at the same time an inhospitable one; a place, moreover, that she may never see fully restored to what it once was – is also the condition and the catalyst for her claiming that position as her own.

Lorde concludes with the following stanza:

> In this alien and temporary haven
> my poisoned fingers
> slowly return to normal
> I read your letter dreaming
> the perspective of a bluefish
> or a fugitive parrot
> watch the chemicals leaving my nails
> as my skin takes back its weaknesses.
> Learning to laugh again.[69]

Here Lorde watches and waits as her body recovers from chemo. In the process of her duration, as she reads Gloria's letter, she imagines a perspective other than her own human one. Perhaps Gloria references a bluefish and parrot in her letter. Or perhaps the animals come to Lorde's mind as being affected by Hugo in their own way. Regardless, reading the letter leads her to dream her way toward the perspective of the animals, grasping her own animal body and form of life as being among many others interrupted or destroyed by the storm. At this point Lorde's sense of her enmeshment with the ecology of the island comes sharply into relief. Her feeling of solidarity with the animals and plants of St. Croix is apparent in her original Hugo journal as well. In it, Lorde pressed two brightly colored bird feathers that, presumably, she found on St. Croix in the months following Hugo – one belonging to an American kestrel, and another a mallard duck.[70] (See Figure 15.2.) The feathers are pressed into pages filled with 1989 Christmas Day reflections, a draft of a letter to Lorde's daughter, Beth, and notes toward a poem.[71]

Lorde's final lines, "[my] skin takes back its weaknesses. / Learning to laugh again," once again reiterate a seeming contradiction: that one could be made sick by the very same place that gives one a feeling of home. This idea permeates Lorde's understanding of place. Whether New York City, St. Croix, or her individual body, all of her "homes" contributed to Lorde's illness, or "weaknesses." But they were also the source of her laughter and joy, a term that elsewhere Lorde uses to describe the sharing of erotic energy with other women that, for her, is the prerequisite for collaborative world building.[72]

I read Lorde as rejecting an idea of "home" tied to normative conceptions of happiness, family, and sexuality, and therefore providing an account of what Sara Ahmed calls "queer unhappiness" (a state that, for

(a)

(b)

Figure 15.2 An American kestrel feather (left) and mallard duck feather (right) that
Lorde pressed in her original Hugo journal. (The phrase "what it means to be
beautiful" would eventually become the title of a poem in *Marvelous Arithmetics*.)
Journal entries, December 24–25, 1989, Audre Lorde Papers, Series 2, Subseries 5,
no. 35, 1989–90, Spelman College Archives, Atlanta, GA.

Lorde, does not preclude self-affirmation or "joy"). In her book *The
Promise of Happiness* (2010), which she dedicates to Lorde, Ahmed explores
what is often the difficulty of "being at home" for queer people. She writes,
"What if the world 'houses' some bodies more than others? . . . Perhaps the
experiences of . . . being stressed, of not being extended by the spaces in
which we reside, can teach us more about happiness [than anything],"
seeming to name precisely Lorde's sentiment at the end of her poem.[73]
Ahmed goes on to suggest that if the heterosexual household is the condition for a "happy ending," then in order to affirm queer love we must tell
stories about queer unhappiness.[74] Ahmed writes, "A revolution of unhappiness might require an unhousing . . . The political energy of unhappy
queers might depend on not being in house."[75]

Lorde's poem articulates her own experience of "not being in house" as a result of hostile, "man-made" environmental conditions. Her physical home on St. Croix was destroyed by an economic system that did not value the lives of people living there. Her body was ravaged by industries that considered her disposable. Earlier, in her *Cancer Journals*, Lorde articulates the absurdity of the pursuit of happiness mandated by the dominant culture, given such inhospitable conditions: "Was I really fighting the spread of radiation, racism, women-slaughter, chemical invasion of our food, pollution of our environment ... merely to avoid dealing with my first and greatest responsibility – to be happy?" She continues, "The idea that happiness can insulate us against the results of our environmental madness is a rumor circulated by our enemies to destroy us."[76] Then, Lorde reflects on how she had worried her mastectomy would alienate her from her body. But in fact, she was able to reclaim the "great well of sexual pleasure" she had associated with her right breast and, through her queer restoration poetics, "attach it anywhere [she wanted] to," because she alone "[owned her] feelings."[77] Similarly, in "Restoration: A Memorial," Lorde explores how after Hugo, returning "home" and becoming happy ("Learning to laugh again") was not possible in any traditional sense, but could be reimagined in queer terms through the attachment of home to whom or whatever she desired – the few still-standing trees, the animals and plants of the island, and, of course, Gloria herself. For Lorde, the queer restoration of home seems to entail embracing vulnerability ("weaknesses") along with all of the unknowns of her life's disjointed time.

Scientific thinking about restoration ecologies can help further illuminate Lorde's restoration poetics. Traditionally restoration has been thought of as the science of assisting the recovery of an ecosystem,[78] through the development of goals that can help achieve a more desirable state for that ecosystem.[79] But in the past decade, ecologists have suggested that we can't necessarily expect a linear model of recovery. Researchers point out that restoration involves "complex webs of interactions and feedbacks among physical, biological, and social factors."[80] As a result, ecosystem dynamics are often unpredictable. In fact, restoration may follow a nonlinear trajectory with interruptions, or "thresholds," along the way. Thresholds are "points where small changes in environmental conditions lead to large or discontinuous changes in other variables that characterize the state of a system."[81] Thresholds can trigger a series of changes that lead to new configurations.[82] Thus, accounting for threshold dynamics requires an openness to contingent, nonlinear processes, as opposed to continuous, progressive ones.

I do not cite research on threshold dynamics to validate the insights of Lorde's restoration poetics; it is not my wish to privilege the insights of the natural sciences. Like Angela Willey, who advocates a "queer feminist critical-materialist" approach to reading, in my reading of Lorde's restoration poetics I hope to "passionately challenge a view of biology as flat and predictable" while also remaining wary of what might be my own impulse to "[romanticize] nature's agency, contingency, self-organization, or plasticity" (as Willey puts it).[83] I want to draw out the ecological nature of Lorde's thinking, while also showing how Lorde's thinking participates in the capacious imagination of ecology.

One might be tempted to align Lorde's ecological thinking with that of recent material feminisms, which have called for bringing the materiality of the human body and environment to the fore of feminist theory, despite the dominance of social constructionist theories.[84] Donna Haraway and Willey, for example, ask how we might think the body in terms of the "naturecultural" (Haraway's term) or "biopossible" (Willey's). That is, how might we resist binaries such as nature/culture and biology/language in order to, as Willey puts it, "queer knowledge" and resist "evidentiary schemas that support fixed ideas of what we are and might become"?[85] But in fact, as Ahmed has pointed out – and as Willey herself suggests through a reading of Lorde in her essay on "biopossibility" – Black feminists such as Lorde have accounted for both material and sociopolitical forces at work on their bodies all along, and it is them to whom today's material feminists owe a debt.[86]

I have shown how Lorde critiques the "man-made" violence of both Hugo and cancer in order to inaugurate a queer restoration poetics, or the queer remaking of home. This restoration poetics exemplifies one approach to environmental justice writing. Through journals and poetry multiply oriented in time, toward the local and transnational, and also toward the biological, cultural, and biocultural, Lorde suggests that the restoration of body, history, and home – however partial, even failed – "might depend on not being in house" (per Ahmed). Through a poem that commits itself to queer environmental navigation, along with practices of home and happiness that do not necessarily correspond with those of the dominant society, Lorde writes her own experience of environmental injustice, resistance, and survival into history. But while poetry serves a documentary function for Lorde, it is by no means a dead artifact. Rather, "poetry makes something happen," as she argues in a posthumously published talk; "poetry is not separate from my living."[87] Thus, a historical approach informed by Lorde's Black feminist environmental justice perspective might assert that to read historically is to read poetry into, or in its, being, despite the structures that try to suppress it. We can read to restore, and thus participate in *ecopoetics*, or home (from *oikos*) making (from *poiesis*), despite what can be the difficulty or seeming impossibility of home in the first place.

Notes

Introduction

1. Scott V. Edwards, Twitter (June 25, 2020), https://twitter.com/ScottVEdward s1. Accessed July 15, 2020.
2. Especially relevant are the lines: "Oh there must be shackles on his feet/ And mother in his eyes/ Stumbling through the devil-dark/ With the hound pack in full cry." Elton John, "Have Mercy on the Criminal," Don't Shoot Me I'm Only the Piano Player (DJM Records, 1973).
3. See, for example, Bridget Alex, "Meet the Harvard Ornithology Professor Biking Across the Country," *Audubon* (June 26, 2020), www.audubon.org/ne ws/meet-harvard-ornithology-professor-biking-across-country.
4. On the redefinition of American literature as drawing from ancient and global sources, see our contributor Wai Chee Dimock's *Through Other Continents: American Literature Across Deep Time* (Princeton, NJ: Princeton University Press, 2008).
5. See Stephen Rust, Salma Monani, and Sean Cubitt (eds.), *Ecomedia: Key Issues* (London: Routledge, 2015).
6. See, for example, the movement from Henry Nash Smith, *Virgin Land: The American West as Symbol and Myth* (New York: Vintage, 1957) to Annette Kolodny, *Lay of the Land* (Chapel Hill, NC: University of North Carolina at Pembroke, 1975).
7. See, for prominent examples, Lawrence Buell's *The Environmental Imagination: Thoreau, Nature Writing and the Formation of American Culture* (Cambridge, MA: Harvard University Press, 1995) and the anthology, Cheryll Glotfelty and Harold Fromm (eds.), *The Ecocriticism Reader: Landmarks in Literary Ecology* (Athens, GA: University of Georgia Press, 1996).
8. See, for an excellent overview of the social expansion of the field, Joni Adamson and Scott Slovic, "The Shoulders We Stand On: An Introduction to Ethnicity and Ecocriticism." *MELUS* 34.2 (2009): 5–24, www.jstor.org/stable/20532676.
9. See Catriona Mortimer-Sandilands and Bruce Erickson (eds.), *Queer Ecologies: Sex, Nature, Politics, Desire* (Bloomington and Indianapolis, IN: Indiana

University Press, 2010) and our contributor Nicole Seymour's *Strange Natures: Futurity, Empathy, and the Queer Ecological Imagination* (Urbana, Chicago, and Springfield, IL: University of Illinois Press, 2013).

10. See Paul Crutzen and Eugene Stoermer, "The 'Anthropocene,'" *Global Change Newsletter* 41 (2000): 17–18. And for an example of an ecocritical response, Timothy Clark, *Ecocriticism on the Edge: The Anthropocene as a Threshold Concept* (New York: Bloomsbury, 2015).

11. Consult the "Posthumanities" book series, edited by Cary Wolfe, at the University of Minnesota Press, for a sample of these orientations; and a recent article by Rosi Braidotti, "A Theoretical Framework for the Critical Posthumanities," *Theory, Culture & Society* 36.6 (November 2019): 31–61.

12. For a related approach, see Donna J. Haraway, *Staying with the Trouble (Experimental Futures)* (Durham, NC: Duke University Press, 2016).

1 Scenes of Human Diminishment in Early American Natural History

1. Ralph Waldo Emerson, *Nature: A Facsimile of the First Edition*, Warner Berthoff (ed.) (San Francisco, CA; Chandler, 1968), 36.

2. Quoted in Edith Emerson Webster Gregg, "Emerson and His Children: Their Childhood Memories," *Harvard Library Bulletin* 28.4 (October 1980): 421.

3. Emerson's source for the assertion that ants do not sleep, not corroborated by contemporary observers and left uncommented in critical editions, is unclear.

4. On the "comic bubbliness" of *Nature*, see Lawrence Buell, *Emerson* (Cambridge, MA: Belknap Press, 2003), 94.

5. Greg Garrard, *Ecocriticism*, 2nd edition (London: Routledge, 2012), 153–154.

6. See Simon L. Lewis and Mark A. Maslin, *The Human Planet: How We Created the Anthropocene* (New Haven, CT: Yale University Press, 2018).

7. Alfred Russel Wallace, *The Geographical Distribution of Animals, with a Study of the Relations of Living and Extinct Faunas as Elucidating Past Changes of the Earth's Surface* (New York: Harper & Brothers, 1876), vol. 1, 150.

8. I have borrowed these terms from James Hanken, "The Art of Life: Depicting the Wonder and Beauty of Animals," *Animal: Exploring the Zoological World* (New York: Phaidon, 2018), 6–9.

9. Charlotte Porter, *The Eagle's Nest: Natural History and American Ideas, 1812–1842* (Tuscaloosa, AL: University of Alabama Press, 1986); Thomas Hallock, *From the Fallen Tree: Frontier Narratives, Environmental Politics, and the Roots of a National Pastoral, 1749–1826* (Chapel Hill, NC: University of North Carolina Press, 2003).

10. See the emphasis on human superiority in Louis Agassiz's inaugural American lecture, given in 1846 in Boston and 1847 in New York, *Introduction to the Study of Natural History*, Christoph Irmscher (ed.) (New York: Springer, 2017).

11. Carlyle to Emerson, 8 July 1851, *The Correspondence of Thomas Carlyle and Ralph Waldo Emerson, 1834–1872*, 2 vols. (Boston, MA: Ticknor & Co., 1888), vol. 2, 198. Emphasis in original.

12. William L. Hedges, "Toward a National Literature," in *The Columbia Literary History of the United States* (New York: Columbia University Press, 1988), 180.

13. Mark Van Doren (ed.), *Travels of William Bartram* (New York: Dover, 1955), 87.

14. Ibid., 88.

15. Ibid., 87.

16. Ibid.

17. Alvin R. Grove, Jr., *The Lure and Lore of Trout Fishing* (London: Stackpole, 2017 [1951]), 46.

18. Van Doren (ed.), *Travels of William Bartram*, 88.

19. See, however, Charles H. Adams on Bartram as an "ironic" or self-conscious writer: "Reading Ecologically: Language and Play in Bartram's *Travels*," *The Southern Quarterly* 32.4 (Summer 1994): 65–74.

20. Larry R. Clarke, "The Quaker Background of William Bartram's View of Nature," *Journal of the History of Ideas* 46.3 (July–September 1985): 435–448.

21. Matthew Wynn Sivils, *American Environmental Fiction, 1782–1847* (New York: Routledge, 2016), 20–21. For a more complex version of the "interconnectedness" argument, see Monique Allewaert, *Ariel's Ecology: Plantation, Personhood, and Colonialism in the Tropics* (Minneapolis, MN: University of Minnesota Press, 2013).

22. Van Doren (ed.), *Travels of William Bartram*, 128.

23. Ian Stapley, "Treaties and the Ecological Perspective of William Bartram and John Burroughs," in David G. Payne (ed.), *Writing the Land: John Burroughs and His Legacy* (Newcastle: Cambridge Scholars, 2008), 76–77.

24. Samuel Taylor Coleridge, "The Rime of the Ancient Mariner," *Lyrical Ballads* (1798), l. 125.

25. Van Doren (ed.), *Travels of William Bartram*, 88.

26. Ibid., 88, 89.

27. Ibid.

28. Ibid.

29. Ibid., 183.

30. John James Audubon to Lucy Audubon, February 17, 1832, cited in Judith Magee, *The Art and Science of William Bartram* (London: Natural History Museum, 2007), 176. Emphasis in original.

31. John James Audubon, *Writings and Drawings*, Christoph Irmscher (ed.) (New York: Library of America, 1999), 250.

32. Emily Dickinson, "A Route of Evanescence," J 1463 (ca. 1879), in Thomas H. Johnson (ed.), *The Complete Poems of Emily Dickinson*, (Boston, MA: Little, Brown and Co., 1951), 619.

33. See Wallace Stevens, *The Necessary Angel: Essays on Reality and the Imagination* (London: Faber and Faber, 1960 [1951]).

34. While McGillivray changes similarly odd phrases in Audubon's manuscript, he left that one intact. For a brief comparison of the manuscript of this essay (at Harvard's Houghton Library) and the revised version, see Christoph Irmscher, *The Poetics of Natural History*, 2nd edition (New Brunswick, NJ: Rutgers University Press, 2019), 210–211.

35. Alan C. Braddock, "The Order of Things," in Karl Kusserow and Alan C. Braddock (eds.), *Nature's Nation: American Art and Environment* (New Haven, CT: Yale University Press, 2018), 62. Braddock is arguing against Jennifer L. Roberts, *Transporting Visions: The Movement of Images in Early America* (Berkeley, CA: University of California Press, 2014), 69–115.

36. Audubon, *Writings and Drawings*, 446.

37. *The Birds of America*, plate 181. Audubon saw a copy of *Napoleon Crossing the Alps* in Rembrandt Peale's exhibition rooms in Philadelphia. Roberta Olson, "Audubon's Innovations and the Traditions of Ornithological Illustration: Some Things Old, Some Things Borrowed, But Most Things New," in *Audubon's Aviary: The Original Watercolors for* The Birds of America*, with an essay by Marjorie Shelley and Contributions by Alexandra Mazzitelli* (New York: Skira Rizzoli, 2012), 50–51.

38. Irmscher, *Poetics*, 222.

39. Susan Fenimore Cooper, *Rural Hours*, Rochelle Johnson and Daniel Patterson (eds.) (Athens, GA: University of Georgia Press, 1998), 286. For a more extended ecocritical reading, see Christoph Irmscher, "Susan Fenimore Cooper's Ecology of Reading," *Partial Answers* 12.1 (January 2014): 41–61.

40. James Fenimore Cooper, *The Pioneers; Or, the Sources of Susquehanna*, 3 vols. (Paris: Braudy, 1825 [1823]), vol. 1,226.

41. Cooper, *Rural Hours*, 149, 169. By 1820, Cooper's home state of New York had become an "ecological war-zone." Two-fifths of the land in Cooper's county alone had been cleared. See Alan Taylor, "The Great Change Begins: Settling the Forest of Central New York," *New York History* 76.3 (July 1995): 265–290.

42. Peter Wohlleben, *The Hidden Life Trees: What They Feel, How They Communicate. Discoveries from a Secret World*, Jane Billinghurst (trans.) (Vancouver, BC: Greystone, 2015), 230–231.

43. Cooper, *Rural Hours*, 128.
44. Ibid.
45. Ibid.
46. Ibid.
47. See Adams, "Reading Ecologically," 73.
48. Henry David Thoreau, "Walking" [1862], in Robert F. Sayre and Elizabeth Hall Witherell (eds.), *Thoreau, Walden, The Maine Woods, and Collected Essays and Poems*, (New York: Library of America College Editions, 2007), 765.
49. James E. Watson, Danielle F. Shanahan, Moreno Di Marco, James Allan, William F. Laurance, Eric W. Sanderson, Brendan Mackey, and Oscar Vente, "Catastrophic Declines in Wilderness Areas Undermine Global Environment," *Current Biology* 26.21 (November 7, 2016): 2929–2934.
50. William Cronon (ed.), "The Trouble with Wilderness; or, Getting Back to the Wrong Nature," in *Uncommon Ground: Rethinking the Human Place in Nature* (New York: Norton, 1996), 69–90.

2 Slavery and the Anthropocene

1. "Extinct Species, Explained," *National Geographic* (February 5, 2019), www.nationalgeographic.com/animals/reference/extinct-species/.
2. Kenneth V. Rosenberg, et. al. "Decline of the North American Avifauna," *Science* 366.6461 (October 2019): 120–124, 120.
3. Scott A. Kulp and Benjamin H. Strauss, "New Elevation Data Triple Estimates of Global Vulnerability to Sea-Level Rise and Coastal Flooding," *Nature Communications* 10.4844 (2019): 1.
4. Robert Glennon, "The Unfolding Tragedy of Climate Change in Bangladesh," *Scientific American* (April 21, 2017), https://blogs.scientificamerican.com/gues t-blog/the-unfolding-tragedy-of-climate-change-in-bangladesh/.
5. Donna J. Haraway, *Staying with the Trouble (Experimental Futures)* (Durham, NC: Duke University Press, 2016), 1.
6. See Amitav Ghosh, *The Great Derangement: Climate Change and the Unthinkable* (Chicago, IL: University of Chicago Press, 2016), for an insightful and accessible discussion of the problems of representing climate change in fiction.
7. For critical discussions about the ways certain forms of Anthropocene discourse can suppress questions of environmental justice and histories of oppression, see Robert Bernasconi (ed.), *Race and the Anthropocene*. Special Issue, *Critical Philosophy of Race* 7.1 (2019), especially Axelle Karera, "Blackness and the Pitfalls of Anthropocene Ethics," 32–56; Nancy Tuana, "Climate Apartheid: The Forgetting of Race in the Anthropocene," 1–31; and Eduardo

Mendieta, "Edge City: Reflections on the Urbanocene and the Plantatiocene," 81–106. Recent book-length works that usefully engage these questions include Haraway's *Staying with the Trouble*, Ghosh's *The Great Derangement*, and Kathryn Yusoff's *A Billion Black Anthropocenes or None* (Minneapolis, MN: University of Minnesota Press, 2018).

8. Karera, "Blackness," 34–35.

9. Donna J. Haraway, *Staying with the Trouble: Making Kin in the Chthulucene* (Durham, NC: Duke University Press, 2016), especially 99–102; Mendieta, "Edge City."

10. This chapter in places draws on arguments I first took up in *Race and Nature from Transcendentalism to the Harlem Renaissance* (New York: Palgrave Macmillan, 2013 [2008]). The first three chapters of that book provide a fuller introduction to those arguments, with a particular focus on the antebellum period.

11. Dipesh Chakrabarty, "The Climate of History: Four Theses," *Critical Inquiry* 35.2 (2009): 197–222.

12. Ibid., 201.

13. Ibid., 205.

14. Ibid., 206–207.

15. For those unfamiliar with this term, the Turing Test is a procedure proposed by Alan Turing in the mid-twentieth century (and used to this day in AI research) for determining if a computer should be deemed intelligent. In the test a (human) judge asks questions of two hidden interlocutors, one of whom is a computer; if the judge is unable to reliably identify the computer on the basis of the responses, Turing asserts that we should consider the computer to be intelligent.

16. Harriet Jacobs, *Incidents in the Life of a Slave Girl, Written by Herself* (Boston, MA: Jacobs, 1861), 128.

17. Frederick Douglass, *My Bondage and My Freedom* (1855), in Henry Louis Gates, Jr. (ed.) *Frederick Douglass: Autobiographies* (New York: Library of America, 1994), 146.

18. Ibid., 147.

19. Jacobs, *Incidents*, 181.

20. Douglass, *My Bondage*, 293.

21. Ibid., 44.

22. Ibid., 50.

23. For a fuller introduction to this terrible history, see Elizabeth Kennedy, "Victim Race and Rape," *The Feminist Sexual Ethics Project* (n.d.), www.brandeis.edu/projects/fse/slavery/united-states/kennedy.html.

24. Bruno Latour, *We Have Never Been Modern*, Catherine Porter (trans.) (Cambridge, MA: Harvard University Press, 1993), 13.

25. Ibid., 32.

26. This is not to say, of course, that the nature/culture distinction originated with the American plantation system.

3 (In)conceivable Futures: Henry David Thoreau and Reproduction's Queer Ecology

1. Madeline Ostrander, "How Do You Decide to Have a Baby When Climate Change Is Remaking Life on Earth?" *The Nation* (March 24, 2016), www .thenation.com/article/archive/how-do-you-decide-to-have-a-baby-when-climate-change-is-remaking-life-on-earth/.
2. Dave Bry, "Does Climate Change Make It Immoral to Have Kids?" *The Guardian* (April 2, 2016), www.theguardian.com/commentisfree/2016/apr/02 /does-climate-change-make-it-immoral-to-have-kids.
3. Child is capitalized as a reference to Lee Edelman's influential claims in *No Future: Queer Theory and the Death Drive* (Durham, NC and London: Duke University Press, 2004). I am not discussing Edelman here because two other contributors to this volume – Min Hyoung Song and Rick Crownshaw – do so at length in their chapters.
4. Roy Scranton, "Raising a Daughter in a Doomed World," in *We're Doomed, Now What?: Essays on Climate Change* (New York: Soho Press, 2018), 324.
5. Ibid., 326.
6. For an ecocritical discussion of reproductive choice in the context of child-free climate activism and nativist policies of population control, see Heather Houser, "Should You Have Kids Despite Climate Change?" *Yes! Magazine* (October 28, 2020), www.ecowatch.com/overpopulation-children-climate-crisis-2648533200.html
7. See Christina Sharpe, *In the Wake: On Blackness and Being* (Durham, NC: Duke University Press, 2016), especially 80–88, where her discussion of what happens to the "meaning of *child* ... as it abuts blackness" (80) traces the contours of what we might deem "reproductive non-futurity" experienced in the wake. For a reading of Edelman's argument in *No Future* in the context of Black feminist theory that traces such reproductive non-futurity, see James Bliss, "Hope Against Hope: Queer Negativity, Black Feminist Theorizing, and Reproduction without Futurity," *Mosaic* 48.1 (March 2015): 83–98.
8. See Andil Gosine, "Non-White Reproduction and Same-Sex Eroticism: Queer Acts Against Nature," in *Queer Ecologies: Sex, Nature, Politics, Desire*, Catriona Mortimer-Sandilands and Bruce Erickson (eds.) (Bloomington, IN: Indiana University Press, 2010): 149–172. In advocating that we disentangle biological reproduction from the nuclear family form, I do not in any

way mean to overlook the way in which a severing of those two paradigms has been a tool of racialized violence, most notably in the production of kinlessness and natal alienation amid legal chattel slavery. Indeed, both biological reproduction and the normative nuclear family model have been implements of institutionalized racism (or racism's institutionalization), from the logic and fallout of the Moynihan Report to the forced sterilization of women of color in the United States. My argument is predicated on the belief that understanding reproduction beyond how it has been *naturalized* (in part by demonstrating the schism between our prevailing definitions/uses of the term and the way in which it functions in the work of one of the preeminent American "nature" writers) can further challenge its normative, disciplinary power, especially as it has been wielded within the context of American environmentalism.

9. Sarah Ensor, "Spinster Ecology: Rachel Carson, Sarah Orne Jewett, and Nonreproductive Futurity," *American Literature* 84.2 (June 2012): 409–435 and Nicole Seymour, *Strange Natures: Futurity, Empathy, and the Queer Ecological Imagination* (Urbana, IL: University of Illinois Press, 2013), 10, emphasis added. Seymour is referring specifically to the queer utopianism of José Esteban Muñoz. In giving a brief overview of field-level tendencies, I don't mean to suggest that queer theorists never think about reproduction in complex ways. See, for example, Valerie Rohy's work on "homosexual reproduction" in *Lost Causes: Narrative, Etiology, and Queer Theory* (Oxford: Oxford University Press, 2015).

10. Henry David Thoreau, *The Writings of Henry D. Thoreau, Journal vol. 4: 1851–1852*, Robert Sattelmeyer, Leonard N. Neufeldt, and Nancy Craig Simmons (eds.) (Princeton, NJ: Princeton University Press, 1992), 145–146.

11. Louis Agassiz and A.A. Gould, *Principles of Zoology* (Boston, MA: Gould and Lincoln, 1853), 162–163.

12. In his analogical reading of Agassiz and Gould, Thoreau also gently alters perhaps the two most problematic elements of their account: their belief in biological "perfectability" yields Thoreau's non-teleological interest in suspension, and their apparent judgment of "barren females" (who must be viewed "merely as nurses") resolves into Thoreau's affirmative investigation of ecological "nurses," which, as we will see, ramifies across his work.

13. Here, we might hear echoes of Kathryn Bond Stockton's *The Queer Child: Growing Sideways in the Twentieth Century* (Durham, NC and London: Duke University Press, 2009), where she coins the term "'sideways growth' to refer to something . . . that locates energy, pleasure, vitality, and (e)motion in the back-and-forth of connections and extensions *that are not reproductive*" (13).

Via Thoreau, I am offering a queer model of sideways movement internal – rather than opposed – to reproduction itself.

14. Henry David Thoreau, "The Succession of Forest Trees," in Walter Harding (ed.), *The Selected Works of Thoreau* (Boston, MA: Houghton Mifflin Company, 1975), 733.

15. Ibid., 737.

16. Henry David Thoreau, Journal Manuscript, vol. 18, http://thoreau .library.ucsb.edu/writings_journals_pdfs/TMS18newTR.pdf.

17. This phrase is Elizabeth Freeman's in "Queer Belongings: Kinship Theory and Queer Theory," in George E. Haggerty and Molly McGarry (eds.), *A Companion to Lesbian, Gay, Bisexual, Transgender, and Queer Studies* (London: Blackwell, 2007), 300.

18. Emily Rapp, "Notes from a Dragon Mom," *New York Times* (October 15, 2011), www.nytimes.com/2011/10/16/opinion/sunday/notes-from-a-dragon-mom.html.

19. Belle Boggs, "The Art of Waiting," *Orion Magazine* (March/April 2012), https://orionmagazine.org/article/the-art-of-waiting/.

20. Rochelle Riley, "Dr. Mona Hanna-Attisha Goes from Doctor to Global Hero," *Detroit Free Press* (April 29, 2016), www.freep.com/story/news/colum nists/rochelle-riley/2016/02/06/dr-mona-hanna-attisha-goes-doctor-global-hero/79772514.

21. Kenrya Rankin, "Black Lives Matter Partners with Reproductive Justice Groups to Fight for Black Women," *Colorlines* (February 9, 2016), www .colorlines.com/articles/black-lives-matter-partners-reproductive-justice-groups-fight-black-women. See also Ruha Benjamin's discussion of reproductive justice in "Black AfterLives Matter: Cultivating Kinfulness as Reproductive Justice," *Boston Review* (July 16, 2018), http://bostonreview .net/race/ruha-benjamin-black-afterlives-matter): "As reproductive justice advocates and analysts like Dorothy Roberts and Charis Thompson have long argued, water, food, education, and healthcare are *all* tools of reproduction, as they impact our life chances in profound and profoundly unequal ways."

22. For more on Cook, see E. Hoover, "Environmental Reproductive Justice: Intersections in an American Indian Community Impacted by Environmental Contamination," *Environmental Sociology* 4.1 (2018): 8–21. The two quotations are from Martine Lappé, Robbin Jeffries Hein, and Hannah Landecker's overview of environmental reproductive justice in "Environmental Politics of Reproduction," *Annual Review of Anthropology* 48 (2019), 6.

23. Sophie Lewis, *Full Surrogacy Now: Feminism Against Family* (London and New York: Verso, 2019), 26.

4 Narrating Animal Extinction from the Pleistocene to the Anthropocene

1. On the Pleistocene colonization, see Tom Dillehay, *The Settlement of the Americas: A New Prehistory* (New York: Basic, 2000); Daniel S. Amick, "Evolving Views on the Late Pleistocene Colonization of North America," *Quaternary International* 431 (2017): 125–51. For a summary account of the extinctions, see Paul S. Martin, *Twilight of the Mammoths: Ice Age Extinctions and the Rewilding of America* (Berkeley, CA: University of California Press, 2005), 10–11, 30–40. Recent reviews of research suggest that human causation was primary. See Anthony D. Barnosky et al., "Assessing the Causes of Late Pleistocene Extinctions on the Continents," *Science* 306 (2004): 70–75; Bernardo B.A. Araujo et al., "Bigger Kill than Chill: The Uneven Roles of Humans and Climate on the Late Quaternary Megafaunal Extinctions," *Quaternary International* 431 (2017): 216–222.

2. For cautious speculation on this possibility, see Roger Echo-Hawk, "Oral Traditions and Indian Origins: A Native American Perspective," in David Hurst Thomas, *Exploring Ancient Native America: An Archaeological Guide* (New York: Macmillan, 1994), 41–42; Echo-Hawk, "Ancient History in the New World: Integrating Oral Traditions and the Archaeological Record in Deep Time," *American Antiquity* 65.2 (April 2000): 267–290; Margaret Bruchac, "Earthshapers and Placemakers: Algonkian Indian Stories and the Landscape," in Claire Smith and H. Martin Wobst (eds.), *Indigenous Archaeologies: Decolonizing Theory and Practice* (New York: Routledge, 2005), 56–80.

3. The term, which alludes to the five mass extinctions that occurred in deep geological time, was apparently coined by Richard Leakey and Robert Lewin in *The Sixth Extinction: Patterns of Life and the Future of Humankind* (New York: Doubleday, 1995).

4. A United Nations-sponsored assessment of global biodiversity conducted by the Intergovernmental Science-Policy Platform on Biodiversity and Ecosystem Services (IPBES) found that around one million species are threatened, and named the causes in descending order as "(1) changes in land and sea use; (2) direct exploitation of organisms; (3) climate change; (4) pollution and (5) invasive alien species." IPBES media release (May 6, 2019), www.ipbes.net/ne ws/Media-Release-Global-Assessment.

5. On Cuvier's work in context, see Martin J.S. Rudwick, *Bursting the Limits of Time: The Reconstruction of Geohistory in the Age of Revolution* (Chicago, IL: University of Chicago Press, 2005), 246–275.

6. The Endangered Species Act was passed in 1973. For a detailed history of activism leading to the passage of the Act, see Mark Barrow, *Nature's Ghosts:*

Confronting Extinction from the Age of Jefferson to the Age of Ecology (Chicago, IL: University of Chicago Press, 2009).

7. So argues Dipesh Chakrabarty in "The Climate of History: Four Theses," *Critical Inquiry* 35 (2009): 197–222. Bruno Latour, in *We Have Never Been Modern* (Cambridge, MA: Harvard University Press, 1993), identifies the separation of nature from culture as modernity's defining operation. On the Enlightenment's will to domination, see Max Horkheimer and Theodore W. Adorno, *The Dialectic of Enlightenment: Philosophical Fragments* (Palo Alto, CA: Stanford University Press, 2002).

8. Timothy Morton, *Hyperobjects: Philosophy and Ecology after the End of the World* (Minneapolis, MN: University of Minnesota Press, 2013), 201.

9. Ibid., 198.

10. Anishinaabe writer Gerald Vizenor revitalized the archaic English word *survivance* in order to shift the understanding of indigenous American presence from mere survival to practices of renewal and continuity into the future. See Vizenor, *Manifest Manners: Postindian Warriors of Survivance* (Hanover, NH: Weslyan University Press, 1994); "Aesthetics of Survivance: Literary Theory and Practice," in Vizenor (ed.), *Survivance: Narratives of Native Presence* (Lincoln, NE: University of Nebraska Press, 2008), 1–23. Here I suggest that Vizenor's usage might be extended to include nonhumans.

11. Buffon's claim consolidated earlier, similar claims regarding climatic difference and sparked a debate that continued through the nineteenth century; see Antonello Gerbi, *The Dispute of the New World: The History of a Polemic, 1750–1900*, Jeremy Moyle (trans.) (Pittsburgh, PA: University of Pittsburgh Press, 1973). For some of what follows, I draw on Timothy Sweet, "The Eighteenth-Century *Archives du Monde*: The Question of Agency in Extinction Stories," in Jonathan Eburne and Judith Roof (eds.), *The Year's Work in the Oddball Archive* (Bloomington, IN: Indiana University Press, 2016), 219–45.

12. George-Louis Leclerc, le Comte de Buffon, *Natural History, General and Particular, by the Count de Buffon*, William Smellie (trans.) (London: Starhand and Cadell, 1791), vol. 5, 131, 137.

13. Remains of both mammoths (genus *Mammuthus*) and mastodons (genus *Mammut*) were found at Big Bone Lick, and it was some time before the genera were disaggregated. I will refer as Jefferson does to the mammoth as including both species.

14. Thomas Jefferson, *Notes on the State of Virginia*, Frank Shuffelton (ed.) (New York: Penguin, 1999), 51.

15. Ibid., 43, 44.

16. Ibid., 55.

17. On Jefferson's hopes for the Lewis and Clark expedition, see Paul Semonin, *American Monster: How the Nation's First Prehistoric Creature Became a Symbol of National Identity* (New York: New York University Press, 2000), 342–44.

18. Julian P. Boyd et al. (eds.), *Papers of Thomas Jefferson* (Princeton, NJ: Princeton University Press, 2002), vol. 29, 297.

19. I am suggesting here, as R. Clifton Spargo does regarding conventional elegy, that a sense of death's injustice forms the ethical basis of elegy's aesthetic reflection. See Spargo, *The Ethics of Mourning: Grief and Responsibility in Elegiac Literature* (Baltimore, MD: Johns Hopkins University Press, 2004).

20. Jefferson, Letter to John Adams, April 11, 1823, in Andrew A. Lipscomb and Albert Ellery Bergh (eds.), *The Writings of Thomas Jefferson* (Washington, DC: Jefferson Memorial Association, 1903), vol. 15, 427.

21. James Buchanan, *Sketches of the History, Manners, and Customs of the North American Indians* (London: Black, Young, and Young, 1824), 40–41.

22. Henry David Thoreau, *A Week on the Concord and Merrimack Rivers; Walden; Maine Woods; Cape Cod* (New York: Library of America, 1985), 712. See also George Catlin, *North American Indians*, Peter Matthiessen (ed.) (New York: Penguin, 1989), 262.

23. Joseph Nicolar, *The Life and Traditions of the Red Man*, Annette Kolodny (ed.) (Durham, NC: Duke University Press, 2007 [1893]), 116, 117–18.

24. Ibid., 119.

25. Ibid., 120.

26. Ibid., 113.

27. Martin, *Twilight of the Mammoths*, 193. On elephants, see 208–209. Gordon Sayre argues that Martin's proposal should be understood in a colonialist context in which mourning for extinct fauna echoes "America's imperial mourning over the vanishing Indian": Sayre, "The Mammoth: Endangered Species or Vanishing Race?" *Journal for Early Modern Cultural Studies* 1.1 (2001), 83. Others however have extended Martin's proposal for refaunation projects to Europe and other continents; for example, Jens-Christian Svenning, "Future Megafaunas: A Historical Perspective on a Wilder Anthropocene," in Anna Tsing et al. (eds.), *Arts of Living on a Damaged Planet* (Minneapolis, MN: University of Minnesota Press, 2017), G67–G86.

28. Charles Mann argues that human predation kept numbers low until the European incursion, which drastically reduced the indigenous human population, at which point the pigeon population increased, ostensibly from lack of predation. See Mann, *1491: New Revelations of the Americas Before Columbus* (New York: Vintage, 2006), 353–357. Some archaeological evidence however suggests a comparatively low population until about 900–1000 CE; see Mark Avery, *A Message from Martha: The Extinction of the*

Passenger Pigeon and Its Relevance Today (New York: Bloomsbury, 2014), 169–171. Other researchers have speculated that the dense forests of eastern North America, which offered an abundance of pigeons' favorite foods such as beechnuts and acorns, were the result of the extinction of Pleistocene Epoch herbivores, which kept forests in check and produced a more diverse landscape of savannah and woodland; see Svenning, "Future Megafaunas."

29. Aldo Leopold, *A Sand County Almanac* (New York: Oxford University Press, 1987 [1949]), 111.

30. Quoted in A.W. Schorger, *The Passenger Pigeon: Its Natural History and Extinction* (Madison, WI: University of Wisconsin Press, 1955), 6.

31. Flights were particularly understood as harbingers of illness, such as yellow fever; see ibid., 12–13.

32. John James Audubon, *Writings and Drawings* (New York: Library of America, 1999), 262.

33. Ibid., 263.

34. Simon Pokagon, "The Wild Pigeon of North America," in W.B. Mershon (ed.), *The Passenger Pigeon* (New York: Outing, 1907), 50.

35. James Fenimore Cooper, *The Pioneers* (New York: Penguin, 1988), 244. Audubon observed that because the migrations are not weather-driven but rather "are entirely owing to the necessity of procuring food," they "do not take place at any fixed period or season of the year," *Writings and Drawings*, 261.

36. Cooper, *Pioneers*, 250.

37. On the environmental implications of this episode, see Timothy Sweet, *American Georgics: Economy and Environment in Early American Literature* (Philadelphia, PA: University of Pennsylvania Press, 2002), 158, 160.

38. Cooper, *Pioneers*, 250.

39. Ibid., 248.

40. Ibid., 247.

41. Several states enacted protective legislation, albeit too late, while public opinion remained largely indifferent; see Schorger, *Passenger Pigeon*, 225–29. Barrow, *Nature's Ghosts*, 97–100, concentrates on hunting as a causal factor.

42. Audubon, *Writings and Drawings*, 267.

43. E.T. Martin, "The Pigeon Butcher's Defense," in Mershon (ed.), Passenger Pigeon, 103.

44. Pokagon, "Wild Pigeon," 54.

45. Gene Stratton-Porter, "The Last Passenger Pigeon," in Bill McKibben (ed.), *American Earth: Environmental Writing Since Thoreau* (New York: Library of America, 2008), 204.

46. For images of the mural, see www.artworkscincinnati.org/mural/martha-the-last-passenger-pigeon. Among recent memorials, a mixed-media work, "...

the sky is darkening ..." by Tuscarora artist Jolene Rickard, is worth remarking upon. This work, which juxtaposes beaded birds made by Haudenosaunee women, collected by the artist over fifty years, against a background photograph of taxidermy pigeons, was part of the exhibit "Hearts of Our People: Native Women Artists," on view at the Minneapolis Institute of Arts, June 2–August 19, 2019.

47. In addition to Avery, *Message from Martha*, see Errol Fuller, *The Passenger Pigeon* (Princeton, NJ: Princeton University Press, 2015); Joel Greenberg, *A Feathered River Across the Sky: The Passenger Pigeon's Flight to Extinction* (New York: Bloomsbury, 2014).

48. Leopold, *Sand County Almanac*, 110.

49. whatismissing.net. While elegy is the most common form of contemporary extinction discourse, other genres such as tragedy, comedy, epic, and encyclopedia are also available, as Ursula Heise demonstrates in *Imagining Extinction: The Cultural Meanings of Endangered Species* (Chicago, IL: University of Chicago Press, 2016).

50. For a history of the project, see Lindsey Davis, "Dematerializing the Memorial: An Interview with Maya Lin," *Art21* (September 28, 2017), magazine.art21.org/2017/09/28/dematerializing-the-memorial-an-interview-with-maya-lin/#.XUxiei2ZNBw.

51. www.whatismissing.net/#add-a-memory.

52. Amitav Ghosh's critique of the modern novel's focus on individual human agency concentrates on the novel's incapacity to deal with catastrophic climate events. Ghosh, *The Great Derangement: Climate Change and the Unthinkable* (Chicago, IL: University of Chicago Press, 2016), 1–84.

53. In 2020, the US Fish and Wildlife Service determined that an Endangered Species listing for the monarch "is warranted but precluded by work on higher-priority listing actions," www.fws.gov/savethemonarch/ssa.html. Its status will be reviewed annually.

54. For example, Patrick Murphy, "Pessimism, Optimism, Human Inertia, and Anthropogenic Climate Change," *Interdisciplinary Studies in Literature and Environment* 21.1 (2014): 149–163; Christopher Lloyd and Jessica Rapson, "'Family Territory' to the "Circumference of the Earth': Local and Planetary Memories of Climate Change in Barbara Kingsolver's *Flight Behaviour*," *Textual Practice* 31.5 (2017): 911–931.

55. Some eastern monarchs overwinter on the Texas Gulf coast. The western population overwinters on the California coast. The USFW status update map shows the populations' ranges: www.fws.gov/savethemonarch/pdfs/Monarch.pdf. Observations since 1998 can be tracked on *The Journey North* website: journeynorth.org/monarchs. On migration and overwintering biology, see

Karen Oberhauser and Michelle Solensky (eds.), *The Monarch Butterfly: Biology and Conservation* (Ithaca, NY: Cornell University Press, 2004), 79–196.

56. Barbara Kingsolver, *Flight Behavior* (New York: Harper Perennial, 2012), 365.

57. Karen Oberhauser, email to the author, April 23, 2019. Although a 2002 storm in Mexico destroyed large numbers, the surviving population returned that fall to their usual Mexican sites and have done so every year since. In spring 2019, they departed slightly early and were observed "behaving normally, dispersing and laying eggs."

58. Kingsolver, *Flight Behavior*, 421.

59. Ibid., 433.

60. Habitat loss includes forest loss in Mexico overwintering sites and loss of milkweed (for larvae) and nectar-bearing plants (for adults) throughout the US.

61. Donna Haraway, *Staying with the Trouble: Making Kin in the Chthulucene* (Durham, NC: Duke University Press, 2016), 141.

62. Ibid., 140.

63. Ibid., 148. Haraway uses *per* as the gender-neutral pronoun.

64. Ibid., 164.

65. See the evidence from radiocarbon dating, archaeological evidence, and Maori story in Atholl Anderson, *Prodigious Birds: Moas and Moa-Hunting in Prehistoric New Zealand* (Cambridge: Cambridge University Press, 1989), 171–187. Similarly, the thylacine became extinct in mainland Australia some 2,000 years ago, long prior to European contact, according to the International Union for Conservation of Nature's Red List of threatened species, www.iucnredlist.org/species/21866/21949291.

66. Barnosky et al., "Assessing the Causes"; Araujo et al., "Bigger Kill than Chill." Not enough data exists for Asia. The correlation is less robust for Europe until 10,000 years ago. The correlation does not hold for prehistoric Africa, where presumably the coevolution of hominids and megafauna sorted the matter long before the evolution of modern humans.

5 Pastoral Reborn in the Anthropocene: Henry David Thoreau to Kyle Powys Whyte

1. The elimination of humanities departments seems to be a world trend. For a broad overview see Ella Delany, "Humanities Studies under Strain around the Globe," *New York Times* (December 1, 2013), www.nytimes.com/2013/12/02/us/humanities-studies-under-strain-around-the-globe.html. For the latest cuts in the US, see Willard Dix, "It's Time to Worry When Colleges Erase Humanities Departments," *Forbes* (March 13, 2018), www.forbes.com/sites/willarddix/2018/03/13/its-time-to-worry-when-colleges-erase-humanities-depart

ments/; and Eric Kelderman, "Can Closing a Humanities College Save a University," *Chronicle of Higher Education* (April 13, 2018), www.chron icle.com/article/Can-Closing-a-Humanities/243113. For far deeper and across-the-board cuts in Japan, see Nash Jenkins, "Alarm over Huge Cuts to Humanities and Social Sciences," *Time* (September 16, 2015), time.com/ 4035819/japan-university-liberal-arts-humanities-social-sciences-cuts/.

2. William Empson, *Some Versions of Pastoral* (New York: New Directions, 1974), 3.

3. Ibid., 19, 22.

4. Raymond Williams, "Pastoral and Counter-Pastoral," in *The Country and the City* (New York: Oxford University Press, 1973), 18, 20.

5. Ibid.

6. Ibid., 32.

7. Paul Alpers, *What Is Pastoral?* (Chicago, IL: University of Chicago Press, 1993), 93.

8. Ibid., 92.

9. Leo Marx, "Does Pastoral Have a Future?" in John Dixon Hunt (ed.), *The Pastoral Landscape* (Washington, DC: National Gallery of Art, 1992), 210.

10. Lawrence Buell, *The Environmental Imagination* (Cambridge: Harvard University Press, 1995), 32.

11. Kenneth Hiltner, *What Else Is Pastoral?* (Ithaca, NY: Cornell University Press, 2011), 7.

12. Seamus Heaney, "Eclogues 'In Extremis': On the Staying Power of Pastoral," *Proceedings of the Royal Irish Academy* 103C.1 (2003): 3, 11, 9.

13. Terry Gifford, "Post-Pastoral as a Tool for Ecocriticism," in Mathilde Skoie and Sonia Bjornstad Velazquez (eds.), *Pastoral and the Humanities* (Exeter: Bristol Phoenix Press, 2006), 15.

14. Henry D. Thoreau, *Walden*, Lyndon Shanley (ed.) (Princeton, NJ: Princeton University Press, 1971), 17.

15. To B.B. Wiley, April 26, 1857, F. B. Sanborn (ed.), *The Writings of Henry David Thoreau, vol. 6, Familiar Letters* (Boston, MA: Houghton Mifflin, 1906), 301–302.

16. Stanley Cavell, *The Senses of Walden: An Expanded Edition* (Chicago, IL: University of Chicago Press, 1992), 19–20.

17. Jeremiah 9:10.

18. According to the Oxford English Dictionary, the adjective, "extinct," referring to "that has died out or come to an end," first appeared in 1581. The word "extinction" appeared shortly thereafter, in 1602.

19. Charles Darwin, *The Origin of Species* (New York: New American Library, 1958), 108–109.

20. Ibid.

21. *The Journals of Henry David Thoreau*, Bradford Torrey and Francis Allen (eds.), 14 vols. (Boston, MA: Houghton Mifflin, 1908), vol. 8, 221.

22. Henry David Thoreau, *The Maine Woods* (New York: Penguin, 1988), 6.

23. Washington Irving, "Traits of Indian Character," in *The Sketch Book* (New York: Signet, 1961 [1820]), 273.

24. Ibid., 280–281.

25. Ibid., 282.

26. Ibid.

27. Herman Melville, *Moby-Dick* (New York: Signet Classics, 1998 [1851]), 82.

28. Ibid., 93.

29. Ibid., 280.

30. Ibid., 535.

31. The Epilogue was added only after English reviewers raised the reasonable objection that, if everyone had perished, as was the case in the English edition, no one should have been left to tell the story.

32. Richard Fleck (ed.), *The Indians of Thoreau: Selections from the Indian Notebooks* (Albuquerque, NM: Hummingbird Press, 1974), 174.

33. Robert Sattelmeyer, *Thoreau's Reading: A Study in Intellectual History with Bibliographical Catalogue* (Princeton, NJ: Princeton University Press, 1988), 107.

34. Fleck, *The Indians of Thoreau*, 185.

35. Joe Leydon, Sundance Film Review, "Rumble: The Indians Who Rocked the World," *Variety* (January 23, 2017), variety.com/2017/film/reviews/rumble-the-indians-who-rocked-the-world-review-1201966605/.

36. Videos of NMAI performances, www.si.edu/spotlight/native-american-music/videos-of-nmai-performances.

37. John Nichols, "No Native American Woman Had Ever Been Elected to Congress – Until Last Year," *Nation* (August 6, 2019), www.thenation.com/p odcast/deb-haaland-next-left/. Both Deb Haaland, a member of the Pueblo of Laguna, and Sharice Davids, a member of the Ho-Chunk nation, were elected in 2018 to the House of Representatives. For the growing importance of the Native American vote, see Delilah Fiedler, "The Rise of the Native American Electorate," *Mother Jones* (August 27, 2019), www.motherjones.com/politics/2 019/08/the-rise-of-the-native-american-electorate/.

38. MIT Indigenous Languages Initiative, linguistics.mit.edu/mitili/.

39. "Native American Language Program offers 8 Indigenous Languages," ygsna.sites.yale.edu/news/native-american-language-program-offers -8-indigenous-languages-spring-2016–0. This program Offers classes conducted via Skype with Cherokee, Choctaw, and Mohawk speakers in Oklahoma and Canada.

40. American Indian Studies Research Institute, https://aisri.indiana.edu. In this context, see also the work of the National Breath of Life Archival Institute for Indigenous Languages, at nationalbreathoflife.org.

41. Standing Rock Lakota/Dakota Language Project, humanitiesforall.org/ projects/standing-rock-lakota-dakota-language-project.

42. Kyle Powys Whyte, "Justice Forward: Tribes, Climate Adaptation and Responsibility," *Climate Change* 120 (March 2013): 517–530, 518; see also Whyte, "Indigenous Climate Change Studies: Indigenizing Futures, Decolonizing the Anthropocene," *English Language Notes* 55 (Fall 2017): 153–162; Whyte, "Indigenous Science (Fiction) for the Anthropocene: Ancestral Dystopias and Fantasies of Climate Change Crises," *Environment and Planning* (March 30, 2018), https://doi.org/10.1177/2514848618777621.

43. Tracey Osborne, "Native Americans Fighting Fossil Fuels," *Scientific American* (April 9, 2018), blogs.scientificamerican.com/voices/native-americans-fighting-fossil-fuels.

44. Hari M. Osofsky, "Climate Change and Dispute Resolution Processes," in Rosemary Gail Rayfuse and Shirley V. Scott (eds.), *International Law in the Era of Climate Change* (Cheltenham: Edward Elgar Publishing, 2012), 353.

45. "Dakota Access Pipeline, What to Know about the Controversy," *Time* (October 26, 2017), time.com/4548566/dakota-access-pipeline-standing-rock-sioux.

46. Matt Egan, "Dakota Access Pipeline Suffers a Minor Leak in April," *CNN Money* (May 10, 2017), money.cnn.com/2017/05/10/investing/dakota-access-pipeline-oil-spill/index.html.

47. Lisa Friedman, "Standing Rock Sioux Tribes Wins a Victory Against the Dakota Access Pipeline," *New York Times* (March 25, 2020), www.nytimes .com/2020/03/25/climate/dakota-access-pipeline-sioux.html.
For the most recent development, see "Dakota Access Pipeline Faces Renewed Legal Bid for Shutdown," *Bloomberg Law* (September 8, 2020), https://news .bloomberglaw.com/environment-and-energy/dakota-access-pipeline-faces-r enewed-legal-bid-for-shutdown.

48. Bill McKibben, "Anti-Pipeline Activists Are Fighting to Stop Line 3. Will They Succeed?" *The Guardian* (June 27, 2018), www.theguardian.com/environment/ commentisfree/2018/jun/27/anti-pipeline-activists-fighting-to-stop-line-3.

6 The Heat of Modernity: *The Great Gatsby* as Petrofiction

1. F. Scott Fitzgerald, *The Great Gatsby* (New York: Scribners and Sons, 1953 [1925]), 105.

2. Ibid., 28, 53, 78, 108.

3. Ibid., 54.

4. To the best of my knowledge, no one has read *The Great Gatsby* as petrofiction. I was inspired to think about oil and the novel during a conversation with Paul Schmidt, doctoral candidate in English at the University of Iowa. During his comprehensive exams, Paul pointed out that the telegraph wires integral to Gatsby's illicit business would have been made out of copper, the very mineral mined by Dan Cody. Thanks to Paul's insightful comment, I began to ponder resource extraction in Fitzgerald's novel. I have also benefited from those critics who have either emphasized Fitzgerald's interest in the Teapot Dome Scandal or examined his relationship to contemporary car culture. For the former, see John H. Randall III, "Jay Gatsby's Hidden Source of Wealth," *Modern Fiction Studies* 13.2 (Summer 1967): 247–257. Randall briefly discusses two citations of oil in the novel (253). For the latter, see Yasuhiro Takeuchi, "Gatsby's Green Light as a Traffic Signal: F. Scott Fitzgerald's Motive Force," *The F. Scott Fitzgerald Review* 14.1 (2016): 198–214; Sarah Churchwell, *Careless People: Murder, Mayhem, and the Invention of the Great Gatsby* (New York: Random House, 2013), 103–106; Peter L. Hays, "Class Differences in Fitzgerald's Works" in Bryant Mangum (ed.), *F. Scott Fitzgerald in Context* (New York: Cambridge University Press, 2013), 221–223; and Leo Marx, *The Machine in the Garden: Technology and the Pastoral Idea in America* (New York: Oxford University Press, 1964), 356–262.

5. Joshua Schuster, "Where Is the Oil in Modernism?" in Imre Szeman and Sheena Wilson (eds.), *Petrocultures: Oil, Energy, Culture* (Montreal: McGill-Queen's University Press, 2017), 204–205.

6. Stephanie LeMenager, *Living Oil: Petroleum Culture in the American Century* (New York: Oxford University Press, 2014), 3.

7. Peter Hitchcock, "Oil in an American Imaginary," *New Formations* 69.4 (2010): 81.

8. Fitzgerald, *The Great Gatsby*, 91.

9. Patricia Yaeger, "Literature in the Ages of Wood, Tallow, Coal, Whale Oil, Gasoline, Atomic Power, and Other Energy Sources," *PMLA* 126.2 (March 2011): 305–326.

10. See Jamie Jones, "Oceans of Oil: Moby-Dick, Energy, and the Environmental Humanities," lecture at the University of Illinois Urbana, January 29, 2020; and Heidi C.M. Scott, *Fuel: An Ecocritical History* (New York: Bloomsbury, 2020).

11. For an important reading of early twentieth-century automotive culture, see Cotten Seiler, *A Republic of Drivers: A Cultural History of Automobility in America* (Chicago, IL: University of Chicago Press, 2009).

12. Hitchcock, "Oil in an American Imaginary," 90. Like Hitchcock, I owe a major debt to Amitav Ghosh's brilliant essay, "Petrofiction," *New Republic* (March 2 1992): 29–34.

13. I take my knowledge of this resource scandal from Laton McCartney, *The Teapot Dome Scandal: How Big Oil Bought the Harding White House and Tried to Steal the Country* (New York: Random House, 2008). For a contemporary account that Fitzgerald may have known, see Marcus Eli Ravage, *The Story of Teapot Dome* (New York: Republic Publishing Company, 1924).

14. In 1924, "the oil scandals were … spread across the front pages of the newspapers," writes Frederick Lewis Allen. See Allen, *Only Yesterday: An Informal History of the 1920's* (New York: Wiley, 2015 [1942]), 116. Allen goes on to argue that the initial furor over oil corruption soon gave way to an overwhelming desire to bury the matter and reaffirm the status quo.

15. Quoted in William Grimes, "There Will Be Scandal: An Oil Stain on the Jazz Age," *New York Times* (February 13, 2000).

16. Fitzgerald, *The Great Gatsby*, 16, 12. It's worth noting that Fitzgerald based the character of Tom Buchanan on William H. Mitchell, a wealthy Chicagoan who later became a director of Texaco, Inc.

17. Fitzgerald, *The Great Gatsby*, 92.

18. Ibid., 108. The linkage of Gatsby's illicit activities to "gas" here may signify in more specific terms. Pointing to Tom Buchanan's assertion that Gatsby has "got something on now" that their common acquaintance Walter is "afraid" to talk about, John H. Randall III has argued that this may be read as a reference to the Teapot Dome Scandal itself (119). See "Jay Gatsby's Hidden Source of Wealth," 250.

19. Fitzgerald, *The Cruise of the Rolling Junk* (London: Hesperus, 2011 [1924]), 59.

20. Ibid., 79.

21. In a projected longer version of this chapter, I plan to address the way in which Fitzgerald enacts this abandonment of civilization by turning to racist discourse while searching for gasoline in the Virginia town.

22. Fitzgerald, *The Great Gatsby*, 60.

23. Ibid., 63, 158.

24. Ibid., 57.

25. Ibid., 82.

26. Ibid., 82. LeMenager, *Living Oil*, 4.

27. Fitzgerald, *The Great Gatsby*, 64.

28. Ibid., 8.

29. For an interesting account of the seismograph's role in earthquake prediction, warfare, and oil speculation, see Daniel Yergin, *The Prize: The Epic Quest for Oil, Money, and Power* (New York: Simon & Schuster, 1990).

30. Indeed, we may speculate that Nick's comment about "the foul dust that floated in the wake of [Gatsby's] dreams" constitutes an inadvertent allusion to the pollution that necessarily followed oil drilling and other forms of resource extraction (8). For an important account of how the contemporary

petroleum industry despoiled one metropole, see Nancy Quam-Wickham, "'Cities Sacrificed on the Altar of Oil': Popular Opposition to Oil Development in 1920s Los Angeles," *Environmental History* 3.2 (April 1998): 189–209.

31. As Chakrabarty elaborates, "Most of our freedoms so far have been energy-intensive": "The Climate of History: Four Theses," *Critical Inquiry* 35.2 (Winter 2009), 208.

32. Fitzgerald, *The Great Gatsby*, 89.

33. Quoted in Michael Watts, "Petro-Violence: Community, Extraction, and Political Ecology of a Mythic Commodity," in Nancy L. Peluso and Michael Watts (eds.), *Violent Environments* (Ithaca, NY and London: Cornell University Press, 2001), 189, 212.

34. Fitzgerald, *The Great Gatsby*, 99.

35. Ibid., 23.

36. Ibid., 23–24.

37. Ibid., 24.

38. Ibid.

39. Ibid., 119.

40. Ibid., 158.

41. Yaeger, "Literature in the Ages," 309.

42. Fitzgerald, *The Great Gatsby*, 71, 55, 122.

43. Even as Tom's boast about making a stable out of a garage may suggest patrician hostility to oil culture, it's important to recognize that this Luddite perspective is itself dependent on a privileged relationship to energy modernity (106).

44. Ibid., 25.

45. Ibid.

46. Ibid., 26.

47. Ibid.

48. The pivotal role of Wilson's garage in the narrative links *The Great Gatsby* to a subgenre of American fiction and film we might call *petro-noir*. Relevant texts include *Sanctuary* (novel, 1931), *The Postman Always Rings Twice* (novel, 1934; film, 1946), and *Out of the Past* (film, 1947).

49. Fitzgerald, *The Great Gatsby*, 27.

50. Ibid.

51. Ibid., 63.

52. See John A. Jakle and Keith A. Sculle, *The Gas Station in America* (Baltimore, MD: Johns Hopkins University Press, 1994).

53. Of course, drilling for oil also relied on labor.

54. Fitzgerald, *The Great Gatsby*, 122.

55. Upton Sinclair, *Oil!* (New York: Penguin, 2007 [1926]), 25.

56. *Time Magazine* (May 11, 1925), 14.
57. Fitzgerald, *The Great Gatsby*, 109.
58. Ibid., 27, 26, 27.
59. Ibid., 109.
60. Ibid., 121.
61. Ibid., 27.
62. Ibid., 110.
63. Ibid., 34.
64. Ibid., 122.
65. Ibid., 141.
66. Ibid.
67. Ibid.
68. This is a revision of Leo Marx's point that "the car proves to be a murder weapon and the instrument of Gatsby's undoing" (*Machine in the Garden*, 358). In *Gatsby*, I would argue, the machine in the garden is also the petroleum in the garden.
69. Edward Said, *Culture and Imperialism* (New York: Vintage, 1994), 188.
70. Ibid.
71. Enda Duffy, *The Speed Handbook: Velocity, Pleasure, Modernism* (Durham, NC: Duke University Press, 2009), 9.
72. To put it another way, "geomodernism" sometimes also signified as *extraction* modernism. For a discussion of the term "geomodernism," see Laura Doyle and Laura Winkiel, "The Global Horizons of Modernism," in *Geomodernisms: Race, Modernism, Modernity* (Bloomington, IN: Indiana University Press, 2005), 1–16.
73. Fitzgerald, *The Great Gatsby*, 89.
74. Ibid., 143, 159, 25.

7 Children in Transit / Children in Peril: The Contemporary US Novel in a Time of Climate Crisis

1. For more information about Alan Kurdi, see Tima Kurdi, *The Boy on the Beach: My Family's Escape from Syria and Our Hope for a New Home* (New York: Simon & Schuster, 2018).
2. Lee Edelman, *No Future: Queer Theory and the Death Drive* (Durham, NC: Duke University Press, 2004), 3.
3. Ibid., 11.
4. Natalia Cecire, "Environmental Innocence and Slow Violence," *WSQ: Women Studies Quarterly* 43.1&2 (2015): 169.
5. Christina Sharpe, *In the Wake: On Blackness and Being* (Durham, NC: Duke University Press, 2016), 80.
6. Jacqueline Bhabha, *Child Migration and Human Rights in a Global Age* (Princeton, NJ: Princeton University Press, 2014), 13.

7. Colin Kelley, Shahrzad Mohtadi, Mark Cane, Richard Seager, and Yochanan Kushnir, "Climate Change in the Fertile Crescent and Implications of the Recent Syrian Drought," *PNAS* 112.11 (2015): 3241.

8. Jonathan Blitzer, "How Climate Change Is Fueling the U.S. Border Crisis," *The New Yorker* (April 3, 2019), www.newyorker.com/news/dispatch/how-climate-change-is-fuelling-the-us-border-crisis.

9. Rebecca Evans, "Fantastic Futures? Cli-Fi, Climate Justice, and Queer Futurity," *Resilience* 4.2&3 (2017): 105.

10. Rebekah Sheldon, *The Child to Come: Life after the Human Catastrophe* (Minneapolis, MN: University of Minnesota Press, 2016), 3.

11. Michael Chabon, *Maps and Legends: Reading and Writing Along the Borderlands* (San Francisco, CA: McSweeney's Books, 2008), 120.

12. John Hillcoat (dir.), *The Road* (Dimension Films, 2009).

13. Cecire, "Environmental Innocence," 169. Also see James Kincaid, *Erotic Innocence: The Culture of Child Molesting* (Durham, NC: Duke University Press, 1998) and Robin Bernstein, *Racial Innocence: Performing American Childhood and Race from Slavery to Civil Rights* (New York: New York University Press, 2011).

14. Cormac McCarthy, *The Road* (New York: Vintage, 2006), 255.

15. Ibid., 257.

16. Ibid., 256.

17. Ibid., 153–154.

18. Cherie Dimaline, *The Marrow Thieves* (Toronto: DCB, 2017), 24.

19. Ibid., 54.

20. Ibid., 86.

21. Ibid., 108.

22. McCarthy, *The Road*, 279.

23. Adeline Johns-Putra, *Climate Change and the Contemporary Novel* (Cambridge: Cambridge University Press, 2019), 68.

24. McCarthy, *The Road*, 277.

25. Dimaline, *The Marrow Thieves*, 231.

26. Ibid., 153.

27. McCarthy, *The Road*, 287.

28. Ibid., 74.

8 Meta-Critical Climate Change Fiction: Claire Vaye Watkins's *Gold Fame Citrus*

1. Rebecca Evans, "Fantastic Futures? Cli-Fi, Climate Justice, and Queer Futurity," *Resilience: A Journal of the Environmental Humanities* 4.2–3 (2017): 99.

2. Andreas Malm, *The Progress of This Storm: Nature and Society in a Warming World* (New York: Verso, 2018), 89.

3. See Timothy Clark, *Ecocriticism on the Edge: The Anthropocene as a Threshold Concept* (New York: Bloomsbury Academic, 2015), 59, 80, 103, 181–182, and Tom Cohen (ed.), "Introduction: Murmurations – 'Climate Change' and the Defacement of Theory," *Telemorphosis: Theory in the Era of Climate Change* (Ann Arbor, University of Michigan Library, MI: Open Humanities Press, 2012), vol. 1, 13–42.

4. See, for example, Adeline Johns-Putra, "'My Job Is to Take Care of You': Climate Change, Humanity, and Cormac McCarthy's *The Road*," *Modern Fiction Studies* 62.3 (2016): 519–540.

5. Lee Edelman, *No Future: Queer Theory and the Death Drive* (Durham, NC: Duke University Press, 2004).

6. Ibid., 12.

7. Claire Vaye Watkins, *Gold Fame Citrus* (New York: Riverhead Books, 2015), 11–12.

8. J. Heather Hicks, "'Smoke Follows Beauty': The Femme Fatale and the Logic of Apocalyptic Affiliation in Claire Vaye Watkins's *Gold Fame Citrus*," *ASAP/Journal* 3.3: 626.

9. Watkins, *Gold Fame Citrus*, 5, 8.

10. Marc Reisner, *Cadillac Desert: The American West and Its Disappearing Water* (New York: Penguin Books, 1993).

11. Hicks, "Smoke Follows Beauty."

12. Watkins, *Gold Fame Citrus*, 77.

13. Hicks, "Smoke Follows Beauty," 626–627, 640.

14. Ibid., 7.

15. Ibid., 333.

16. Rebekah Sheldon, *The Child to Come: Life After Human Catastrophe* (Minneapolis, MN: University of Minnesota Press, 2016), 3–4.

17. Ibid., 20.

18. Ibid., 17, 5.

19. Kath Weston, *Animate Planet: Making Visceral Sense of Living in a High-Tech, Ecologically Damaged World* (Durham, NC: Duke University Press, 2017), 4, 31, 7–8, 21.

20. Sheldon, *The Child to Come*, 118–220, 20.

21. Ibid., 5–6.

22. Watkins, *Gold Fame Citrus*, 232.

23. Ibid., 339.

24. Ibid., 85.

25. Ibid., 118.

26. Ibid., 85.

27. Ibid., 124.

28. Stacy Alaimo, *Bodily Natures: Science, Environment, and the Material Self* (Bloomington, IN: Indiana University Press, 2010), 2.
29. Watkins, *Gold Fame Citrus*, 4.
30. Ibid., 124–125.
31. Ibid., 153.
32. Ibid., 184–185.
33. Ibid., 193–200.
34. Ibid., 202.
35. Ibid., 284.
36. Jane Bennett, *Vibrant Matter: A Political Ecology of Things* (Durham, NC: Duke University Press, 2009),viii–ix.
37. Ibid., xvii.
38. Ibid., xviii, 23–24.
39. Ibid., 37.
40. Ibid., 117.
41. David Farrier, *Anthropocene Poetics: Deep Time, Sacrifice Zones, and Extinction* (Minneapolis, MN: University of Minnesota Press, 2019), 17.
42. Thomas Lemke, "An Alternative Model of Politics? Prospects and Problems of Jane Bennett's *Vital Materialism*," *Theory, Culture & Society* 35.6 (2018): 42.
43. Ibid., 45.
44. Ibid., 41–42.
45. Watkins, *Gold Fame Citrus*, 117.
46. Ibid., 120.
47. Ibid.
48. Ibid., 252.
49. Ibid., 72, 252, 207.
50. Ibid., 254.
51. John Beck, *Dirty Wars: Landscape, Power, and Waste in Western American Literature* (Lincoln, NE: University of Nebraska Press, 2009), 26, 41.
52. Ibid., 20–22.
53. Ibid., 22–23, 28–29, 34–35.
54. Watkins, *Gold Fame Citrus*, 114–117.
55. Ibid., 117.
56. Jan Zalasiewicz, Colin N. Waters, Colin P. Summerhayes, Alexander P. Wolfe, Anthony D. Barnosky, Alejandro Cearreta, Paul Crutzen, et al. "The Working Group on the Anthropocene: Summary of Evidence and Interim Recommendations," *Anthropocene* 19 (2017): 55–60.
57. Watkins, *Gold Fame Citrus*, 113–114.
58. Derek Woods, "Scale Critique for the Anthropocene," *The Minnesota Review* 83 (2014): 137.
59. Clark, *Ecocriticism on the Edge*, 23, 149.

60. Watkins, *Gold Fame Citrus*, 113–114.

61. See Woods, "Scale Critique," 138.

62. Farrier, *Anthropocene Poetics*, 6–8.

63. Watkins, *Gold Fame Citrus*, 153–154.

64. Farrier, *Anthropocene Poetics*, 22.

65. See EPA, "What Is the Yucca Mountain Repository?" www.epa.gov/radi ation/what-yucca-mountain-repository.

66. Sandia National Laboratories, "Expert Judgment on Markers to Deter Inadvertent Human Intrusion into the Waste Isolation Pilot Plant" (1993), prod-ng.sandia.gov/techlib-noauth/access-control.cgi/1992/921382.pdf.

67. Watkins, *Gold Fame Citrus*, 220–223.

68. Rob Nixon, *Slow Violence and the Environmentalism of the Poor* (Cambridge, MA: Harvard University Press, 2013), 2, 6.

69. Watkins, *Gold Fame Citrus*, 222.

70. Ibid., 219–223.

71. Ibid., 224.

72. See e.g., Western Shoshone, Submission to the United Nations Periodic Review ICCPR (January 14, 2019), https://static1.1.sqspcdn.com/static/f/356 082/28091890/1551972983713/1+14+19+UN_CERD_ICCPR_1-14-2019.pdf?to ken=LZCGk%2FP4ebCcAmk%2B5begIQobBwk%3D; and John Sadler, "Native American Tribe Claims Nuclear Waste Can't Be Stored on Its Land," *Las Vegas Sun* (August 15, 2019), https://lasvegassun.com/news/2019/aug/15/nati ve-american-tribe-claims-nuclear-waste-cant-be/.

73. Ibid.

74. Kathryn Yusoff, *A Billion Black Anthropocenes or None* (Minneapolis, MN: University of Minnesota Press, 2019).

75. Ibid., 51.

9 *Junk* Food for Thought: Decolonizing Diets in Tommy Pico's Poetry

1. March 5, 2020 visit to California State University, Fullerton.

2. Tommy Pico, Twitter (n.d.), https://twitter.com/heyteebs/status/59815988259 7048320. Accessed June 24, 2019.

3. Tommy Pico, *Junk* (New York: Tin House Books, 2018), 58.

4. Tommy Pico, *Nature Poem* (New York: Tin House Books, 2017), 2.

5. For a brief etymology of "treehugger," see Braxton Bridgers, "#CCRewind: What It Means to Be Called a Tree Hugger" (June 19, 2018), www.newamerica.org/mi llennials/dm/ccrewind-what-it-means-be-called-tree-hugger/.

6. Jean-Thomas Tremblay, "On Queer Ecopoetics and the Natures We Cannot Disavow," *Dispatches from the Poetry Wars* (April 30. 2020), www.dispatchespoetrywars.com/commentary/on-queer-ecopoetics-and-the-natures-we-cannot-disavow.

7. Jacqueline Ardam, "Canoodling with Junk Food: On Tommy Pico's 'Junk,'" *Los Angeles Review of Books* (May 10, 2018), lareviewofbooks.org/article/canoodling-with-junk-food-on-tommy-picos-junk.

8. *IRL* and *Nature Poem* also contain allusions to Ammons's *Garbage*. While *IRL* and *Nature* also reference food, and fast/junk food in particular, they do so rather sparingly compared to *Junk*'s sustained attention.

9. Mishuana Goeman, "Indigenous Interventions and Feminist Methods," in Chris Anderson and Jean M. O'Brien (eds.), *Sources and Methods in Indigenous Studies* (New York: Routledge, 2016), 191.

10. Kyle Powys White, "What Do Indigenous Knowledges Do for Indigenous Peoples?" in Melissa K. Nelson and Daniel Shilling (eds.), *Traditional Ecological Knowledge: Learning from Indigenous Practices for Environmental Sustainability* (Cambridge: Cambridge University Press, 2018), 59.

11. Luz Calvo and Catriona Rueda Esquibel, *Decolonize Your Diet* (Vancouver: Arsenal Pulp Press, 2015), 22.

12. White, "What Do Indigenous Knowledges Do," 70–71.

13. Jen Miller, "Frybread," *Smithsonian Magazine* (July 2008), www.smithsonianmag.com/arts-culture/frybread-79191.

14. Ibid.

15. Considering a different geographical location in the so-called Americas, Calvo and Rueda Esquibel report that "foods, such as amaranth in Mesoamerica and quinoa in the Andes, were outlawed because of their use in indigenous religious ceremonies," *Decolonize Your Diet*, 23.

16. Bryant Terry, "Foreword," in ibid., 9.

17. See Nicole Seymour, *Bad Environmentalism: Irony and Irreverence in the Ecological Age* (Minneapolis, MN: University of Minnesota Press, 2018), especially 152–153.

18. Kimberly TallBear, "Shepard Krech's *The Ecological Indian*: One Indian's Perspective," *The Ecological Indian Review*, International Institute for Indigenous Resource Management (September 2000), iiirm.org/publications/Book%20Reviews/Reviews/Krech001.pdf, 2.

19. Sarah Jaquette Ray, *The Ecological Other: Environmental Exclusion in American Culture* (Tucson, AZ: University of Arizona Press, 2013), 85.

20. www.maskmagazine.com/the-dropout-issue/work/tommy-pico. Accessed April 17, 2018.

21. Sherman Alexie, *Face* (New York: Hanging Loose Press, 1996), 116.

22. Kyle Bladow, "Pitching Camp in the City: Tommy Pico's Recalcitrant Ecopoetics." Paper presented at the Native American and Indigenous Studies Association Annual Conference, May 19, 2018, InterContinental Hotel, Los Angeles, CA.

23. Seymour, *Bad Environmentalism*, 166.

24. Pico, *Nature Poem*, 67.

25. Hannah Burdette, *Revealing Rebellion in Abiayala: The Insurgent Poetics of Contemporary Indigenous Literature* (Tucson, AZ: University of Arizona Press, 2019), 131.

26. I wrote about this situation for *Edge Effects* digital magazine, as someone who cited Alexie fairly extensively in a book that was going to press just as these accusations came to light. See Seymour, "Citation in the #MeToo Era," *Edge Effects* (September 11, 2018), edgeeffects.net/metoo-era-citation.

27. To offer just one example: Teebs recalls of a former boyfriend, "The first charming thing / you said to me was that when you walk behind a woman at / night you walk slower farther away so she doesn't think yr / tryin to run up on her," *Junk*, 45.

28. The wave to which I'm referring arguably includes Pico as well as Billy Ray Belcourt (Driftpile Cree Nation), Terese Mailhot (Seabird Island), Tommy Orange (Cheyenne and Arapaho), Arielle Twist (Cree), Joshua Whitehead (Oji-Cree), and more. Many of these writers attended the Institute of American Indian Arts, an institution that Mailhot has described as shaping a new Indigenous literary "renaissance": Mailhot, *Heart Berries* (Berkeley, CA: Counterpoint Press, 2018), 58.

29. My colleague Salma Monani and I recently published a related piece that extends these ideas. See Monani and Seymour, "How Wendy Red Star Decolonizes the Museum with Humor and Play," *Edge Effects* (September 30, 2020), https://ed geeffects.net/wendy-red-star/edgeeffects.net/wendy-red-star/

30. The Little Big Horn College Library reports that "[t]he Crow call this dance the Hot Dance, because when they received it they were instructed not to eat as poor people. That is, to eat well, to eat fresh hot meat. The Crow therefore called it Baatawéelissuua, the Hot Dance." See also Jonathan Holmes, "Ponca Hethuska Society" (July 31, 2012), www.powwows.com/ponca-hethuska-society.

31. Ashley Stull Myers, "Interview with Wendy Red Star," *Daily Serving* (March 14, 2017), www.dailyserving.com/2017/03/interview-with-wendy-red-star.

32. Pico, *Junk*, 7.

33. Ibid., 16.

34. Ibid., 23.

35. Ibid., 44.

36. Ibid., 29.

37. Ibid., 10.
38. Ibid., 45.
39. Salma Monani, *Indigenous Ecocinema: Decolonizing Media Landscapes* (Morgantown, WV: West Virginia University Press, forthcoming).
40. US Department of Health and Human Services Department of Minority Health, "Obesity and American Indians/Alaska Natives," minorityhealth. hhs.gov/omh/browse.aspx?lvl=4&lvlid=40. Accessed August 18, 2021.
41. Elizabeth Hoover and Devon A. Mihesuah, "Introduction," in *Indigenous Food Sovereignty in the United States: Restoring Cultural Knowledge, Protecting Environments, and Regaining Health* (Norman, OK: University of Oklahoma Press, 2019), 4. Mihesuah is a foundational figure in the concept and practice of dietary decolonization; see her cookbook, *Recovering Our Ancestors' Gardens: Indigenous Recipes and Guide to Diet and Fitness* (Lincoln, NE: University of Nebraska Press, 2005).
42. Scott Beattie, "Bear Arts Naked: Queer Activism and the Fat Male Body," in Cat Pausé, Jackie Wykes, and Samantha Murray (eds.), *Queering Fat Embodiment* (Farnham, Surrey: Ashgate, 2014), 123; Patrick Giles, "A Matter of Size," in Dawn Atkins (ed.), *Looking Queer: Body Image and Identity in Lesbian, Bisexual, Gay and Transgender Communities* (New York: Harrington Park Press, 1998), 355–357. See also Gioncarlo Valentine, "Fatima Jamal's New Documentary Celebrates Being Fat, Black, and Trans" (March 20, 2018), www.them.us/story/jamal-lewis-new-documentary-celebrates-being-fat-black-and-trans.
43. Jeffry J. Iovannone, "Toxic Gay Masculinity in Hulu's Shrill," *Medium* (April 9, 2019), medium.com/th-ink/toxic-gay-masculinity-in-hulus-shrill-aac5b4f48ad5. Lindy West published her perspective here: West, "Hello, I Am Fat," *The Stranger* (February 11, 2011), www.thestranger.com/slog/archives/2011/02/11/hello-i-am-fat. The fact that Patrick Giles first published on gay male fatphobia over twenty years before the West–Savage battle took place suggests just how entrenched these attitudes are.
44. Pico, *Junk*, 11.
45. Phillip Joy and Matthew Numer, "Constituting the Ideal Body: A Poststructural Analysis of 'Obesity' Discourses among Gay Men," *Journal of Critical Dietetics* 4.1 (2018): 55.
46. Lucas Crawford, "Slender Trouble," *GLQ* 23.4 (2017): 447.
47. Ibid., 450.
48. See Olivia Petter, "The Truth about What Soya Does to Men's Bodies," *Independent* (June 12, 2018), www.independent.co.uk/life-style/health-and-families/soya-male-body-health-side-effects-truth-milk-sexual-function-a8382976.html.
49. Elspeth Probyn, *Carnal Appetites: FoodSexIdentities* (New York: Routledge, 2000), 59.

50. Ibid., 69.

51. Ibid., 9, 128.

52. Pico, *Junk*, 1.

53. Ibid.

54. Qwo-Li Driskill, Chris Finley, Brian Joseph Gilley, and Scott Lauria Morgensen (eds.), *Queer Indigenous Studies: Critical Interventions in Theory, Politics, and Literature* (Tucson, AZ: University of Arizona Press, 2011), 3.

55. Pico, *Junk*, 21, 25, 40, 54, etc.

56. Mark Rifkin, "The Erotics of Sovereignty," in Driskill et al., *Queer Indigenous Studies*, 179.

57. Tom Hertweck, "A Hunger for Words: Food Affects and Embodied Ideology," in Kyle Bladow and Jennifer Ladino (eds.), *Affective Ecocriticism: Emotion, Embodiment, Environment* (Lincoln, NE: University of Nebraska Press, 2018), 135.

58. Driskill et al., *Queer Indigenous Studies*, 19.

59. See Hertweck, "A Hunger for Words," 135 and Heather Ashbach, "Where Does Fat Phobia Come From?" University of California News (August 15, 2019), www.universityofcalifornia.edu/news/fat-phobia?utm_source=fiat-lu x&utm_medium=internal-email&utm_campaign=article-general&utm_content=img.

60. See Abby Phillip, "'Fat Shaming' Doesn't Work, a New Study Says," *Washington Post* (September 11, 2014), www.washingtonpost.com/ne ws/to-your-health/wp/2014/09/11/fat-shaming-doesnt-work-a-new-study-says.

61. Craig Santos Perez, "SPAM's carbon footprint," Poets.org (2010), https://p oets.org/poem/spams-carbon-footprint.

62. For more on the literatures of SPAM, see Caitlin Yuri Yamamoto, "Emergent Voices of (Neo)Colonial Resistance: The Contemporary Literatures, Cultures, and Histories of 'Micronesia,'" PhD thesis, University of California San Diego (2016), escholarship.org/content/qt2gd447sm/qt2gd447sm.pdf?t=oi1ibq.

63. Calvo and Rueda Esquibel, *Decolonize Your Diet*, 17.

64. Ibid.

65. Crawford, "Slender Trouble," 451.

66. Pico, *Junk*, 45.

67. Pico, *Nature Poem*, 25. *IRL* also alludes to Pico/Teebs being given "peanut butter cups n onion rings" to stop fighting with his cousins, followed by the observation, "I mean, there's / no grocery store on the rez," 67. The poem also references his dad driving him to the fast food chain Jack in the Box "bc

worms in the commod / oatmeal that arrives on gov't / trucks each month," 45.

68. Alethea Arnaquq-Baril's 2016 documentary *Angry Inuk* documents how predominately White animal rights activists have deprived Inuit peoples of a source of food and income by waging a PR campaign against seal hunting. Some of the Inuit youth protestors featured in the documentary take a humorous tack, chanting, "Seals are yummy … in my tummy!" While seal is a healthy food and junk food is, well, junk, I see some overlap between this tack and Pico's, in terms of the unapologetic and humorous approach to food politics.

69. Quoted in Soleil Ho, "The Bay Area's Most Intriguing New Pop-Up Highlights Precolonial California Cuisine," *San Francisco Chronicle* (March 28, 2019), www.sfchronicle.com/restaurants/article/The-Bay-Area-s-most-intriguing-new-pop-up-13724206.php. On the appropriation and whitewashing of ethnic foods, see, for example, Lena Felton, "Alison Roman's Comments about Chrissy Teigen and Marie Kondo Lit a Fire. Here's Why It's Still Burning," *The Lily* (May 11, 2020), www.thelily.com/a lison-romans-comments-about-chrissy-teigen-and-marie-kondo-lit-a-fire-heres-why-its-still-burning/. See also Kyla Wazana Tompkins's work on food, race, and sexuality.

70. Pico, *Junk*, 72.

71. Ardam, "Canoodling with Junk Food," (n.p.).

72. While I don't have time to discuss it here, Pico has also referred to *Junk* as a breakup poem, prompting Ardam to observe that, "for Pico, the couple/(t) is a form to work against, not within," (n.p.).

73. Calvo and Rueda Esquibel, *Decolonize Your Diet*, 15.

74. Ibid., 17.

75. We might trace the germ of this ethos to Teebs's declaration in *IRL*, "Stop fucking posting about 'veggies,' truly / America's most disgustingly perky word," 87.

76. Hertweck, "A Hunger For Words," 138.

77. Ibid., 147.

78. Tara Kenny, "Meet Tommy Pico, the Native American, Beyoncé-Loving Poet," *Interview Magazine* (March 27, 2018), www.interviewmagazine.com/culture/tommy-pico-native-american-beyonce-loving-poet.

79. See Will Clark's review, "'Let Go': On Tommy Pico's 'Feed,'" *Los Angeles Review of Books* (November 19, 2019), lareviewofbooks.org/article/let-go-on-tommy-picos-feed.

10 Tender Woods: Looking for the Black Outdoors with Dawoud Bey

1. Angela Tucker (dir.), *Black Folk Don't* series (2011–2016), https://blackpublic media.org/, www.youtube.com/watch?v=cdgkXhzvqKA.

2. Unnamed interviewees, "Black Folk Don't Camp," *Black Folk Don't* series, season 2, episode 3 (July 2, 2012), https://Blackpublicmedia.org/episodes/ Black-folk-dont-camp-season-2-episode-3/.

3. See Christopher Martin, "Apartheid in the Great Outdoors: American Advertising and the Reproduction of a Racialized Outdoor Leisure Identity," *Journal of Leisure Research* 36.4 (2004): 513–535, 516, 517.

4. See Joni Adamson, Mei Mei Evans, and Rachel Stein (eds.), *The Environmental Justice Reader: Politics, Poetics, and Pedagogy* (Tuscon, AZ: University of Arizona Press, 2002).

5. For a sample of scholarship that analyzes this dual formation, see, for example, Joyce Chaplin, *Subject Matter: Technology, the Body, and Science on the Anglo-American Frontier, 1500–1676* (Cambridge, MA: Harvard University Press, 2003); Paul Outka, *Race and Nature from Transcendentalism to the Harlem Renaissance* (New York: Palgrave, 2008); Susan Scott Parrish, *American Curiosity: Cultures of Natural History in the Colonial British Atlantic World* (Chapel Hill, NC: University of North Carolina Press, 2006).

6. Sophie Sapp Moore, Monique Allewaert, Pablo F. Gomez, and Gregg Mittman, "Plantation Legacies," *Edge Effects* (January 22, 2019), edgeeffects.net/plantation-legacies-plantationocene. This group conducted a John E. Sawyer seminar on "The Plantationocene" at the University of Wisconsin from February 2019 to May 2020.

7. Camille Dungy, *Black Nature: Four Centuries of African American Nature Poetry* (Athens, GA: University of Georgia Press, 2009), xxi.

8. Kimberly Ruffin, *Black on Earth: African American Ecoliterary Traditions* (Athens, GA: University of Georgia Press, 2010), 4, 2, 16, 20.

9. Carolyn Finney, *Black Faces, White Spaces: Reimagining the Relationship of African Americans to the Great Outdoors* (Chapel Hill, NC: University of North Carolina Press, 2014), 7, xiii, 9.

10. See J. Kameron Carter and Sarah Cervenak, "The Black Outdoors: Humanities Futures After Property and Possession," which describes the concept, the working group, and now the book series at Duke University Press: humanitiesfutures.org/papers/the-Black-outdoors-humanities-futures-after-property-and-possession.

11. Monique Allewaert, *Ariel's Ecology: Plantations, Personhood, and Colonialism in the American Tropics* (Minnesota, MN: University of Minnesota Press, 2013), 6.

12. The scholarship on early African American plantation experience is extensive; please see the footnotes in Chapter 7 of Parrish, *American Curiosity* for further reading.

13. Lanham made this statement in an online piece for "Outdoor Afro": outdoorafro.com/2011/11/birding-while-Black-does-it-really-matter/. See also *Orion Magazine* (October 23, 2013), orionmagazine.org/article/9-rules-for-the-Black-birdwatcher.

14. See www.fledgingbirders.org/.

15. See outdoorafro.com; a 2017 "1A with Joshua Johnson" episode aired a conversation among a number of these outdoor activists; consult the episode, https://outdoorafro.com/ 1a.org/segments/2017–12–18-get-out-nurturing-a-bond-between-Black-people-and-nature/, which begins by asking "Is nature a white thing?"

16. It should be said that Black visual artists have for centuries been studying American environments. Consider, for example, nineteenth-century landscape painters Robert S. Duncanson (1821–1872), who painted both US and European landscapes (americanart.si.edu/artist/robert-s-duncanson-1353) and Edward Mitchell Bannister (1828–1901), who concentrated on New England scenes (americanart.si.edu/artist/edward-mitchell-bannister-226).

17. Frantz Fanon, *Black Skin, White Masks* (New York: Grove Atlantic, 1967), 112.

18. On slavery as a "peculiarly *ocular* institution," see Jasmine Nichole Cobb, *Picture Freedom: Remaking Black Visuality in the Early Nineteenth Century* (New York: New York University Press, 2015), 31.

19. Nicole R. Fleetwood, *Troubling Vision: Performance, Visuality, and Blackness* (Chicago, IL: University of Chicago Press, 2011), 13.

20. See Albert Boime, *The Magisterial Gaze: Manifest Destiny and American Landscape Painting, c.1830–1865* (Washington, DC: Smithsonian Institution Press, 1991) and Martin A. Berger, *Sight Unseen: Whiteness and American Visual Culture* (Berkeley, CA: University of California Press, 2005), Chapter 2, on the racialization of nature through visual media.

21. Susan Buck-Morss, "Aesthetics and Anaesthetics: Walter Benjamin's Artwork Essay Reconsidered," *October* 62 (1992): 5. Emphasis in original.

22. W.M. Hunt, "Dawoud Bey, 'Night Coming Tenderly, Black'" (September 5, 2018), 2018.frontart.org/2018/09/05/dawoud-bey-night-coming-tenderly-Black-front-international-cleveland-triennial-for-contemporary-art/.

23. Dawoud Bey, Artist Statement, *Night Coming Tenderly, Black* 2018.frontart. org/artists/dawoud-bey/.

24. Hunt, "Dawoud Bey, 'Night Coming Tenderly, Black.'"

25. Langston Hughes, "Dream Variations," in *The Collected Poems of Langston Hughes* (New York: Vintage, 1995), 40.

26. William Meyers, "'Dawoud Bey: Night Coming Tenderly, Black' Review: Out of Darkness; Dawoud Bey's Large-scale Photographs Dve Into Art And Literary History While Trying To Re-create The Experience Of Slaves Fleeing on the Underground Railroad," *Wall Street Journal* (January 14, 2019). According to Meyers, Bey also drew on Faulkner's "Red Leaves" (1930) which is, frankly, a confusing source, given the enslaved fugitive's seemingly fateful, circular return and self-delivery to his Chickasaw captors in that story.

27. Frederick Douglass, *My Bondage and My Freedom* (New Haven, CT: Yale University Press, 2014 [1855]), 55, 40.

28. Sharon Block, *Colonial Complexions: Race and Bodies in Eighteenth-Century America* (Philadelphia, PA: University of Pennsylvania Press, 2018), 86, 5; Hannah Walser, "Under Description: The Fugitive Slave Advertisement as Genre," *American Literature* 92.1 (March 2020): 69, 78.

29. For a description of photographic practices during lynchings, see Leon F. Litwack, "Hellhounds," in James Allen (ed.), *Without Sanctuary: Lynching Photographs in America* (Santa Fe, NM: Twin Palms Publishers, 2000), 11.

30. Buck-Morss, "Aesthetics and Anaesthetics," 6, 11.

31. In *Troubling Vision*, Fleetwood explains that "*Non-iconicity* is an aesthetic and theoretical position that lessens the weight placed on the black visual to do so much," including produce iconic Black figures (9). Bey does this both for the Black figure and the American landscape.

32. Dawoud Bey, quoted in Maurice Berger, "Escaping to Freedom, in the Shadows of the Night," *New York Times* (July 5, 2018), www.nytimes.com /2018/07/05/lens/escaping-to-freedom-in-the-shadows-of-the-night.html.

33. Dawoud Bey, quoted in ibid.

34. Unnamed interviewee, "Black Folk Don't Camp."

11 Urban Narrative and the Futures of Biodiversity

1. See Raymond Williams, *The Country and the City* (Oxford: Oxford University Press, 1973); Henry Nash Smith, *Virgin Land* (Cambridge, MA: Harvard University Press, 1974); Roderick Nash, *Wilderness and the American Mind* (New Haven, CT: Yale University Press, 1973); William Cronon (ed.), "The Trouble with Wilderness; or, Getting Back to the Wrong Nature," in *Uncommon Ground: Rethinking the Human Place in Nature* (New York: Norton, 1995), 69–90.

2. See UNDESA (United Nations Department of Economic and Social Affairs), Population Division, *World Urbanization Prospects: The 2007 Revision* (New York: United Nations, 2008), www.ipcc.ch/apps/njlite/srex/njlite_down load.php?id=5849.

3. Nik Heynen, Maria Kaika, and Erik Swyngedouw, "Urban Political Ecology," in Nik Heynen, Maria Kaika, and Erik Swyngedouw (eds.), *In the Nature of Cities: Urban Political Ecology and the Politics of Urban Metabolism* (Abingdon: Routledge, 2006), 11.

4. The Australian ecologist Richard Hobbs and his collaborators originally coined the term "novel ecosystem" for a different context: areas that have been altered by human intervention and then left to their own ecological development, such as abandoned mines, agricultural fields, or forests after timber extraction. Clearly, cities, which undergo constant human maintenance, do not fit this definition. But the term "novel ecosystem" has gradually expanded its meaning to include urban areas.

5. Jennifer Price, "Thirteen Ways of Seeing Nature in L.A.," in William Deverell and Greg Hise (eds.), *Land of Sunshine: An Environmental History of Metropolitan Los Angeles* (Pittsburgh, PA: University of Pittsburgh Press, 2005), 222.

6. Ibid., 221.

7. Lawrence Buell, "Toxic Discourse," in *Writing for an Endangered World: Literature, Culture and Environment in the U.S. and Beyond* (Cambridge, MA: Harvard University Press, 2001), 36–43.

8. Ibid., 37.

9. Ibid., 43–44.

10. For a more detailed analysis of urban climate change narratives from a comparative perspective, see Ursula K. Heise, "Urban Narrative and Climate Change," in Stuart Cooke and Peter Denney (eds.), *Transcultural Ecocriticism: Indigenous, Romantic and Global Perspectives* (London: Bloomsbury, 2021), 21–40.

11. Jennifer Wolch, "Zoöpolis," in Jennifer Wolch and Jody Emel (eds.), *Animal Geographies: Place, Politics, and Identity in the Nature-Culture Borderlands* (London: Verso, 1998), 135.

12. Jennifer Wolch, "Anima Urbis," *Progress in Human Geography* 26.6 (2002): 733–734.

13. See Thom Van Dooren, *Flight Ways: Life and Loss at the Edge of Extinction* (New York: Columbia University Press, 2014), and Van Dooren and Deborah Bird Rose, "Storied Places in a Multispecies City," *Humanimalia* 3.2 (2012): 1–27.

14. See nhm.org/community-science-nhm/rascals.

15. Scott Slovic, *Seeking Awareness in American Nature Writing* (Salt Lake City, UT: University of Utah Press, 1998).

16. Lydia Millet, *How the Dead Dream: A Novel* (Berkeley, CA: Counterpoint, 2008), 197, 216. For a more detailed analysis of *How the Dead Dream*, see Heise, *Imagining Extinction: The Cultural Meanings of Endangered Species* (Chicago, IL: University of Chicago Press, 2016), Chapter 2.

17. Kim Stanley Robinson, *New York 2140* (New York: Orbit, 2017), 285, 279.

18. Ibid., 33.
19. Ibid., 33.
20. Ibid., 319–320.
21. Joanne Gottlieb, "Darwin's City, or Life Underground: Evolution, Progress, and the Shapes of Things to Come," in Michael Bennett and David W. Teague (eds.), *The Nature of Cities: Ecocriticism and Urban Environments* (Tucson, AZ: University of Arizona Press, 1999), 246.
22. Menno Schilthuizen, *Darwin Comes to Town: How the Urban Jungle Drives Evolution* (New York: Picador, 2018), 2–5.
23. Ibid., 7.
24. Paolo Bacigalupi, *The Windup Girl* (San Francisco, CA: Nightshade Books, 2009), 1.
25. Harryette Mullen, *Urban Tumbleweed: Notes from a Tanka Diary* (Minneapolis, MN: Graywolf Press, 2013), viii.
26. For a more detailed exploration of this aspect of Mullen's volume, see Heise, "Terraforming for Urbanists," *Novel: A Forum for Fiction* 49.1 (2016): 21–23.
27. Mullen, *Urban Tumbleweed*, x.
28. Ibid., 5.
29. Ibid., 122.
30. Ibid., 7.
31. Ibid., 19.
32. Ibid., 64.
33. Ibid., 119.

12 Japanese American Incarceration and the Turn to Earth: Looking for a Man Named Komako in *Bad Day at Black Rock*

1. Throughout this piece, I use the romanization of the name as it appears in the film's shooting script. The actors, however, pronounce the name "Ko*mo*ko." It's also worth noting that "Komako" is neither a typical Japanese family name, nor a male given name, so even their existence in name is a fairly spectral one. Hara Komako (原⊠子), however, was a prominent silent film actress in Japan during the 1920s and 1930s, though Komako is still her given name, not her family name. "Komoko" is also not a real Japanese name; and neither is "Kamotka," the name Howard Breslin used in the original short story upon which *Black Rock* is based, titled "Bad Time at Honda." See Howard Breslin, "Bad Time at Honda," *The American Magazine* 143 (January–June, 1947): 40–43, 136–138.
2. Don McGuire (adapter), *Bad Day at Black Rock (1955): Continuity Script.* Written by Millard Kaufman and Howard Breslin (Alexandria, VA: Alexander Street Press, 2004), 2.

3. See Walter Benjamin, "Theses on the Philosophy of History", in Hannah Arendt (ed.), Harry Zohn (trans.), *Illuminations* (New York: Shocken Books, 1969).

4. Throughout this chapter, I will adopt the cinematographic terminologies used by the shooting script for *Bad Day at Black Rock*.

5. Wyatt Earp was a frontiersman of the Wild West – lawman, gambler, and gunslinger, among many other roles. He is best known for his feud, which escalated to become the gunfight at the O.K. Corral in 1881. Both this gunfight and Earp's exploits at large have been told, retold, and referenced across all eras of tales of the wild west, including *Black Rock* director John Sturges's *Gunfight at the O.K. Corral* (1957).

6. Though not the focus of this chapter, *The Magnificent Seven* is itself an interesting product of the post-World War II Western, given that it was adapted from an Akira Kurosawa script.

7. The OPA was established shortly after the United States' entrance into World War II. The OPA set price ceilings on goods and also had the authority to ration scarce items.

8. Indeed, producer Dore Schary originally intended the film to be scoreless. In his autobiography, he describes his vision for the film's opening scene, carried by ambient sound, without musical accompaniment: "First the quiet speck of a station in the heart of desolation. A wind blowing, a yowl of a coyote, the far-off-horn of a diesel engine, then the roar of the train. The music department hated me" (quoted in Rob Nixon, "Behind the Camera on *Bad Day at Black Rock*" in *Turner Classic Movies*, www.tcm.com/this-month/art icle/288809%7C296104/Behind-the-Camera-Bad-Day-at-Black-Rock.html, accessed October 12, 2020). Schary, however, ultimately decided the scene didn't work without the score, and so the final cut of the film carried the orchestral, anxious bombast described earlier.

9. Dana Polan (audio commentary), *Bad Day at Black Rock*, John Sturges (dir.) (Metro-Goldwyn Meyer, 1955).

10. Neil Campbell, "Mourning in America: The Lusty Men (1952) and Bad Day at Black Rock", in *Post-Westerns: Cinema, Region, West* (Lincoln, NE: University of Nebraska Press, 2013), 96.

11. Taunya Lovell Banks, "Outsider Citizens: Film Narratives About the Internment of Japanese Americans," *Suffolk University Law Review* 269.4 (2009): 782.

12. Ibid., 775.

13. Marita Sturken, "Absent Images of Memory: Remembering and Reenacting Japanese American Internment," *positions* 5.3 (1997): 697.

14. McGuire, *Continuity Script*, 44.

15. The studio that currently holds the distribution rights to *Bad Day at Black Rock* only allows for the reprinting of their films' official promotional stills. Unfortunately, establishing shots of *Black Rock*'s black rocks did not make the cut. The scenes in question are timestamped between seconds 00:36 and 00:52 of the first minute of the film.

16. Deborah A. Carmichael (ed.), "Introduction," in *The Landscapes of Hollywood Westerns: Ecocriticism in an American Film Genre* (Salt Lake City, UT: University of Utah Press, 2006), 1.

17. Iyko Day, *Alien Capital: Asian Racialization and the Logic of Settler Colonial Capitalism* (Durham, NC: Duke University Press, 2016), 117–118.

18. Polan, *Bad Day at Black Rock*.

19. See John Beck, *Dirty Wars: Landscape, Power, and Waste in Western American Literature* (Lincoln, NE: University of Nebraska Press, 2009); Stephen Hong Sohn, "These Desert Places: Tourism, the American West, and the Afterlife of Regionalism in Julie Otsuka's *When the Emperor Was Divine*," *MFS Modern Fiction Studies* 55.1 (2009): 163–188; and Connie Chiang, *Nature Behind Barbed Wire: An Environmental History of the Japanese American Incarceration* (Oxford: Oxford University Press, 2018).

20. See Marita Sturken, "Absent Images of Memory: Remembering and Reenacting the Japanese Internment," *positions* 5.3 (Winter 1997): 687–707. William Deverell also mentions *Black Rock*'s setting "in the California desert" in "Fighting Words: The Significance of the American West in the History of the United States," *Western Historical Quarterly* 24.2 (1997): 185–206.

21. McGuire, *Continuity Script*, 7.

22. See Rea Tajiri (dir.), *History and Memory: For Akiko and Takashige* (Women Make Movies, 1991). John Streamas also discusses *Black Rock* and Poston in "'Patriotic Drunk': To Be Yellow, Brave, and Disappeared in *Bad Day at Black Rock*," *American Studies* 44.1/2 (2003): 99–114.

23. John Walton, "Conquest and Incorporation," in *Western Times and Water Wars: State, Culture, and Rebellion in California* (Berkeley, CA: University of California Press, 1992), 13.

24. Ibid., 18.

25. See www.manzanardiverted.com/.

26. Ruth Okimoto, *Sharing a Desert Home: Life on the Colorado River Indian Reservation, Poston, Arizona, 1942–1945* (Berkeley, CA: Heyday Books, 2001), 7.

27. National Park Service, "California: Parker Dam," *Discover Our Shared Heritage Travel Itinerary Series* (January 13, 2017), www.nps.gov/articles/california-parker-dam.htm.

28. Okimoto, *Sharing a Desert Home*, 7.

29. The OIA undermined the authority of the tribal council by authorizing the construction of Poston prior to their acquiescence, essentially making the decision for them. After World War II, the Poston facilities were repurposed to house Hopi and Navajo from eastern Arizona, in a further bid to consolidate Indigenous presence in Arizona to the CRIR. See Bernard L. Fontana, "The Hopi-Navajo Colony on the Lower Colorado River: A Problem in Ethnohistorical Interpretation," *Ethnohistory* 10.2 (1963): 164.

30. Karl Lillquist, "Farming the Desert: Agriculture in the World War II-era Japanese American Relocation Centers," *Agricultural History* 84.1 (Winter 2010): 81.

31. R.L. Nicholson, Letter to Charles F. Doyle (March 23, 1942), Box 92, RG499 Western Defense Command and Fourth Army Wartime Civil Control Administration and Civil Affairs Division Central Correspondence 1942–1946. National Archives and Records Administration – College Park.

32. Charles F. Ernst, *Welcome to Topaz*, Doren Benjamin Boyce Papers, Special Collections, Brigham Young University Harold B. Lee Library, MSS 7980.

33. Quoted in Brian Niiya, "Japanese American Creed," *Densho Encyclopedia*, encyclopedia.densho.org/Japanese_American_Creed/.

34. Kristen Michaud, "Japanese American Internment Centers on United States Indian Reservations: A Geographic Approach to the Relocation Centers in Arizona, 1942–1945." Unpublished MA Thesis in Geography, University of Massachusetts Amherst (2008), 26.

13 Leisure over Labor: Latino Outdoors and the Production of a Latinx Outdoor Recreation Identity

1. Latino Outdoors, "Yo Cuento Outdoors-The Stories Of Latino Outdoors. Part 3" (October 9, 2017), http://latinooutdoors.org/2017/10/yo-cuento-outdoorsthe-stories-of-latino-outdoors-part-3/. Emphasis in original.

2. Latino Outdoors, "2019: Un Año Outdoors" (2019), https://latinooutdoors.org/wp-content/uploads/2020/01/2019-Un-A%C3%B1o-Outdoors.pdf.

3. Sarah Maslin Nir, "How 2 Lives Collided in Central Park, Rattling the Nation," *New York Times* (June 14, 2020), www.nytimes.com/2020/06/14/ny region/central-park-amy-cooper-christian-racism.html.

4. Carolyn Finney, "The Perils of Being Black in Public: We Are All Christian Cooper and George Floyd," *The Guardian* (June 3, 2020), www.theguardian.com/commentisfree/2020/jun/03/being-black-public-spaces-outdoors-perils-christian-cooper.

5. Sarah Jaquette Ray, *The Ecological Other: Environmental Exclusion in American Culture* (Tucson, AZ: University of Arizona Press, 2013).

6. On Indigenous outdoor equity work, see Ashley Reis, "#Equity Outdoors: Public Lands and the Decolonial Mediascape," *Western American Literature* 54.1 (Spring 2019): 63–78.

7. Latino Outdoors, https://latinooutdoors.org/; Green Latinos, www .greenlatinos.org/.

8. Outdoor Afro, https://outdoorafro.com/; Black Girls Trekkin', https://black girlstrekkin.com/.

9. William Cronon (ed.), "The Trouble with Wilderness," in *Uncommon Ground: Rethinking the Human Place in Nature* (New York: W.W. Norton & Company, 1995), 69–90; Carolyn Finney, *Black Faces, White Spaces: Reimagining the Relationship of African Americans to the Great Outdoors* (Chapel Hill, NC: University of North Carolina Press, 2014); Karl Jacoby, *Crimes against Nature: Squatters, Poachers, Thieves, and the Hidden History of American Conservation* (Berkeley, CA: University of California Press, 2001); Jake Kosek, *Understories: The Political Life of Forests in Northern New Mexico* (Durham NC and London: Duke University Press, 2006); Paul Outka, *Race and Nature from Transcendentalism to the Harlem Renaissance* (London: Palgrave Macmillan, 2008); Mark David Spence, *Dispossessing the Wilderness: Indian Removal and the Making of the National Parks* (Oxford: Oxford University Press, 1999).

10. Gail Bederman, *Manliness and Civilization: A Cultural History of Gender and Race in the United States, 1880–1917* (Chicago, IL: University of Chicago Press, 1996); Ray, *The Ecological Other*; Dorceeta E. Taylor, *The Rise of the American Conservation Movement: Power, Privilege, and Environmental Protection* (Durham WC and London: Duke University Press, 2016); Alexandra Minna Stern, *Eugenic Nation: Faults and Frontiers of Better Breeding in Modern America* (Berkeley, CA: University of California Press, 2005).

11. I am drawing from Derek Christopher Martin, "Apartheid in the Great Outdoors: American Advertising and the Reproduction of a Racialized Outdoor Leisure Identity," *Journal of Leisure Research* 36.4 (2004): 513–535.

12. Outdoor Alliance, "Human Powered Recreation On Public Lands," www .outdooralliance.org/recreation-reports.

13. Stephen Davis, *In Defense of Public Lands: The Case Against Privatization and Transfer*(Philadelphia, PA: Temple University Press, 2018), 10.

14. Ibid., 2.

15. Ibid.

16. Roderick Nash, *Wilderness and the American Mind* (New Haven, CT: Yale University Press, 2001 [1965]); Ramachandra Guha, "Radical American Environmentalism and Wilderness: A Third World Critique," *Environmental Ethics* 11.1 (1989):71–83; Cronon, "The Trouble with Wilderness," 496.

17. Kari Mari Norgaard, *Salmon and Acorns Feed Our People: Colonialism, Nature, and Social Action* (New Brunswick, NJ; Rutgers University Press, 2019), 15.

18. Ibid., 73.

19. The Wilderness Act, Public Law 88–577 (16 U.S.C. 1131–1136) 88th Congress, Second Session, September 3, 1964, www.nps.gov/orgs/1981/upload/W-Act_508.pdf.

20. Dennis Martinez, "Redefining Sustainability through Kincentric Ecology: Reclaiming Indigenous Land, Knowledge, and Ethics," in Melissa K. Nelson and Dan Shilling (eds.), *Traditional Ecological Knowledge: Learning from Indigenous Practices for Environmental Sustainability* (Cambridge: Cambridge University Press, 2018), 139–174; Enrique Salmón, "Kincentric Ecology: Indigenous Perspectives of the Human-Nature Relationship," *Ecological Applications* 10.5 (2000): 1327–1332; Kyle Powys Whyte, "Our Ancestors' Dystopia Now: Indigenous Conservation and the Anthropocene," in Ursula Heise, Jon Christensen, and Michelle Neimann (eds.), *Routledge Companion to the Environmental Humanities* (London: Routledge, 2017), 206–215.

21. Spence, *Dispossessing the Wilderness* and Jacoby, *Crimes against Nature.*

22. Norgaard, *Salmon and Acorns*, 10.

23. Dina Gilio-Whitaker, *As Long as Grass Grows: The Indigenous Fight for Environmental Justice from Colonization to Standing Rock* (Boston, MA: Beacon Press, 2019), 97.

24. J.M. Bacon, "Settler Colonialism as Eco-Social Structure and the Production of Colonial Ecological Violence," *Environmental Sociology* (2019): 1–11.

25. Norgaard, *Salmon and Acorns*, 20.

26. Ibid., 62.

27. Ramachandra Guha, *Unquiet Woods: Ecological Change and Peasant Resistance in the Himalaya*, expanded edition (Berkeley, CA: University of California Press, 2000 [1989]); Amitav Ghosh, *The Hungry Tide* (Boston, MA: Mariner Books, 2006); Mark Dowie, *Conservation Refugees: The Hundred Year Conflict Between Global Conservation and Native Peoples* (Cambridge: MIT Press, 2011).

28. Gilio-Whitaker, *As Long as Grass Grows*, 152–153. Rebecca Robinson, *Voices from Bears Ears: Finding Common Ground on Sacred Land* (Tucson, AZ: University of Arizona Press, 2018); Bears Ears Inter-tribal Coalition, https://bearsearscoalition.org/.

29. April Anson, "The President Stole Your Land: Public Lands and the Settler Commons," *Western American Literature* 54.1 (2019): 49–62.

30. Ibid.; Nick Estes, *Our History Is the Future: Standing Rock Versus the Dakota Access Pipeline and the Long History of Indigenous Resistance* (New York: Verso Books, 2019); Elizabeth Hoover, *The River Is in Us: Fighting Toxics in*

a Mohawk Community (Minneapolis, MN: University of Minnesota Press, 2017); Julie Sze, *Environmental Justice in a Moment of Danger* (Berkeley, CA: University of California Press, 2020); Gilio-Whitaker, *As Long as Grass Grows*.

31. Davis, *In Defense*; Margaret Grebowicz, *The National Park to Come* (Palo Alto, CA: Stanford University Press, 2015); Jennifer Ladino, *Memorials Matter: Emotion, Environment, and Public Memory at American Historical Sites* (Reno, NV: University of Nevada Press, 2019); Stephanie LeMenager and Marsha Weiseger, "Revisiting the Radical Middle (What's Left of It)," *Western American Literature* 54.1 (2019): 1–18; Terry Tempest Williams, *The Story of an Hour: A Personal Topography of America's National Parks* (London: Picador, 2016).

32. Latino Outdoors, "Yo Cuento Blog," https://latinooutdoors.org/blog/.

33. Latino Outdoors, "2019: Un Año Outdoors."

34. Latino Outdoors, "A Guide to Writing Your Yo Cuento Blog Post," https://latinooutdoors.org/blog/a-guide-to-writing-your-yo-cuento-blog-post/.

35. Latino Outdoors, "Yo Cuento Outdoors, The Stories of Latino Outdoors, Part 4," (November 7, 2017), https://latinooutdoors.org/2017/11/yo-cuento-outdoorsthe-stories-of-latino-outdoors-part-3-2/.

36. Jasmine Antonía Estrada, "In Your Blood," Latino Outdoors (November 20, 2019), https://latinooutdoors.org/2019/11/in-your-blood/.

37. Luis Villa, "Hiking, Car Hopping, and Unconventional Recreation," Latino Outdoors, (August 7, 2019), https://latinooutdoors.org/2019/08/hiking-car-hopping-and-unconventional-outdoor-recreation/.

38. In researching this piece, I read "Yo Cuento" blogs from 2015 to 2020.

39. Priscilla Solis Ybarra, *Writing the Goodlife: Mexican American Literature and the Environment* (Tucson, AZ: University of Arizona Press, 2016).

40. Ibid., 7.

41. José G. González, "¡Estamos Aquí! Opening America's Public Lands and Green Spaces," Latino Outdoors (January 20, 2017), http://latinooutdoors.org/2017/01/estamos-aqui-opening-americaspublic-lands-and-green-spaces/.

42. Josie Gutierrez, "Yo Cuento Outdoors ~ The Stories of Latino Outdoors. Part 7," Latino Outdoors (August 14, 2018), https://latinooutdoors.org/2018/08/yo-cuento-outdoors-the-stories-of-latino-outdoors-part-7/.

43. See Ybarra, *Writing the Goodlife*.

44. Randy J. Ontiveros, *In the Spirit of a New People: The Cultural Politics of the Chicano Movement* (New York: New York University Press, 2014).

45. Denis Cosgrove, "Habitable Earth: Wilderness, Empire, and Race in America" in D. Rothenberg (ed.), *Wild Ideas* (Minneapolis, MN: University of Minnesota Press, 1995), 36.

46. Lisa Park and David Naguib Pellow, *The Slums of Aspen: Immigrants vs. the Environment in America's Eden* (New York: New York University Press, 2011).

47. Latino Outdoors, "Latino Outdoors 2020: Connecting *Cultura* and Community with the Outdoors" (September 2017), https://latinooutdoors .org/wp-content/uploads/2017/10/LO_Strategic_Plan_508.pdf.
48. Go RVing (sponsor content), "A New Notion of Nature. How Latino Outdoors Is Rethinking the Ways Their Community Gets Outside," *Outside* (August 10, 2018), www.outsideonline.com/2296666/new-notion-nature.
49. Latino Outdoors, "Yo Cuento Outdoors . . . Part 3."
50. David Flores and Karmon Kuhn, "Latino Outdoors: Using Storytelling and Social Media to Increase Diversity on Public Lands," *Journal of Park and Recreation Administration* 36 (2018): 47–62.
51. Finney, *Black Faces, White Spaces.*
52. Laura Pulido, *Environmentalism and Economic Justice: Two Chicano Struggles in the Southwest* (Tucson, AZ: University of Arizona Press, 1996).
53. Ray, *Ecological Other.*
54. This argument developed from conversations with Mireya Loza. Sarah D. Wald, *The Nature of California: Race, Citizenship, and Farming since the Dustbowl* (Seattle, WA: University of Washington Press, 2016).
55. U.S. Bureau of Labor Statistics, "Hispanics and Latinos in Industries and Occupations," *The Economics Daily* (October 9, 2015), www.bls.gov/opub/t ed/2015/hispanics-and-latinos-in-industries-and-occupations.htm.
56. Villa, "Hiking, Car Hopping."
57. Richard White, "Are You an Environmentalist or Do You Work for a Living?" in Cronon (ed.), Uncommon Ground, 171–185.
58. Mario Jimenez Sifuentez, *Of Forests and Fields: Mexican Labor in the Pacific Northwest* (New Brunswick, NJ: Rutgers University Press, 2016); Anna Tsing, *The Mushroom at the End of the World: On the Possibility of Life in Capitalist Ruins* (Princeton, NJ: Princeton University Press, 2015).
59. Estrada, "In Your Blood."

14　Sanctuary: Literature and the Colonial Politics of Protection

1. Nanjala Nyabola, "The End of Asylum," *Foreign Affairs* (October 10, 2019), www.foreignaffairs.com/articles/2019-10-10/end-asylum.
2. This statistic is a composite of the UNHCR's estimate of 70 million political refugees and displaced people (www.unhcr.org) and the Internal Displacement Monitoring Centre's estimate of 22 million people displaced by climate (www .internal-displacement.org/sites/default/files/inline-files/2019-mid-year-figures_for %20website%20upload.pdf).
3. As Nyabola notes, the enactment of this liberal global order was self-contradictory from the beginning as, for example, the United Nations provision of rights for

refugees was coincident with its support for the founding of Israel and the displacement or destruction of hundreds of thousands of Palestinians.

4. Stephanie LeMenager, "The Humanities after the Anthropocene," in Ursula Heise, Jon Christensen, and Michelle Neiman (eds.), *The Routledge Companion to the Environmental Humanities* (London: Routledge Press, 2017), 476.

5. See Demetrius Eudell, "Landscapes of Man: Ecological and Cultural Change before Hurricane Katrina," in Bernd Sommer (ed.), *Cultural Dynamics of Climate Change and the Environment in North America* (Leiden: Brill Press, 2015), 159–186 and Kyle Powys Whyte, "Our Ancestors' Dystopia Now: Indigenous Conversation and the Anthropocene," in Heise et al. (eds.), *Routledge Companion to the Environmental Humanities*, 206–215.

6. Lisa Lowe, *The Intimacies of Four Continents* (Durham, NC: Duke University Press, 2015), 3.

7. Wallace Stegner, "The Best Idea We Ever Had: An Overview," *Wilderness Magazine*, Winter 1983. Henry David Thoreau, "Walking," in Elizabeth Hall Witherall (ed.), *Henry David Thoreau: Collected Essays and Poems* (New York: Library of America, 2001), 239.

8. See Mark Dowie, *Conservation Refugees: The Hundred-Year Conflict Between Global Conservation and Native Peoples* (Cambridge, MA: MIT Press, 2015).

9. See Philip J. Deloria, *Playing Indian* (New Haven, CT: Yale University Press, 1998), 4–5.

10. Lawrence Buell, *Writing for an Endangered World: Literature, Culture, and Environment in the U.S. and Beyond* (Cambridge, MA: Harvard University Press, 2003), 13.

11. Ibid.

12. Lowe, *Intimacies of Four Continents*, 4.

13. Angela Naimou, *Salvage Work: U.S. and Caribbean Literatures amid the Debris of Legal Personhood* (New York: Fordham University Press, 2015), 158.

14. Theodore Roosevelt, "Speech of President Roosevelt at the laying of the cornerstones of gateway to Yellowstone National Park, Gardiner, Montana, April 24, 1903" (Theodore Roosevelt Papers Library of Congress Digital Library), www.theodorerooseveltcenter.org/Research/Digital-Library/Record?lIbid=0289720.

15. Peter Mancina, "Sanctuary Cities and Sanctuary Power," in Reece Jones (ed.), *Open Borders: In Defense of Free Movement* (Athens, GA: University of Georgia Press, 2019), 251–252.

16. Paul M. Jakus and Sherzod B. Akhundjanov, "The Antiquities Act, National Monuments and the Regional Economy," *Journal of Environmental Economics and Management* 95 (2019): 103.

17. Terry Tempest Williams, *Refuge: An Unnatural History of Family and Place* (New York: Vintage, 1992), 21.
18. Ibid., 248.
19. Ibid., 4.
20. Ibid., 287.
21. Ibid., 289.
22. Ibid., 290.
23. Alyosha Goldstein, "By Force of Expectation: Colonization, Public Lands and the Property Relation," *UCLA Law Review Discourse* 65 (2018): 124–140.
24. Mark Rifkin, *When Did Indians Become Straight? Kinship, the History of Sexuality, and Native Sovereignty* (Oxford: Oxford University Press, 2011), 48, 239.
25. Eve Tuck and K. Wayne Yang, "Decolonization Is Not a Metaphor," *Decolonization: Indigeneity, Education, & Society* 1.1 (2012): 11.
26. Williams, *Refuge*, 13.
27. Jared Farmer, *On Zion's Mount: Mormons, Indians, and the American Landscape* (Cambridge, MA: Harvard University Press, 2010), 109.
28. Williams, *Refuge*, 69.
29. Farmer, *On Zion's Mount*, 90.
30. Randy Lippert, *Sanctuary, Sovereignty, Sacrifice: Canadian Sanctuary Incidents, Power, and Law* (Vancouver: University of British Columbia Press, 2005), 89–140.
31. Williams, *Refuge*, 239.
32. Lippert, *Sanctuary*, 2.
33. Williams, *Refuge*, 244.
34. Ibid., 252.
35. Ibid., 264–265.
36. Jodi Byrd, *The Transit of Empire: Indigenous Critiques of Colonialism* (Minneapolis, MN: University of Minnesota Press, 2010), xiii.
37. Nicole Waligora-Davis, *Sanctuary: African-Americans and Empire* (Oxford and New York: Oxford University Press, 2011), 56, xvi.
38. Joan Naviyuk Kane, *The Straits* (New Orleans, LA: Voices of the American Land, 2015), 34.
39. Ibid.
40. Joan Naviyuk Kane, *Milk Black Carbon* (Pittsburgh, PA: University of Pittsburgh Press, 2017), 42.
41. Kane, *Milk Black Carbon*, 22–23.
42. Jen Bagelman, *Sanctuary City: A Suspended State* (London: Palgrave, 2016), 8.
43. Kane, *Milk Black Carbon*, 49.
44. Ibid., 3.
45. Kane, *The Straits*, 34.

15 The Queer Restoration Poetics of Audre Lorde

1. Audre Lorde, "Of Generators and Survival – Hugo Letter 12/89," in Gloria I. Joseph and Hortense M. Rowe (eds.), *Hell Under God's Orders: Hurricane Hugo in St. Croix – Disaster and Survival* (St. Croix: Winds of Change Press, 1990), 205.

2. Audre Lorde, "A Burst of Light: Living With Cancer," in Rudolph P. Byrd, Johnnetta Betsch Cole, and Beverly Guy-Sheftall (eds.), *I Am Your Sister: Collected and Unpublished Writings of Audre Lorde* (Oxford: Oxford University Press, 2009), 119.

3. Audre Lorde, *The Cancer Journals: Special Edition* (San Francisco: Aunt Lute Books, 1980), 70.

4. Audre Lorde, "Uses of the Erotic," in *Sister Outsider: Essays and Speeches* (Berkeley, CA: Crossing Press, 2007), 55.

5. Lorde, *Cancer Journals*, 20. See also Audre Lorde, "Poetry Makes Something Happen," in *I Am Your Sister*, 186; and Adrienne Rich, "An Interview with Audre Lorde," *Signs: Journal of Women in Culture and Society* 6.4 (Summer 1981): 730.

6. "Restoration, n.," OED Online, www.oed.com. Accessed September 2019.

7. "Restore, v.," ibid.

8. See "resurgence, n." and "resilience, n.," ibid.

9. For critiques of "cure" and related notions in disability theory, see Alison Kafer, *Feminist Queer Crip* (Bloomington, IN: Indiana University Press, 2013); Sara Ahmed, *Willful Subjects* (Durham, NC: Duke University Press, 2014); Eli Claire, *Brilliant Imperfection* (Durham, NC: Duke University Press, 2017); and Leah Lakshmi Piepzna-Samarasinha, *Care Work: Dreaming Disability Justice* (Vancouver: Arsenal Pulp Press, 2018).

10. See Joni Adamson, Rachel Stein, Simon Ortiz, Teresa Leal, Devon Peña, and Terrell Dixon, "Environmental Justice: A Roundtable Discussion," *ISLE: Interdisciplinary Studies in Literature and Environment* 7.2 (Summer 2000): 155; and Joni Adamson, Mei Mei Evans, and Rachel Stein (eds.), "Environmental Justice Politics, Poetics, and Pedagogy," in *The Environmental Justice Reader: Politics, Poetics, and Pedagogy* (Tucson, AZ: University of Arizona Press, 2002), 4.

11. Ibid.

12. "Principles of Environmental Justice," First National People of Color Environmental Leadership Summit, October 24 to 27, 1991, Washington, DC. The document is available at the Natural Resource Defense Council, www.nrdc.org.

13. See Walter D. Mignolo, *The Darker Side of Western Modernity: Global Futures, Decolonial Options* (Durham, NC: Duke University Press, 2011), xv, for more on what he names "the 'colonial matrix of power.'"

14. See Lawrence Buell, "Toxic Discourse," *Critical Inquiry* 24.3 (Spring 1998): 639–665.

15. Stacy Alaimo, *Bodily Natures: Science, Environment, and the Material Self* (Bloomington, IN: Indiana University Press, 2010).

16. Rob Nixon, *Slow Violence and the Environmentalism of the Poor* (Cambridge, MA: Harvard University Press, 2011), 2.

17. Dr. June Jackson Christmas, "Black Women and Health Care in the 80s," *Spelman Messenger* 100.1 (1984): 8 (a printed version of her keynote address).

18. Ibid., 9.

19. Byllye Avery and Sybil Shainwald, letters to conference participants, First National Conference on Black Women's Health Issues Program, June 24–26, 1983, 1–2. Black Women's Health Imperative Records, Sophia Smith Collection, SSC-MS-00487, Smith College Special Collections, Northampton, MA.

20. Byllye Avery, "Breathing Life into Ourselves: The Evolution of the National Black Women's Health Project," in Evelyn White (ed.), *The Black Women's Health Book: Speaking for Ourselves* (Seattle, WA: Seal Press, 1990), 4–10.

21. Byllye Avery, "Empowerment Through Wellness," *Yale Journal of Law & Feminism* 4.1 (1991): 150.

22. Audre Lorde, "Difference and Survival: An Address at Hunter College," in *I Am Your Sister*, 201.

23. Lorde, *Cancer Journals*, 14–15.

24. Ibid., 61.

25. Lorde, "A Burst of Light," 114.

26. Audre Lorde, "On My Way Out I Passed Over You and the Verrazano Bridge," in *The Collected Poems of Audre Lorde* (New York: W.W. Norton & Company, 1997), 403.

27. Lorde, *Cancer Journals*, 20.

28. See Gloria I. Joseph, *The Wind Is Spirit: The Life, Love and Legacy of Audre Lorde* (New York: Villarosa Media, 2016) for a chronicle of Lorde's travels.

29. Lorde, "A Burst of Light," 140, 122.

30. Ibid., 132.

31. Joseph, *The Wind Is Spirit*, 65.

32. Resources, Community, and Economic Development Division, United States General Accounting Office, "Disaster Assistance: Federal State, and Local Responses to Natural Disasters Need Improvement," March 6, 1991, 12, www.gao.gov/products/RCED-91-43.

33. Jeffrey Schmalz, "3 Weeks After Storm, St. Croix Still Needs Troops," *New York Times* (October 9, 1989), www.nytimes.com/1989/10/09/us/3-wee ks-after-storm-st-croix-still-needs-troops.html?pagewanted=all.

34. Resources, Community, and Economic Development Division, "Disaster Assistance," 45.

35. Ibid., 33.

36. Schmalz, "3 Weeks After Storm."

37. Lorde, "Of Generators," 202.

38. Ibid., 202.

39. Ibid., 203.

40. Ibid., 204–205.

41. Ibid., 202.

42. Audre Lorde, Journal entry, September 19, 1989, Audre Lorde Papers, Series 2, Subseries 5, no. 35, 1989–90, Spelman College Archives, Atlanta, GA.

43. Lorde, "Of Generators," 204.

44. Resources, Community, and Economic Development Division, "Disaster Assistance," 25.

45. Ibid., 33.

46. Ibid., 45.

47. Lorde, "Of Generators," 204.

48. Quoted in Michael York, "St. Croix's Climate Proved Explosive After Hurricane Hugo Hit the Island," *Washington Post* (October 1, 1989), www.washingtonpost.com/archive/politics/1989/10/01/st-croixs-climate-proved-explosive-after-hurricane-hugo-hit-the-island/5e8f3186-82bb-4800-9ca5-aa8249ca0927/.

49. Lorde, "Of Generators," 210.

50. Ibid., 211.

51. Ibid., 205.

52. Ibid., 206.

53. Ibid., 207.

54. Emerging in the late 1970s and coming to fruition in the 1980s, ecofeminism argues that the ideologies that oppress women are the same as those that sanction environmental degradation.

55. For more on ecofeminist perspectives, see Val Plumwood, *Feminism and the Mastery of Nature* (New York: Routledge, 1993) and Greta Gaard, "Toward a Queer Ecofeminism," *Hypatia* 12.1 (Winter 1997): 114–137.

56. Gaard, "Toward a Queer Ecofeminism," 132.

57. Lorde, "Of Generators," 214.

58. Ibid., 215.

59. Ellen Samuels, "Six Ways of Looking at Crip Time," *Disability Studies Quarterly* 37.3 (2017), dsq-sds.org/article/view/5824/4684.

60. Lorde, "Restoration: A Memorial – 9/18/91," in *Collected Poems*, 456.

61. See Dagmar Schultz, "Preface," and "[Reading at] Haus der Kulturen der Welt," March 11, 1990, Berlin, Germany, Sarah Schnier (trans.), in Mayra A. Rodríguez Castro (ed.), *Audre Lorde: Dream of Europe, Selected Seminars and Interviews 1984–1992* (Chicago, IL: Kenning Editions, 2020), 9–10, 240–241.

62. "Authenticity, n.," OED Online, www.oed.com. Accessed September 2019.

63. Lorde, journal entry, September 19, 1989.

64. Notably, Lorde's conception of time contrasts with the compressed "lyric still life" that Sharon Cameron has influentially argued characterizes much poetry of the Western tradition. See Cameron, *Lyric Time* (Baltimore, MD: Johns Hopkins University Press, 1981), 240, 247.

65. Lorde, "Restoration: A Memorial," 456.

66. Lorde, journal entry, September 19, 1989.

67. Lorde, "Restoration: A Memorial," 456.

68. Ibid., 457.

69. Ibid.

70. Thank you to David Bonter from the Cornell Lab of Ornithology for identifying these feathers.

71. Lorde, journal entries, December 24–25, 1989.

72. Lorde, "Uses of the Erotic," 56.

73. Sara Ahmed, *The Promise of Happiness* (Durham, NC: Duke University Press, 2010), 12.

74. Ibid., 90, 94.

75. Ibid., 106.

76. Lorde, *Cancer Journals*, 77.

77. Ibid., 79.

78. Society for Ecological Restoration (SER), *The SER International Primer on Ecological Restoration* (Washington, DC: SER International Science & Policy Working Group, 2004), 1.

79. Michael L. Cain, William D. Bowman, and Sally D. Hacker, *Ecology: Second Edition* (Sunderland, MA: Sinauer Associates, Inc., 2011), 518.

80. Elizabeth G. King and Steven Whisenant, "Thresholds in Ecological and Linked Social-Ecological Systems: Application to Restoration," in Richard J. Hobbs, Katharine N. Suding, and Society for Ecological Restoration International (eds.), *New Models for Ecosystem Dynamics and Restoration* (Washington, DC: Island Press, 2008), 63.

81. Ibid., 64.

82. Ibid.

83. Angela Willey, "Biopossibility: A Queer Feminist Materialist Science Studies Manifesto, with Special Reference to the Question of Monogamous Behavior," *Signs: Journal of Women in Culture and Society* 41.3 (2016): 555.

84. Stacy Alaimo and Susan Hekman, "Introduction: Emerging Models of Materiality in Feminist Theory," in *Material Feminisms* (Bloomington, IN: Indiana University Press, 2008), 1.

85. See Donna Haraway, *When Species Meet* (Minneapolis, MN: University of Minnesota Press, 2008), 249; and Willey, "Biopossibility," 555.

86. See Sara Ahmed, "Imaginary Prohibitions: Some Preliminary Remarks on the Founding Gestures of the 'New Materialism,'" *European Journal of Women's Studies* 15.1 (2008): 23–39.

87. Lorde, "Poetry Makes Something Happen," 184.

Index

www.ingramcontent.com/pod-product-compliance
Ingram Content Group UK Ltd.
Pitfield, Milton Keynes, MK11 3LW, UK
UKHW010032140625
459647UK00012BA/1338